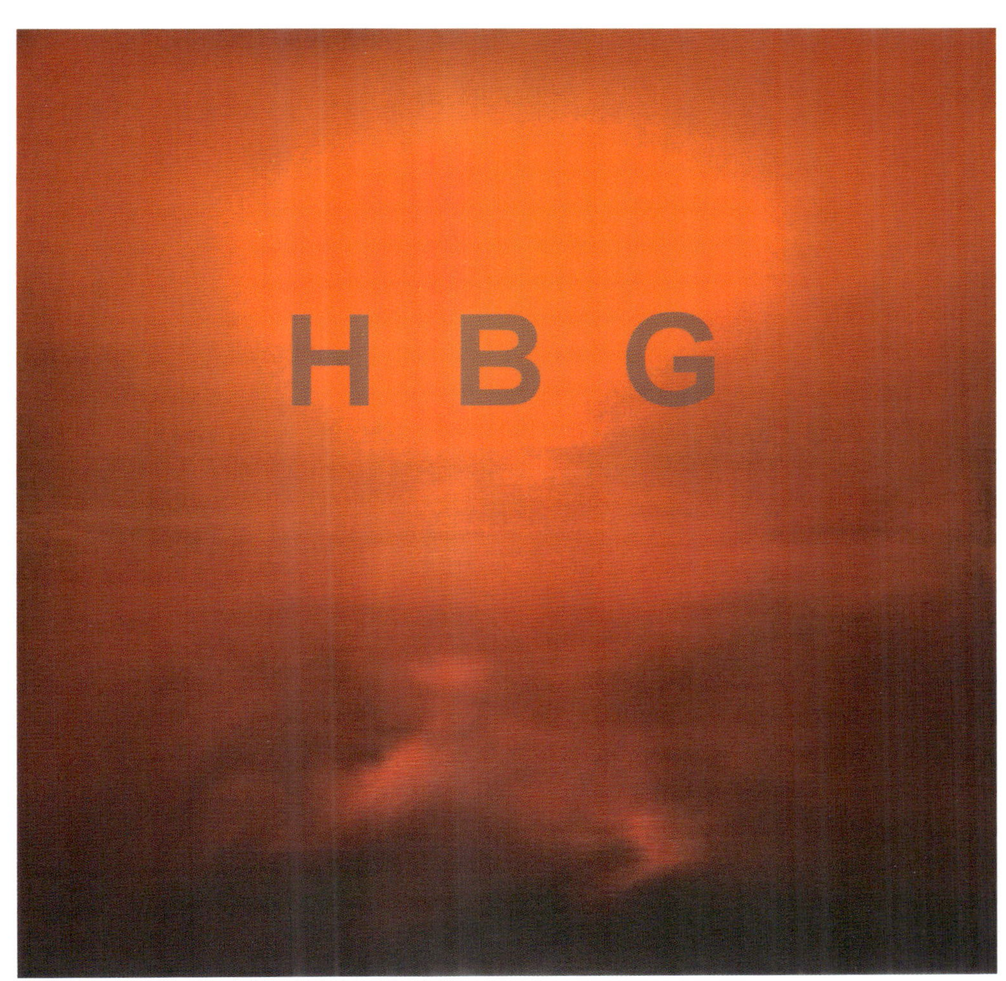
H B G

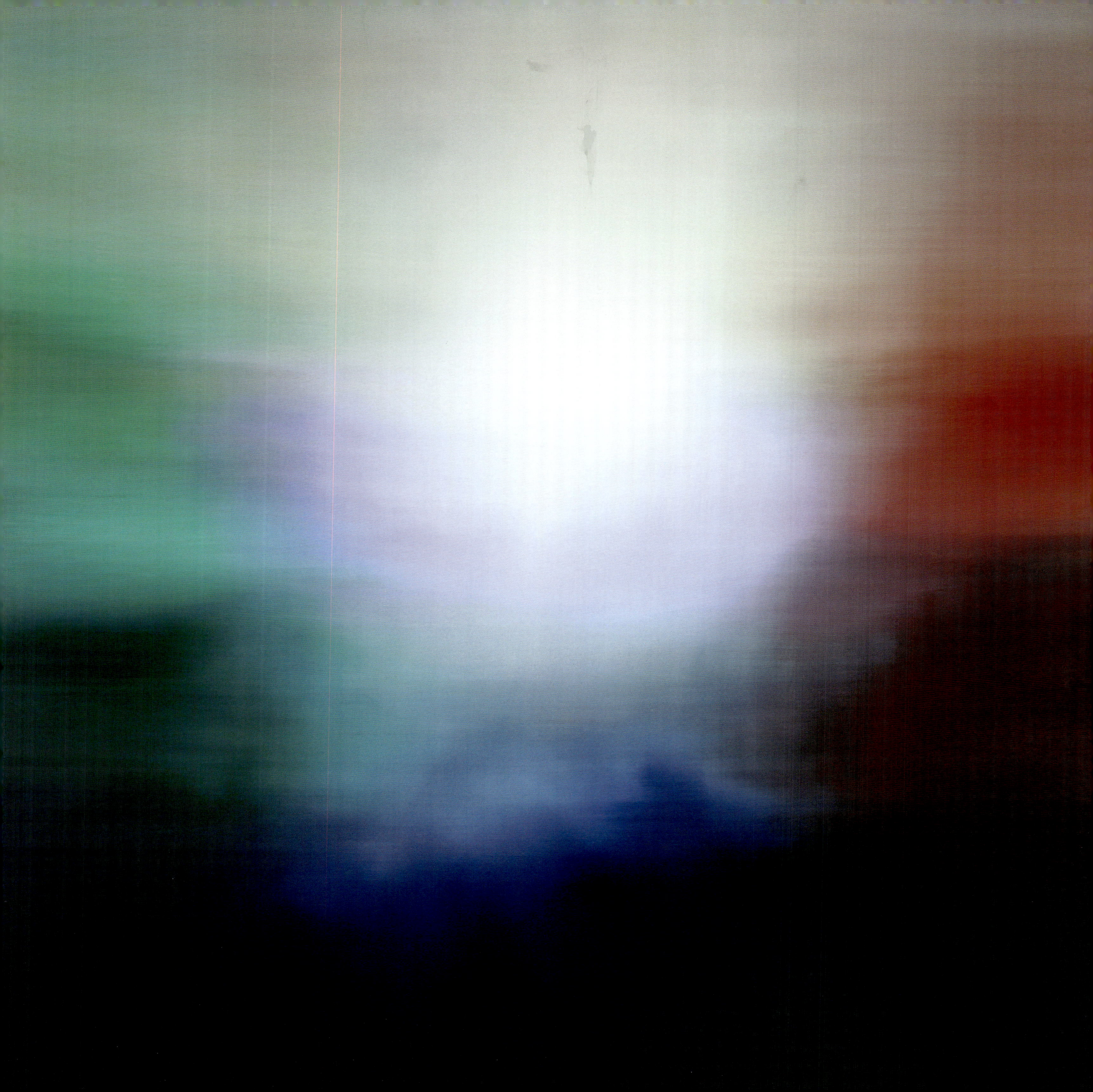

Helene B. Grossmann

Share the Light

HIRMER

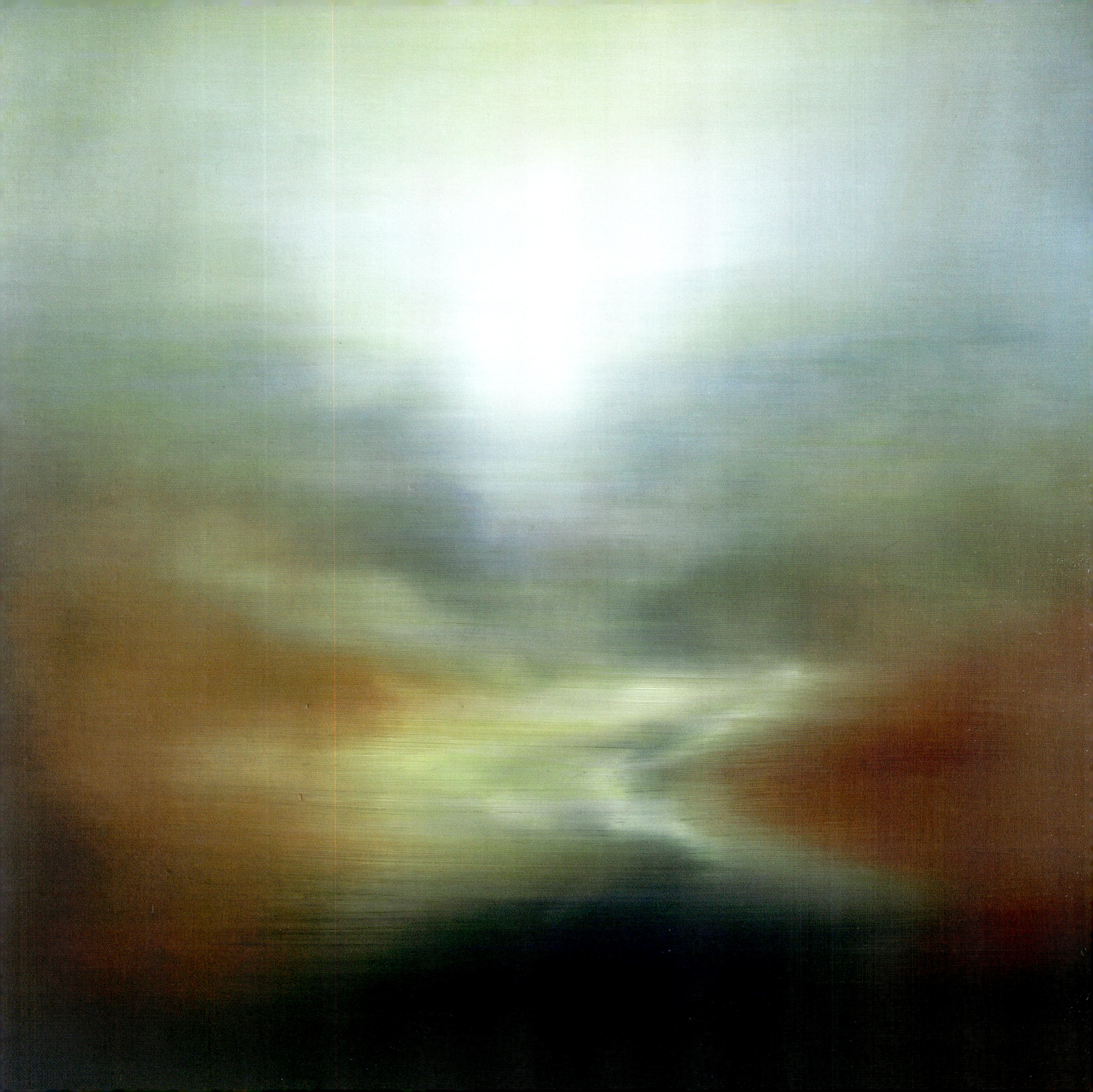

Content | Inhalt

Christoph Vitali
zu Helene B. Grossmann

Schon seit geraumer Zeit verfolge ich das Leben und Schaffen von Helene B. Grossmann mit der allergrößten Aufmerksamkeit und Bewunderung. Ich bin in den letzten Jahren zu allen ihren Ausstellungen gereist, nach Küssnacht an der Rigi, nach Basel und ganz kürzlich erst nach Zug.

Was ist es, das die Künstlerin so bedeutsam, so wichtig macht? Fraglos ist es ihre großartige und atemberaubende Darstellung des Lichts. In zahllosen Bildern hat sie dieses Licht gemalt, in Grau, Rot und vor allem Blautönen, in kleinen und sehr großen Formaten.

Mein Münchner Kollege und Freund, Raimund Thomas, vergleicht sie deshalb zu Recht mit Seurat, Tiepolo, Turner und Monet ... Ich will noch weiter gehen. Helene B. Grossmann gelingt es immer wieder von Neuem, das Licht in ihre Malerei hineinzunehmen, es zum dominierenden Punkt zu machen. So stehen wir dann ergriffen vor ihrem Werk und staunen immer wieder aufs Neue über ihre bedeutsame Kraft.

Das Curriculum Vitae der Künstlerin zeigt, an wie vielen wichtigen Ausstellungen in Deutschland und in der Schweiz sie schon teilgenommen hat. Möge sie so fortfahren und uns lange erhalten bleiben. Dies wünsche ich ihr und uns von ganzem Herzen.

Christoph Vitali ist ein schweizerischer Ausstellungskurator, Museumsdirektor und Kunstautor. Von 1985–1993 war er Direktor der Kunsthalle Schirn. 1994 wechselte er als Direktor an das Haus der Kunst in München (bis 2004). 2004 wurde er Direktor der Fondation Beyeler in Riehen/Basel. 2008 ging er als Direktor der Kunst- und Ausstellungshalle der Bundesrepublik Deutschland nach Bonn. Christoph Vitali lebt in Zürich.

Christoph Vitali
on Helene B. Grossmann

For some considerable time now I have been following the life and work of Helene B. Grossmann with the greatest attention and admiration. I have been to see all her exhibitions in recent years, in Küssnacht an der Rigi, in Basel, and most recently in Zug.

What is it that makes this artist so important, so significant? Without a doubt, it is her magnificent and breathtaking depiction of light. She has painted this light in numerous pictures: in grey, red and above all blue tones, in small-scale works and in very large ones.

It is for this reason that my colleague and friend from Munich, Raimund Thomas, rightly compares her to Seurat, Tiepolo, Turner and Monet … I would go even further. Helene B. Grossmann succeeds, time and again, in bringing light into her painting, making it the dominant feature. And so we stand in front of her work, deeply moved, constantly amazed at the force of her images.

The artist's biography shows how many important exhibitions in Germany and Switzerland have featured her works. May she continue in this vein and remain with us for a long time. This is my heartfelt wish for her and for all of us.

Christoph Vitali is a Swiss exhibition curator, museum director and art writer. From 1985 to 1993 he was director of the Schirn Kunsthalle, Frankfurt. In 1994 he was appointed director of the Haus der Kunst in Munich until 2004, when he became director of the Beyerler Foundation in Riehen near Basel. He moved to Bonn in 2008 to become director of the Kunst- und Ausstellungshalle der Bundesrepublik Deutschland. Christoph Vitali now lives in Zurich.

Raimund Thomas
zu Helene B. Grossmann

Bilder anzusehen, sind wir gewohnt, aber Helene B. Grossmanns Bilder anzusehen, ist ein Erlebnis völlig anderer Art. Bereits seit dem allerersten Blickkontakt vergisst der Betrachtende seine Position des Beobachters. Er wird augenblicklich tief im Inneren berührt und magisch in die tiefe, beglückende und lichterfüllte Unendlichkeit hinein- oder besser noch hinausgenommen.

Und meine Seele spannte
weit ihre Flügel aus,
flog durch die stillen Lande,
als flöge sie nach Haus.

So sagte es Eichendorff in dem Gedicht *Mondnacht*. Zweifellos hat er solche Bilder mit seiner intuitiven Wahrnehmung gesehen. Wenn ich mich als Betrachter dann doch wieder zurückhole, sehe ich Wolken, vielleicht Wasser und Nebel, auf alle Fälle eine Ahnung einer Landschaft, die aber sofort wieder zur Basiserscheinung wird, im übertragenen wie im wörtlichen Sinne. Was erneut und umso mehr gefangen nimmt, ist das zentrale Licht, teils gebündelt und blendend, teils gestreut und hindurchscheinend.

Wahrhaftig! Helene B. Grossmann gelingt es, Licht zu malen, dieses unfassbare, nicht zu materialisierende, flüchtige und doch so kraftvolle Fluidum. Licht! Was für ein Thema! Also nicht das Licht von Rembrandt oder Georges de la Tour. Es geht hier nicht um einen Lampenschein. Es geht um diese letzte Essenz im tiefen Sein, der sich Seurat in seinen Schwarz-Weiß-Zeichnungen genähert hat, oder wie sie bei einigen wenigen der ganz Großen der europäischen Malkultur so faszinierend formuliert werden konnte, ich meine Tiepolo, ich meine Turner und Monet.

Wie viele Maler ringen seit Beginn des 20. Jahrhunderts darum, reine Farbe ohne die Zwangsjacke der Form darzustellen. Mir ist niemand bekannt, der es gewagt hätte, das noch weitaus flüchtigere und weit dahinter liegende Medium Licht über den Weg des Malens zum Betrachter bringen zu wollen, ja, wie eingangs schon gesagt, ihn selbst ins Licht mit hineinzunehmen und zu erhellen. Das geht nur vor dem Hintergrund einer intuitiven Schau, einer ehrlichen Bescheidenheit, einer eruptiven Kraft und eines gereiften Könnens.

Raimund Thomas ist ein deutscher Galerist und Kunsthändler für moderne und zeitgenössische Kunst in München.

Raimund Thomas
on Helene B. Grossmann

We are accustomed to looking at pictures, but looking at Helene B. Grossmann`s pictures is an experience of an entirely different kind. From our first eye contact, we forget our role as viewers. We are immediately touched to the soul and magically drawn into, or rather out of, profound, gratifying and light-filled infinity.

And my soul spread
wide its wings
and flew o'er the silent lands
as if it were flying home.

Thus wrote Joseph Freiherr von Eichendorff (1788–1857) in his poem "Mondnacht" ("Moonlit Night"). He had doubtless also seen such pictures in his mind's eye. But if as the viewer I return to reality, I see clouds, perhaps water and mist, and in all cases the impression of a landscape, which however immediately turns back into a basic manifestation, both figuratively and literally.

What repeatedly and increasingly captivates me is the central light, partly concentrated and dazzling, partly diffuse and translucent. Incredibly, Helene B. Grossmann actually manages to paint light, this incomprehensible fluid that is so volatile and yet so powerful and impossible to materialise. Light! What a subject! It is not the light of Rembrandt or Georges de la Tour. The light here is not lamplight but the ultimate essence in its profound being. Seurat came close to it in his black-and-white drawings, and it was fascinatingly achieved by just a few really great European painters such as Tiepolo, Turner and Monet.

How many painters have struggled since the start of the twentieth century to represent pure colour without the strait-jacket of form? I do not know anyone who has attempted to convey the much more volatile and distant medium of light to viewers, or, as I suggested at the beginning, to draw them into it and to illuminate them. That is possible only against the background of an intuitive show, an honest modesty, an eruptive force and a mature ability.

Raimund Thomas is a Munich-based German art dealer and gallery owner specialising in modern and contemporary art.

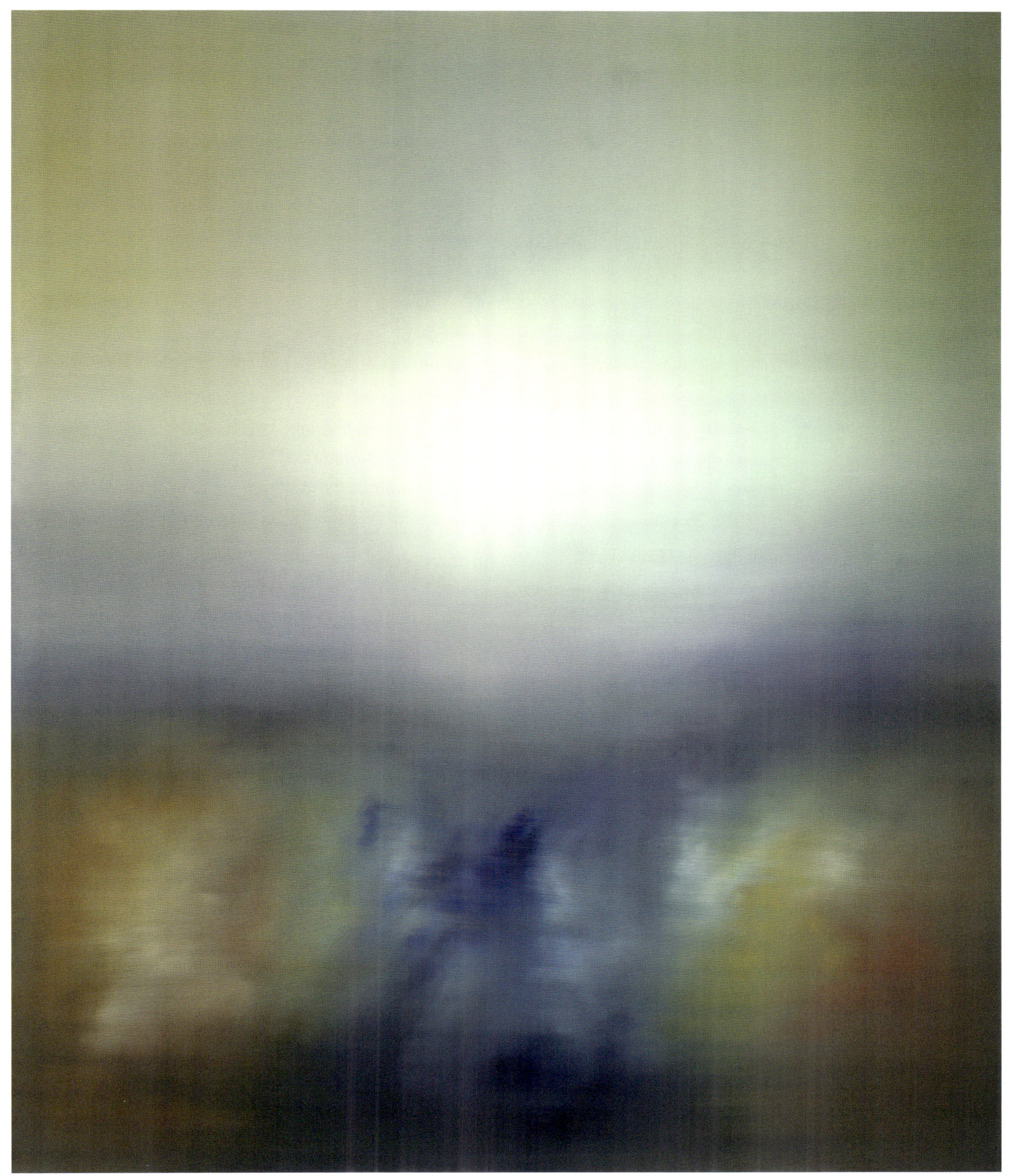

4 *IV-VIII-08*, 2008

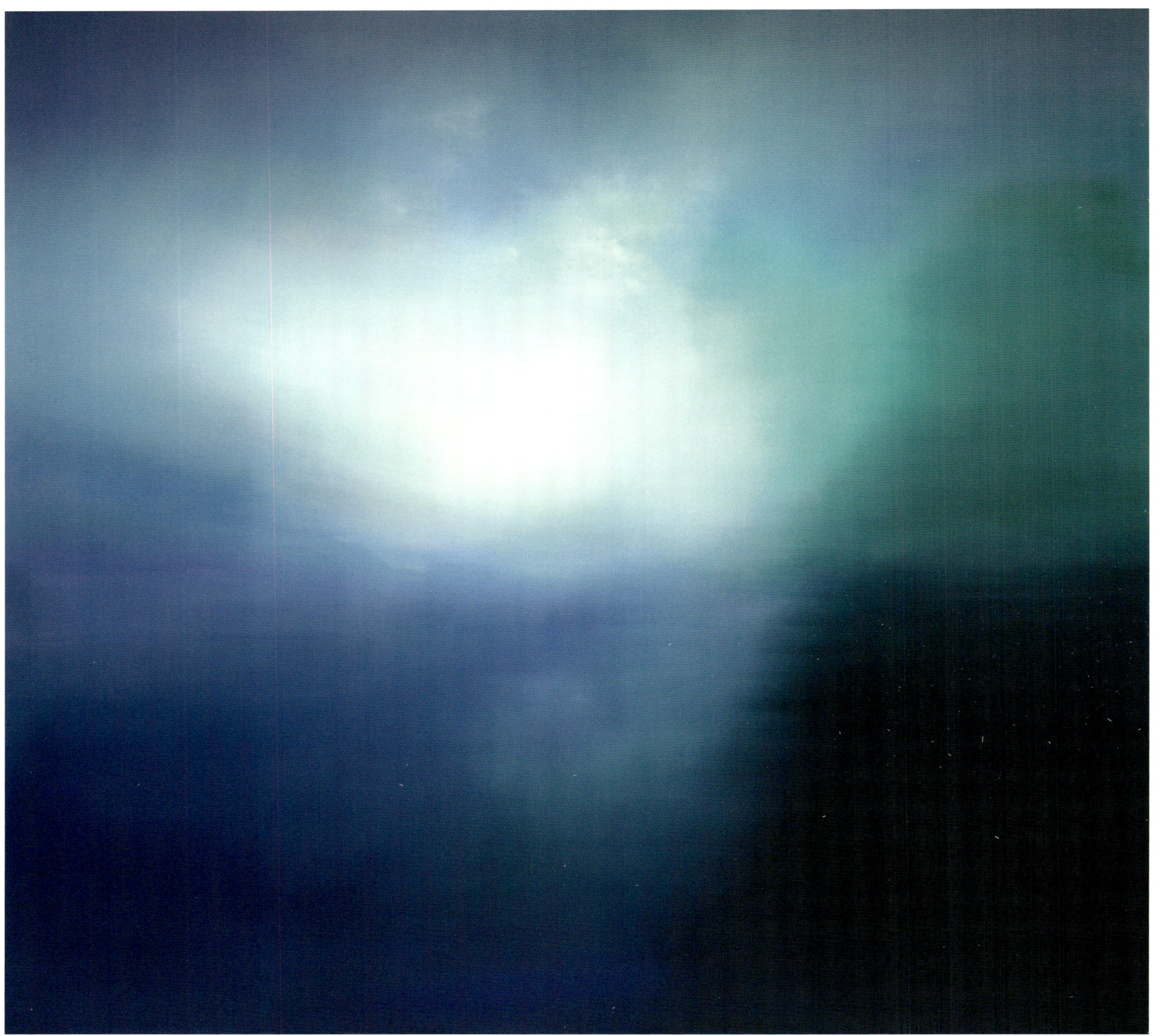

5 *XIX-VII-08*, 2008

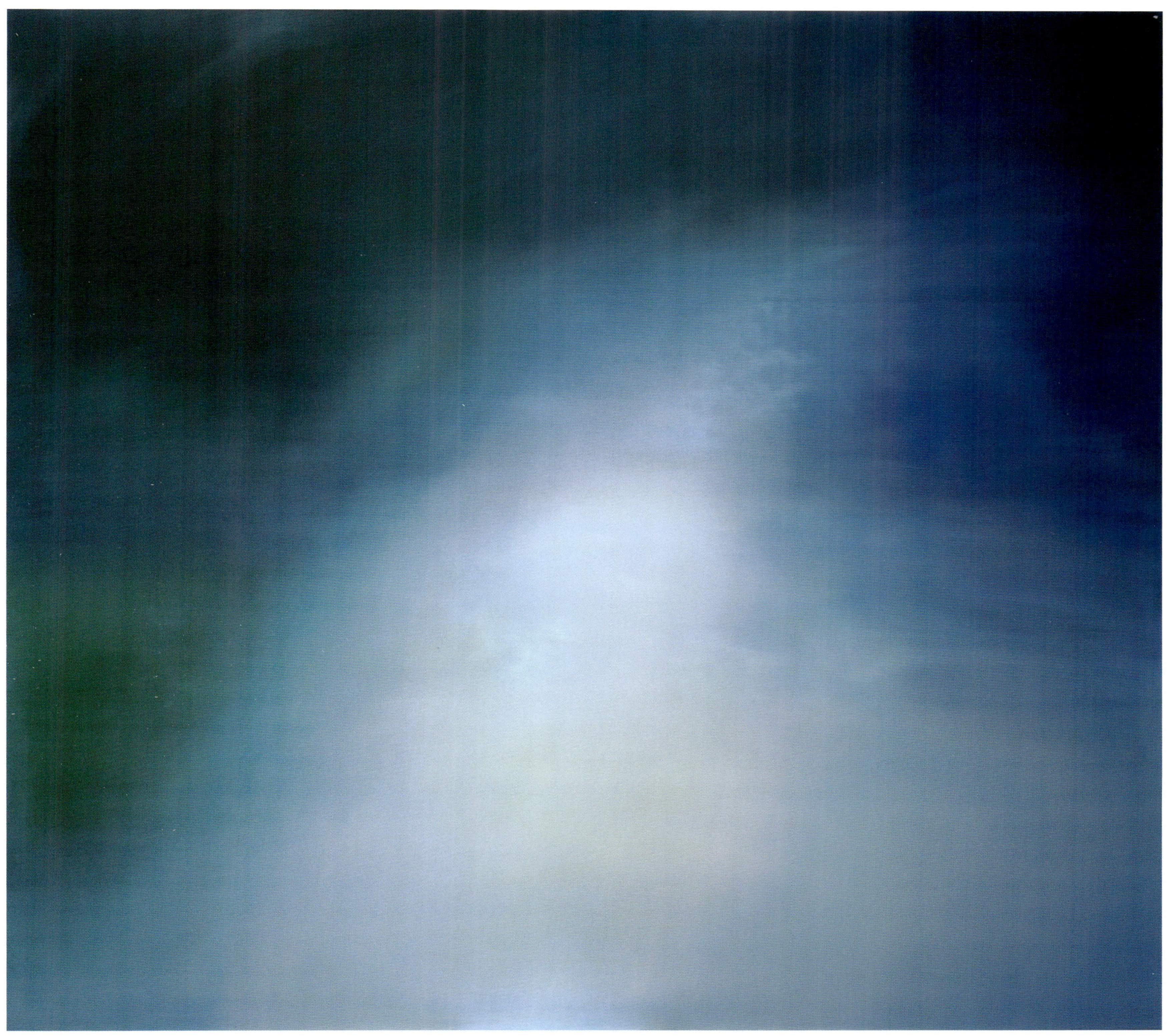

6 *XXX-VII-08*, 2008

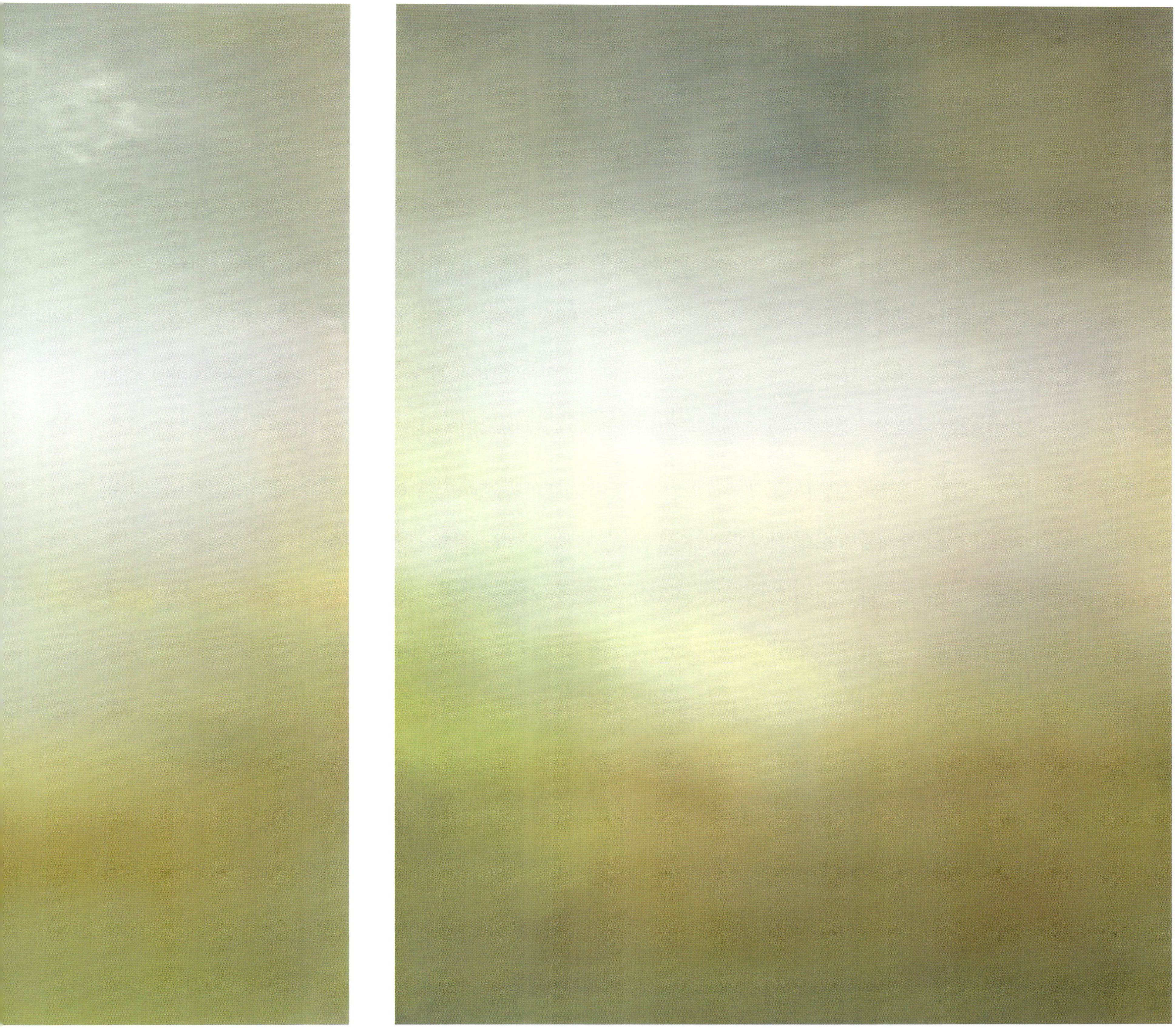

7 *XXI-I-08*, 2008

8 *VII-III-16*, 2016
9 *Poetry of Light I / Poesie des Lichts I,* 2015

10 *Dual I*, 2015
11 *Dual II*, 2015

12 *XV-IX-14*, 2014

13 *Poetry of Light II / Poesie des Lichts II*, 2015
14 *Poetry of Light III / Poesie des Lichts III*, 2015

15 *Poetry of Light IV* / *Poesie des Lichts IV*, 2015

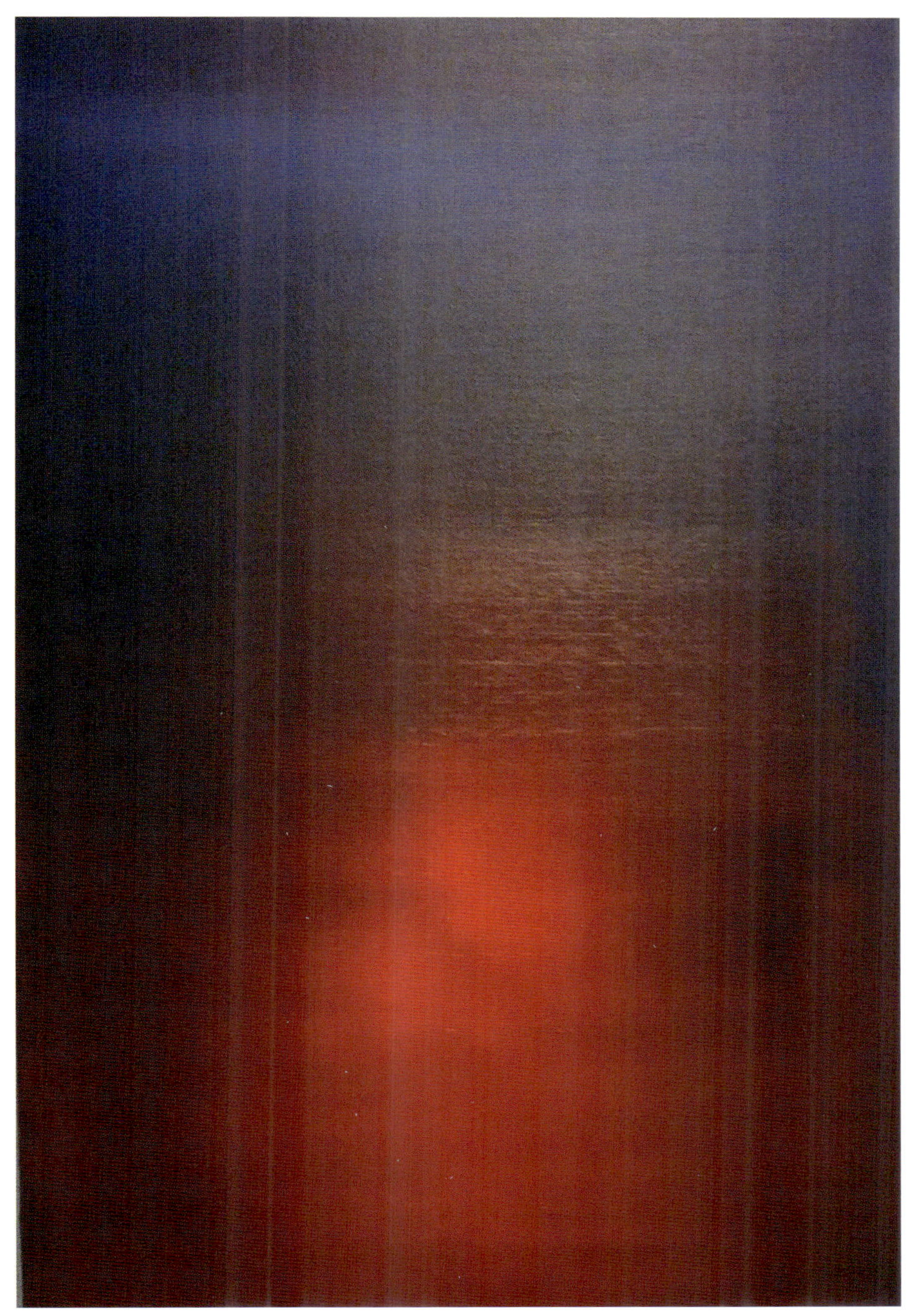

16 *Still Light / Noch Licht*, 2016

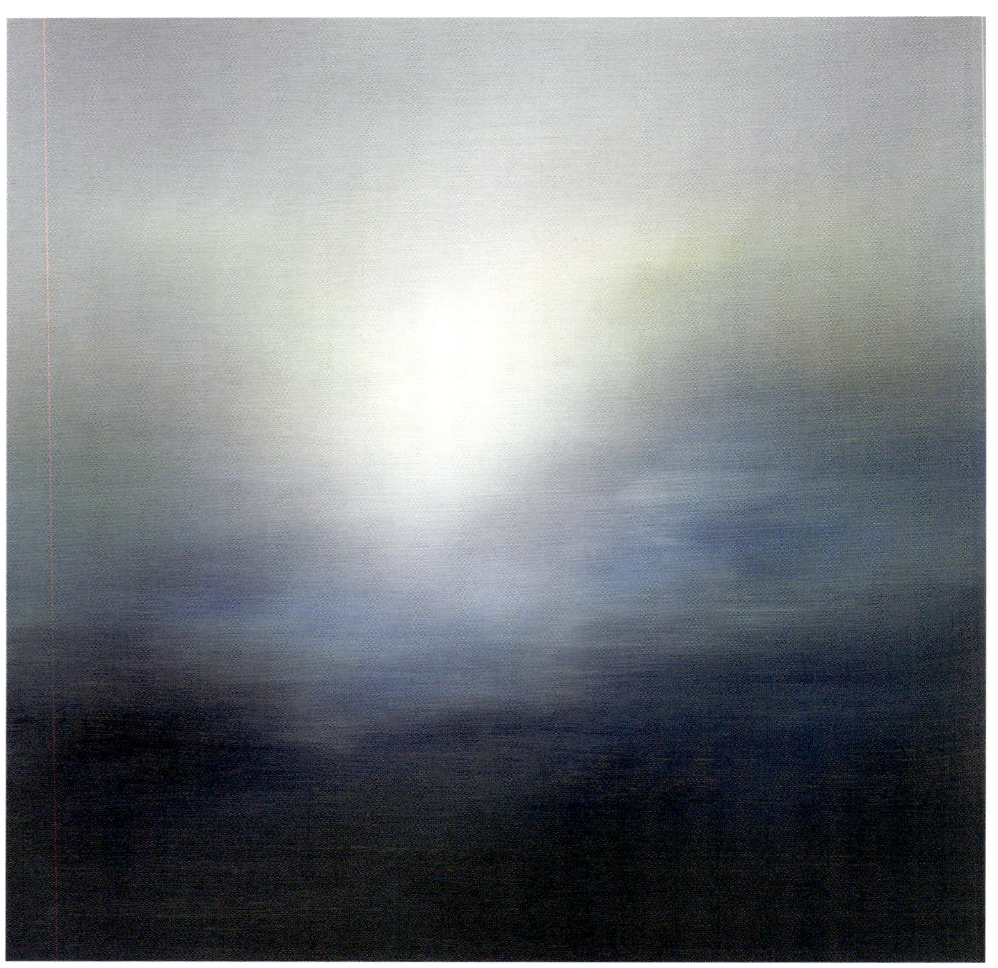

17 *XXVII-II-13*, 2013
18 *XXX-VIII-13*, 2013

Following double-page spread / folgende Doppelseite
19 *Aurora I, X-VII-13*, 2013
20 *Aurora II, X-VII-13*, 2013

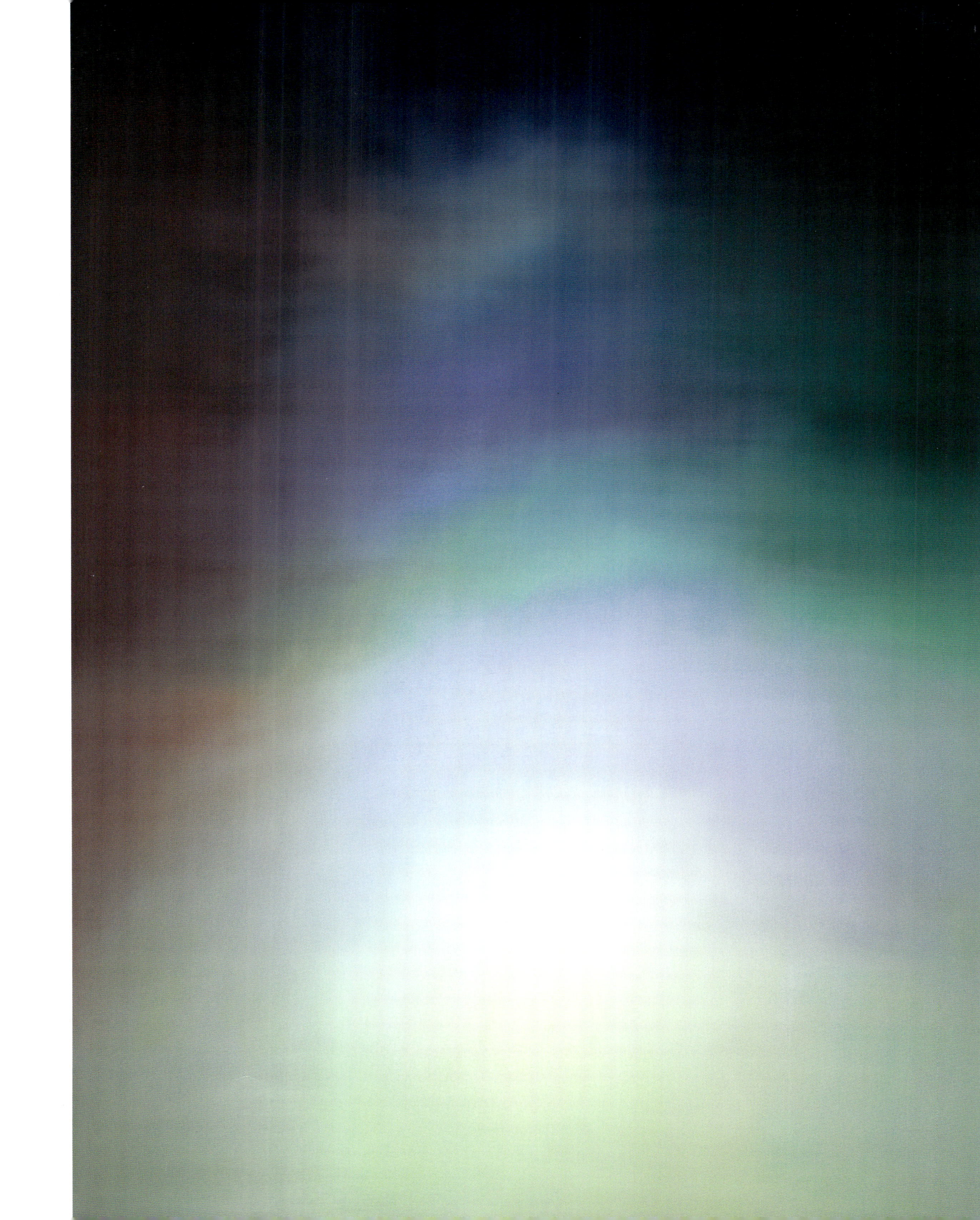

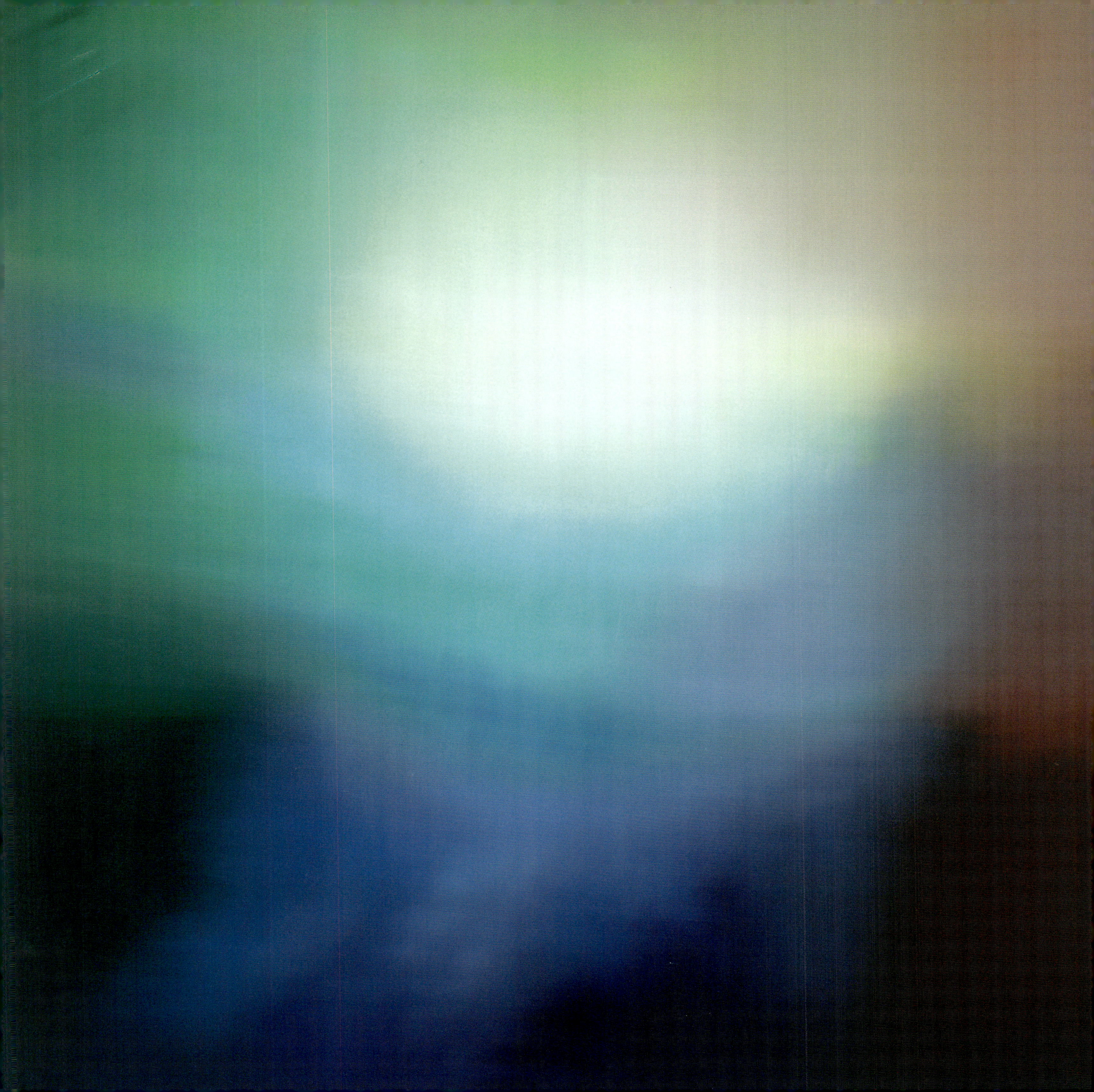

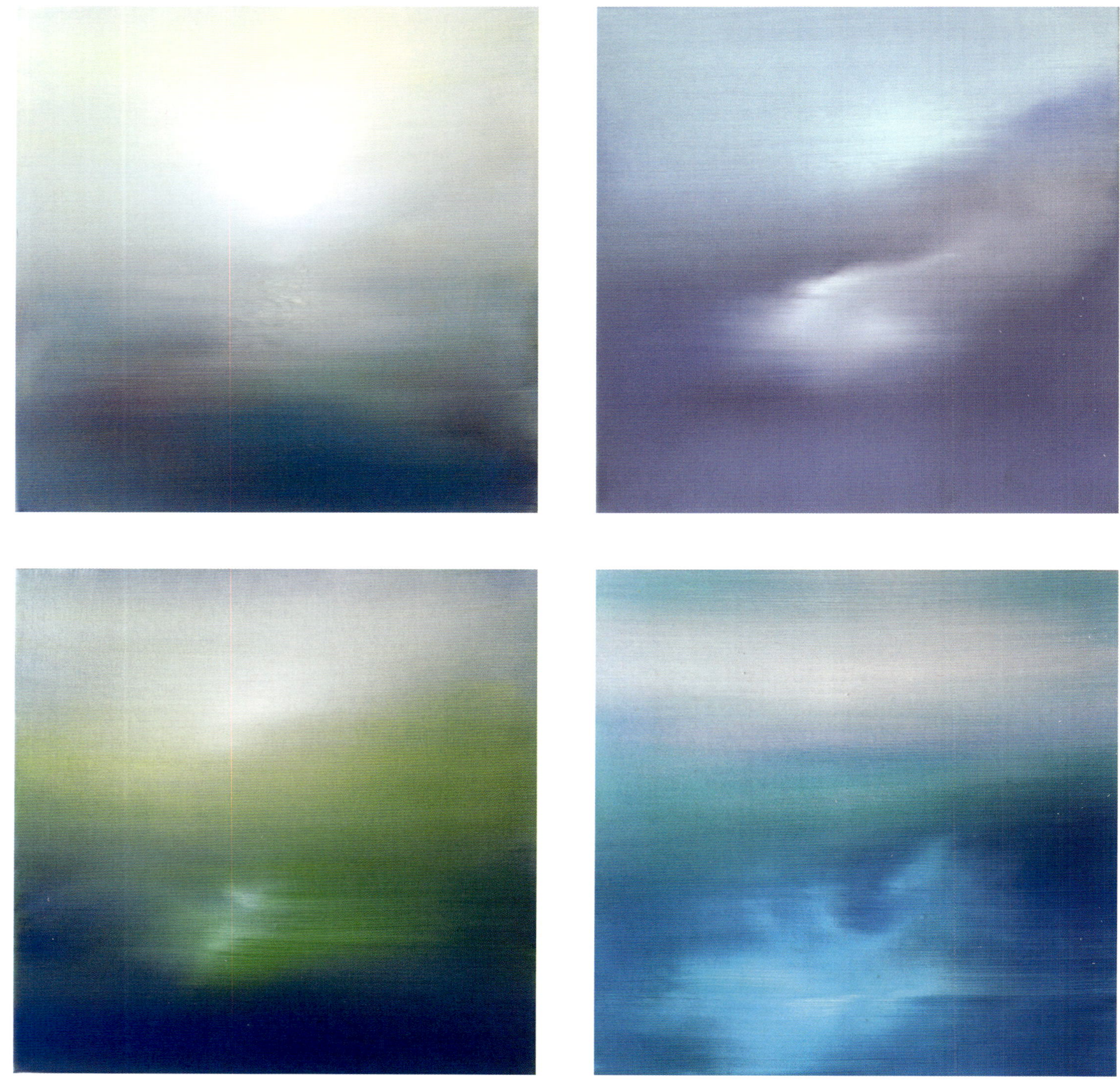

21 *Dance of the Hay Girls* / Tanz der Heumädchen, 2013

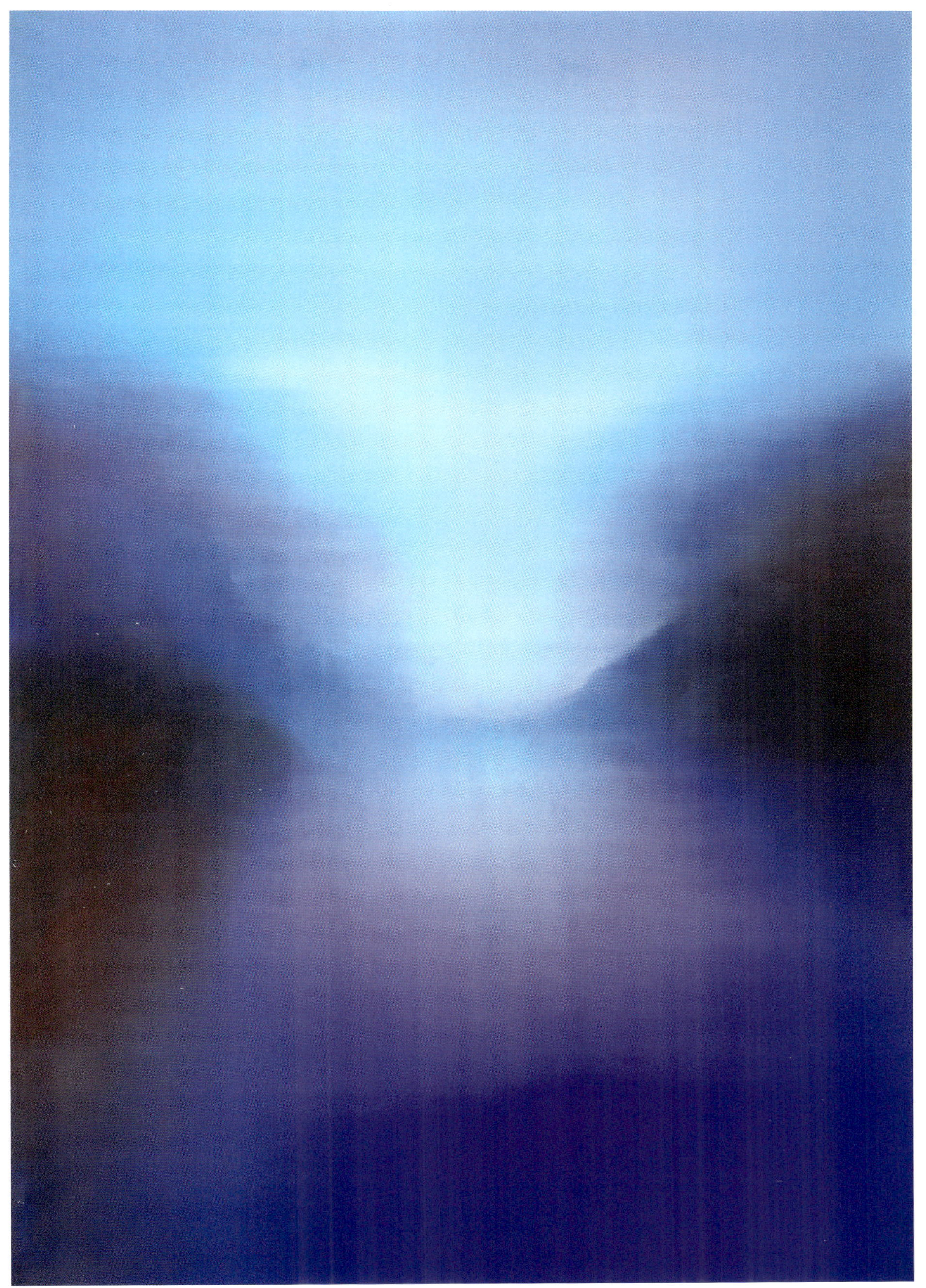

22 *Light Blue*, 2016

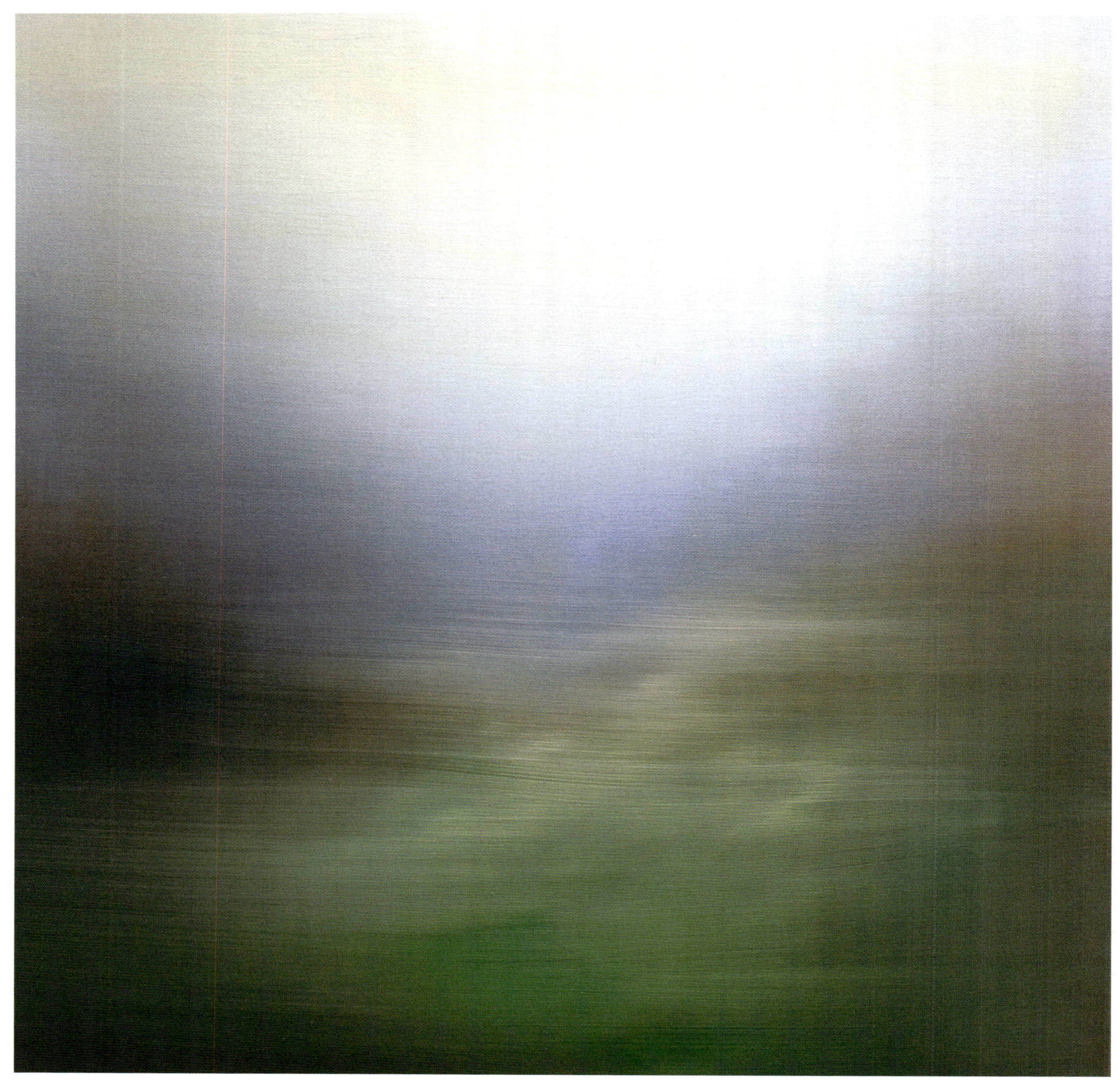

23 *XXXI-V-13*, 2013

24 *XXV-II-11*, 2011

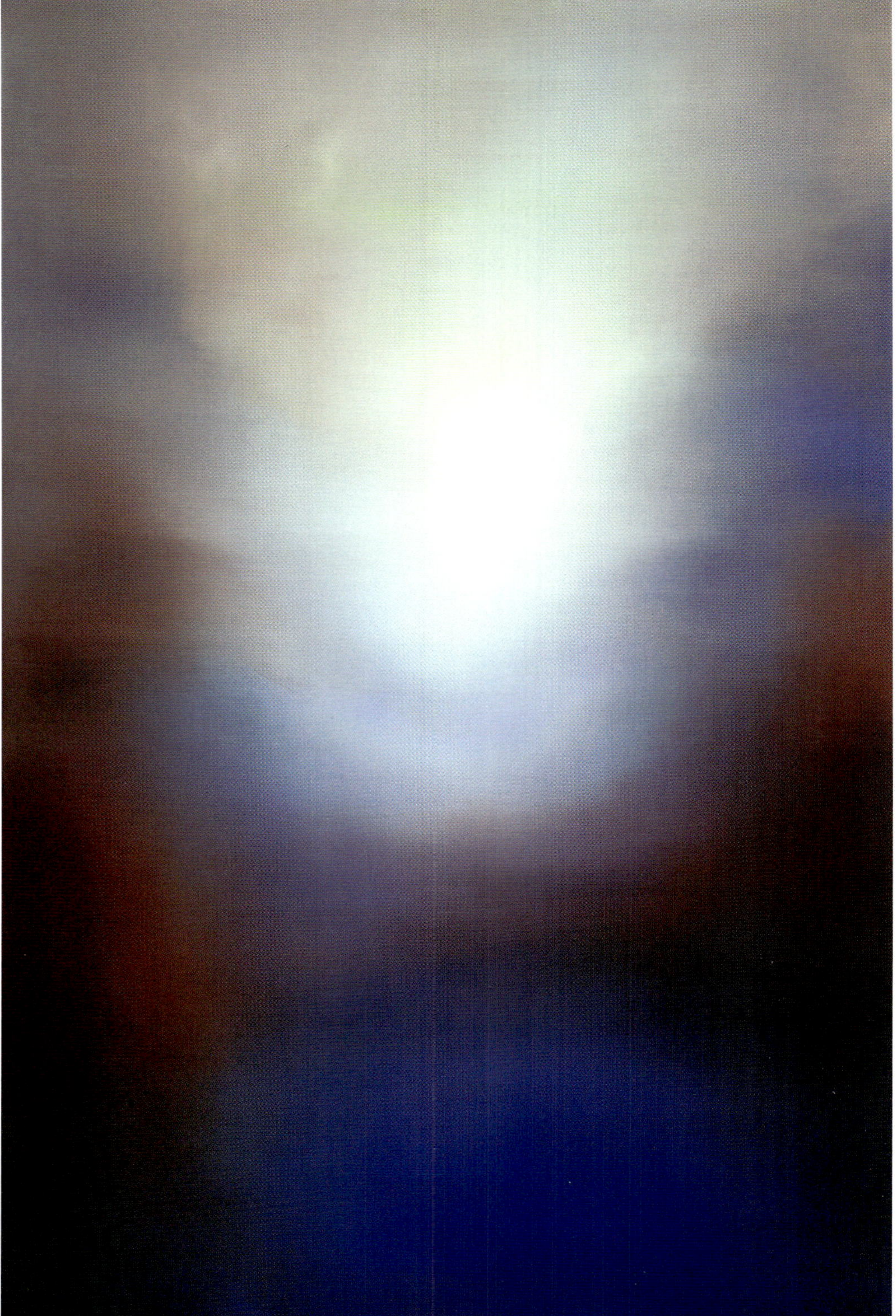

25 *The Vltava after Smetana / Die Moldau nach Smetana*, 2015

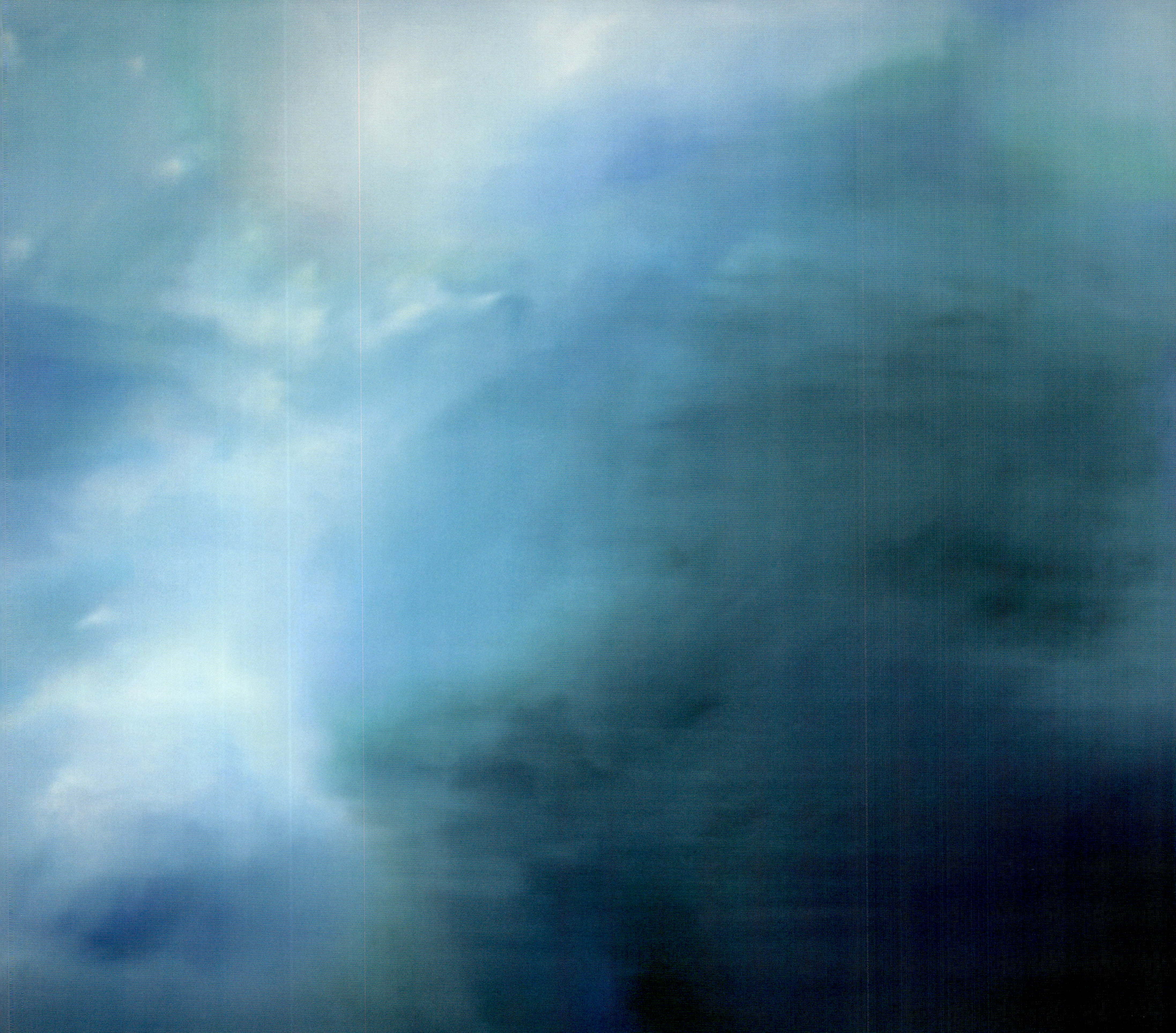

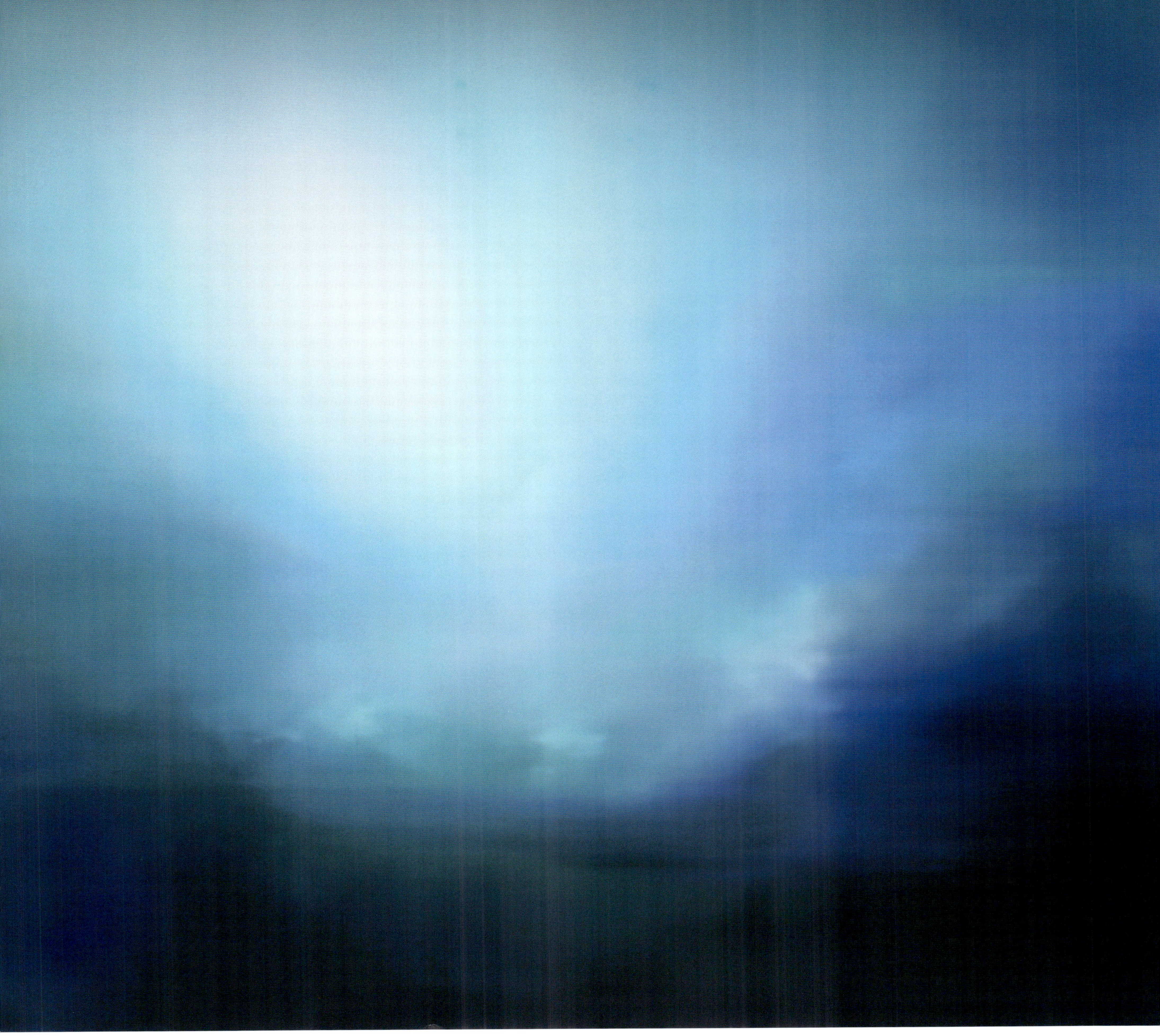

26 *Wave / Welle*, 2009

27 *Light II* / *Licht II*, 2015

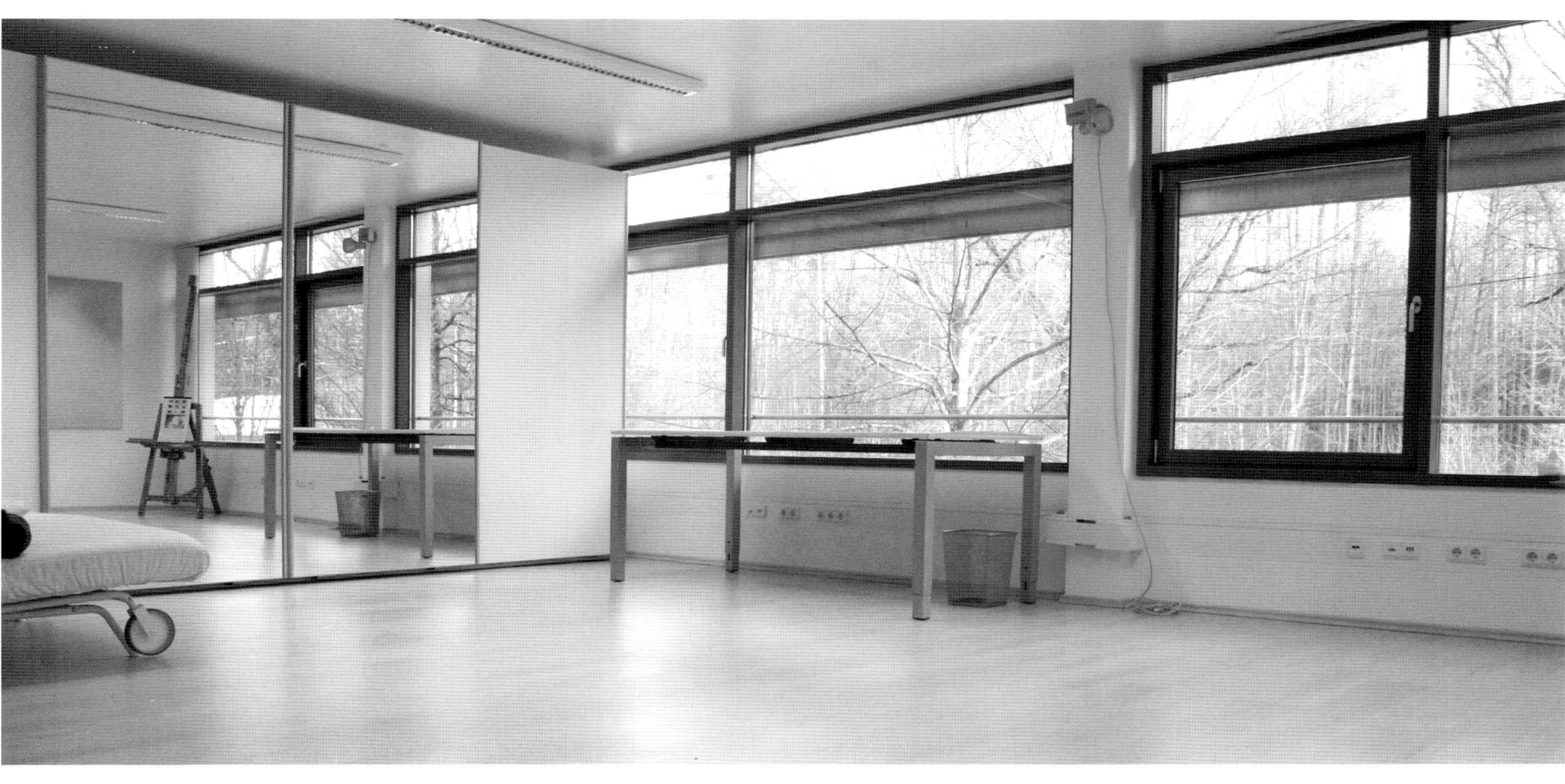

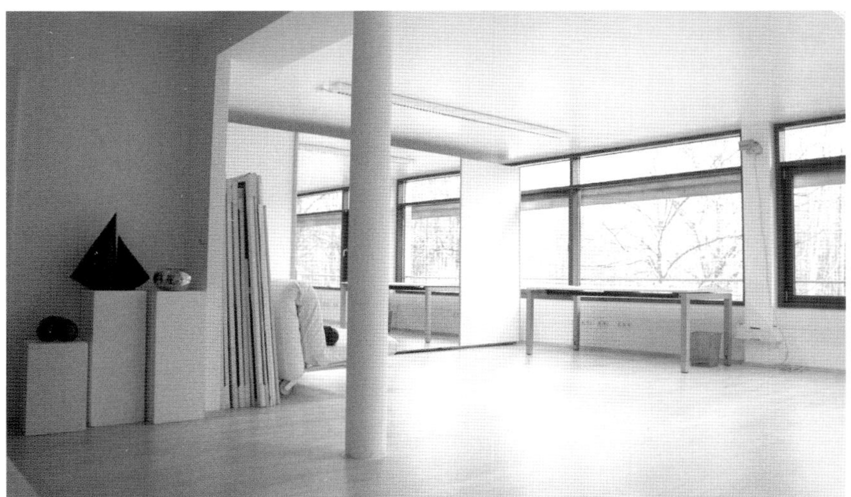
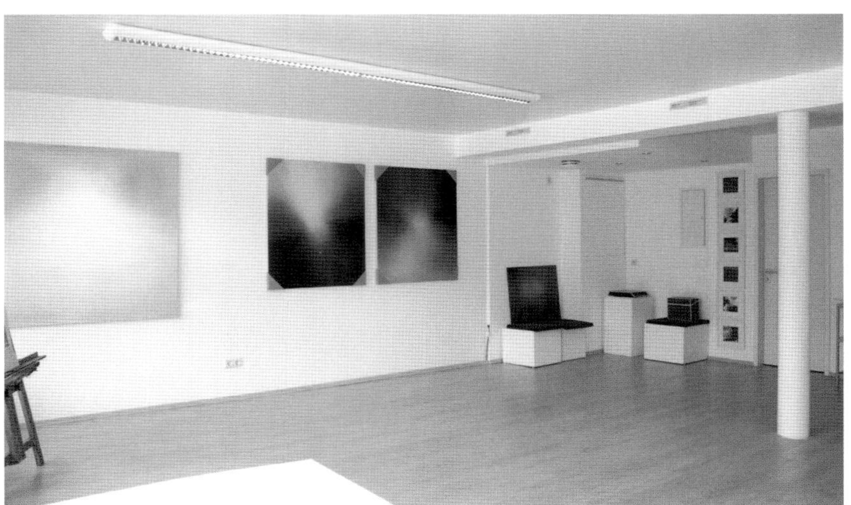

Studio in Munich
Atelier in München

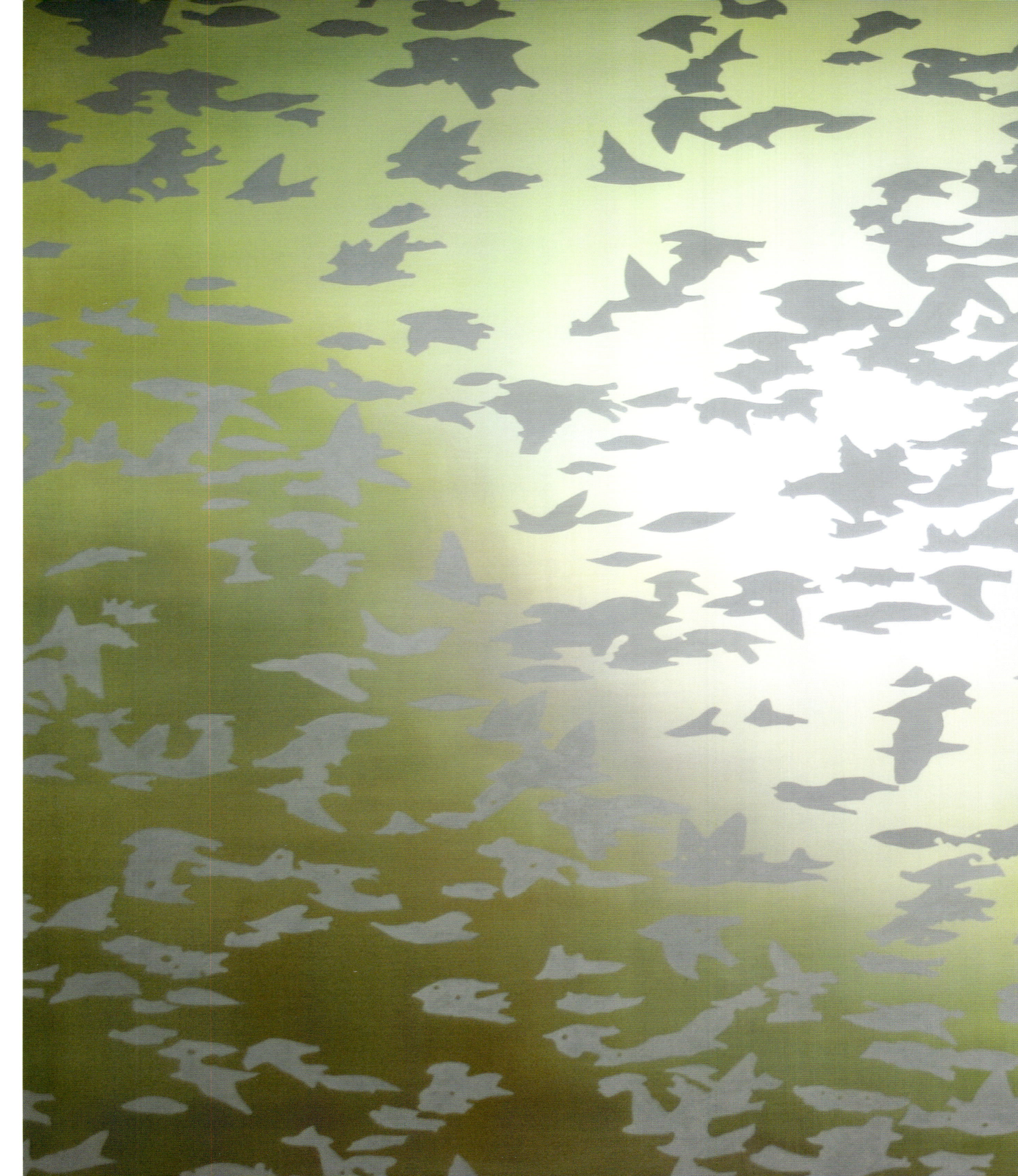

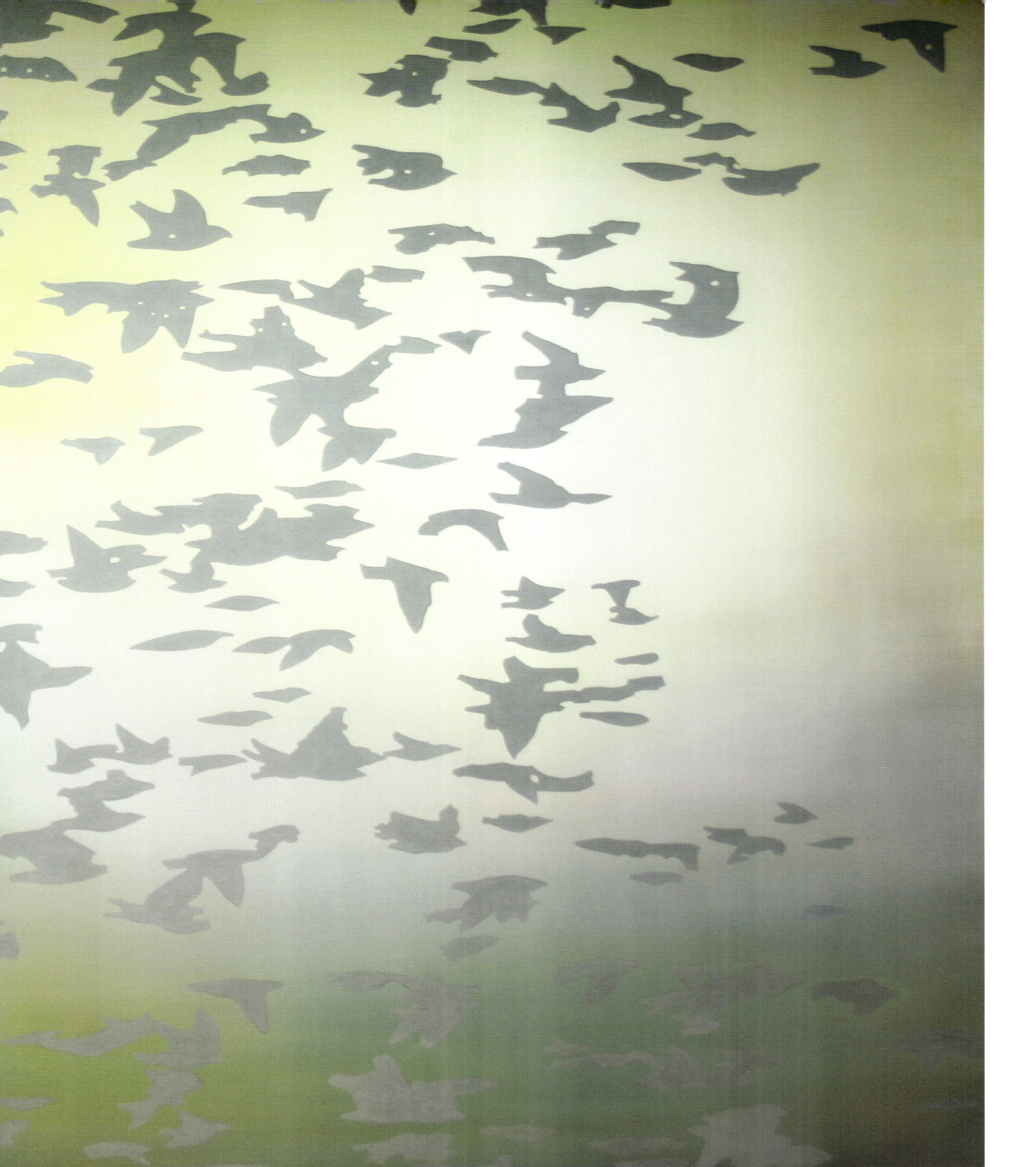

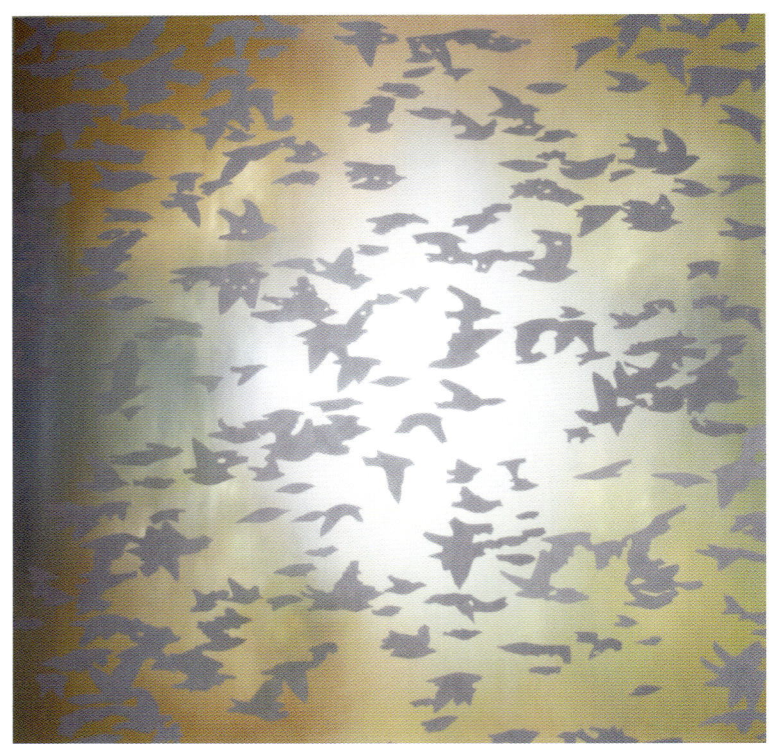

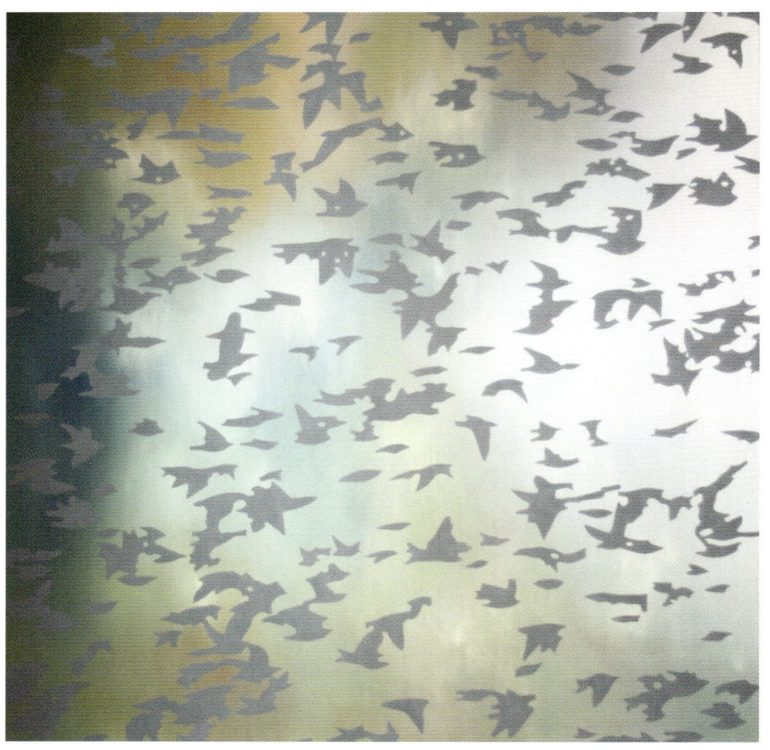

Previous double-page spread / vorherige Doppelseite
28 *Without Borders I* / *Ohne Grenzen I*, 2007

29 *Without Borders II* / *Ohne Grenzen II*, 2007
30 *Without Borders III* / *Ohne Grenzen III*, 2007

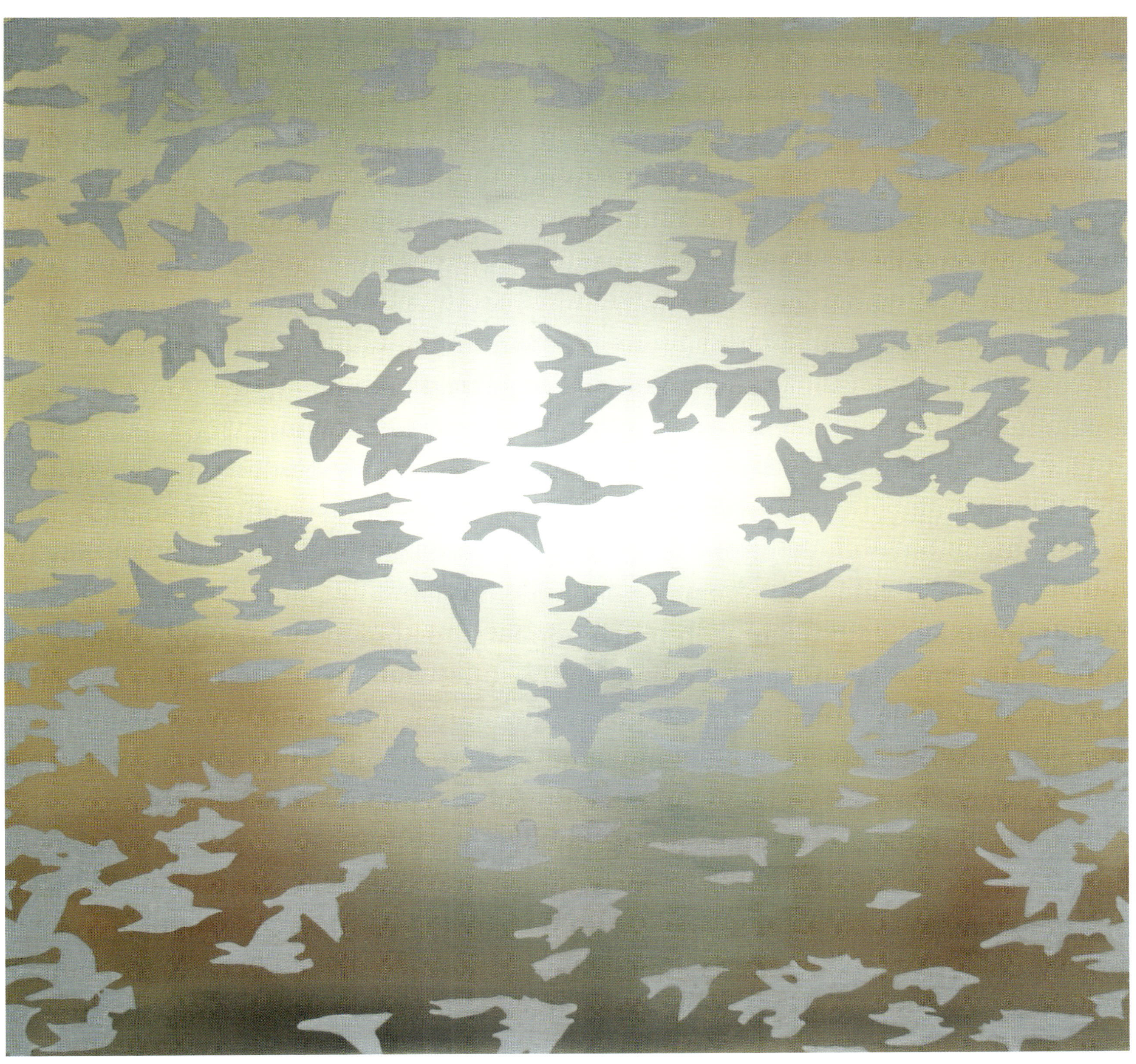

31 *Without Borders IV / Ohne Grenzen IV*, 2007

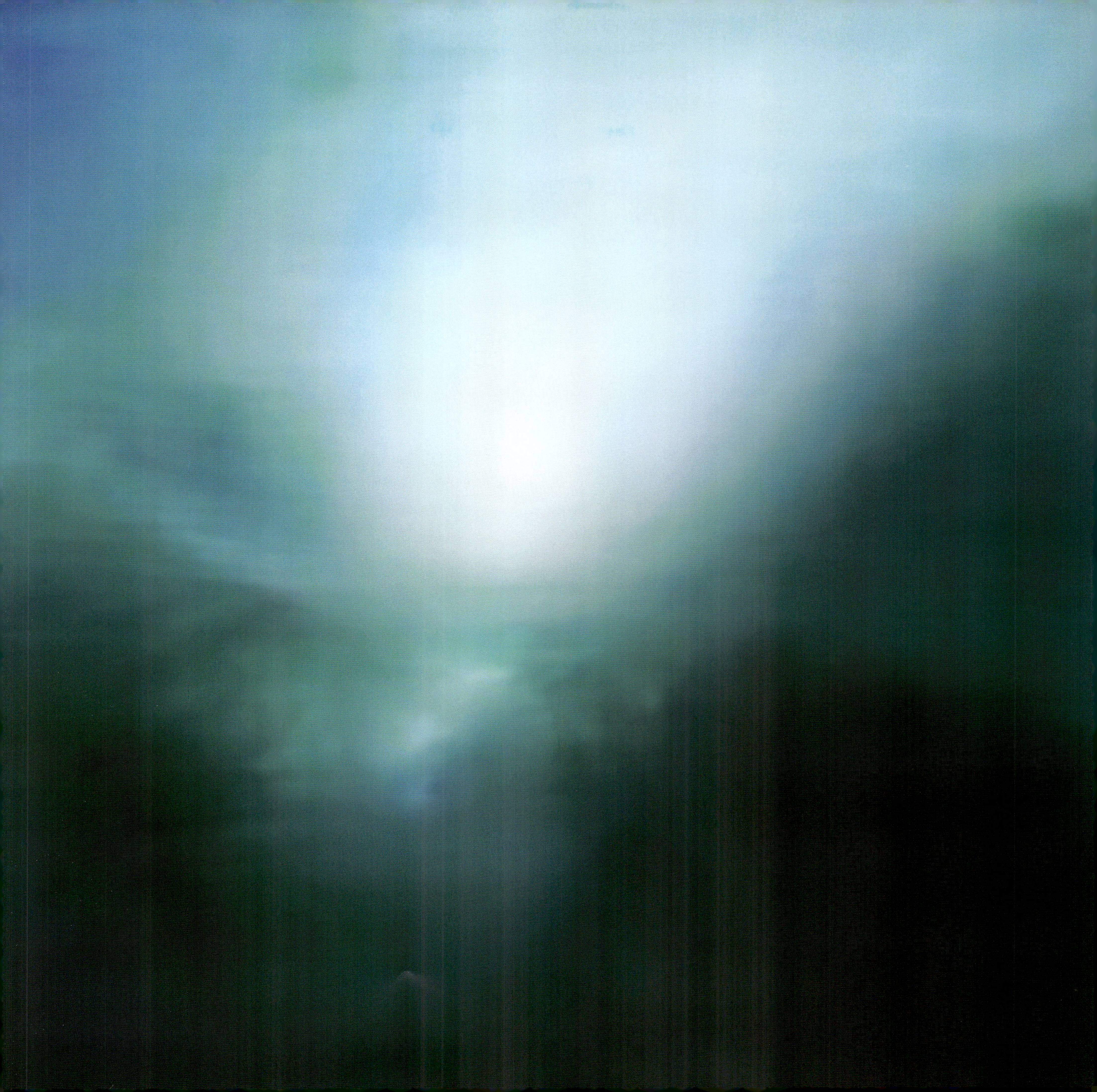

33 *XV-VIII-16*, 2016

34 *XVI-VIII-16*, 2016
35 *XVII-VIII-16*, 2016
36 *XVIII-VIII-16*, 2016
37 *XIX-VIII-16*, 2016

38 *XXVIII-VII-13*, 2013
39 *Sisters / Schwestern*, 2013

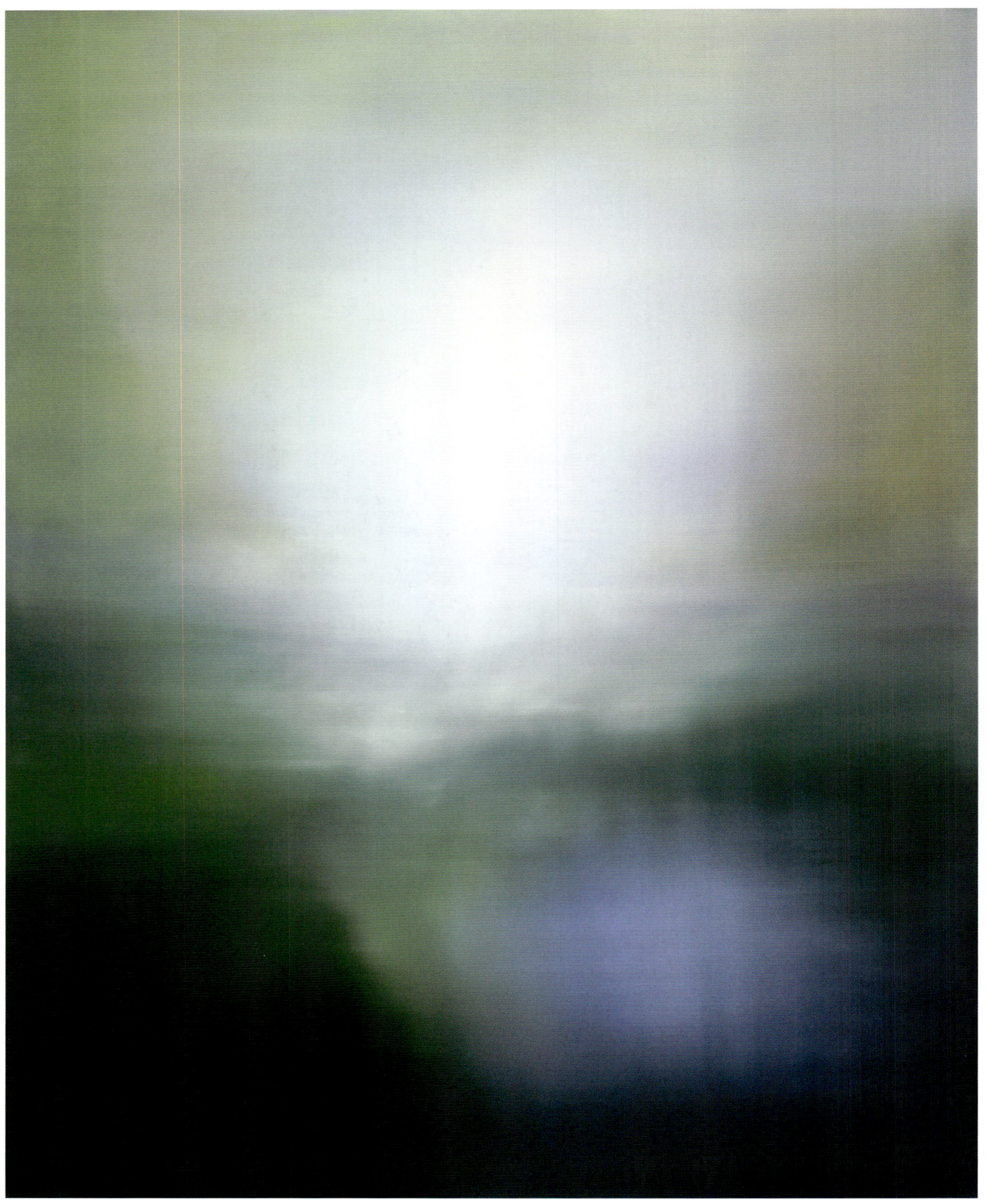

40 *Swiss Impressions II* / *Schweizer Impressionen II*, XXI-I-11, 2011

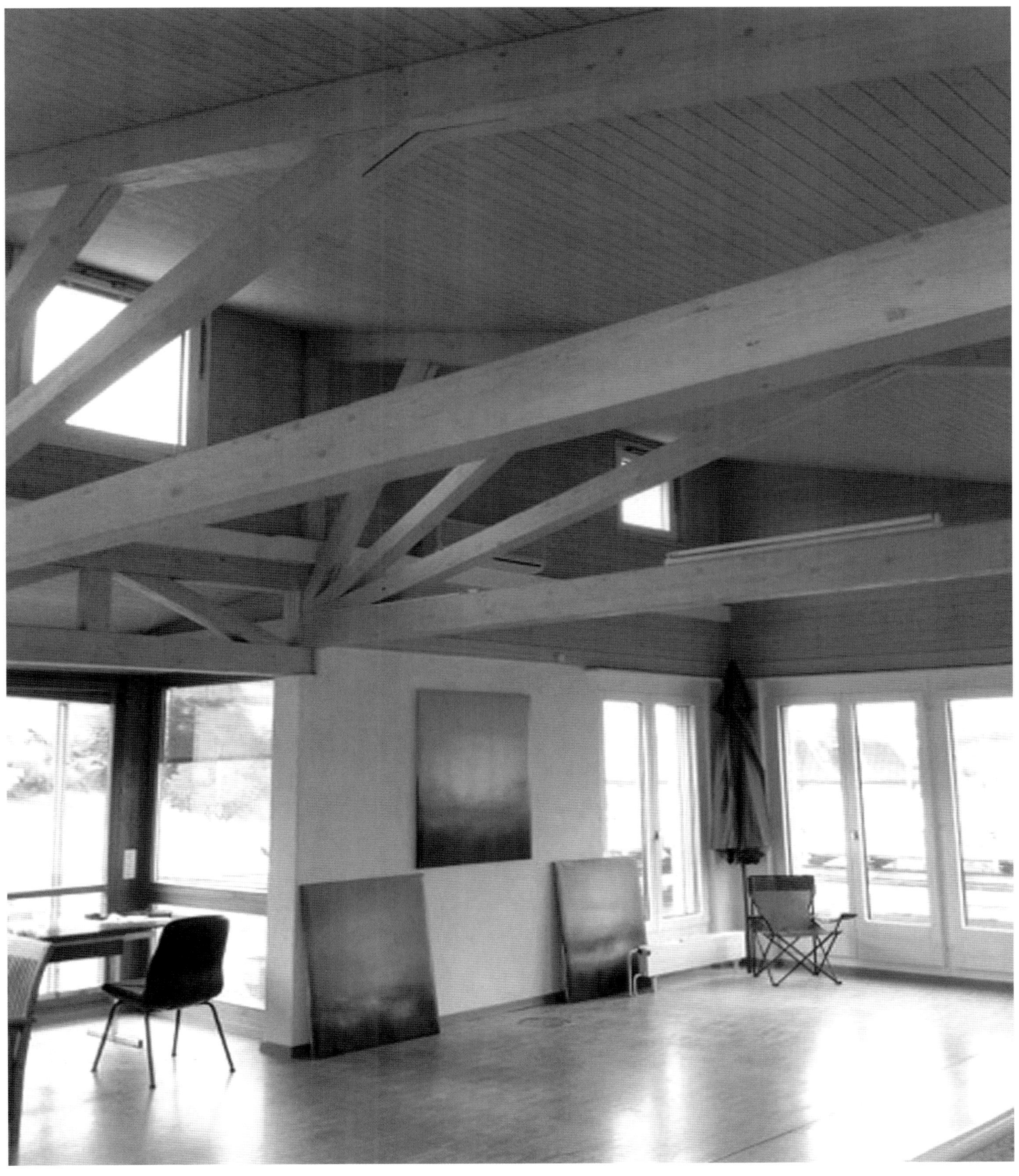

Studio in Switzerland
Atelier in der Schweiz

41 *XX-VII-03*, 2003

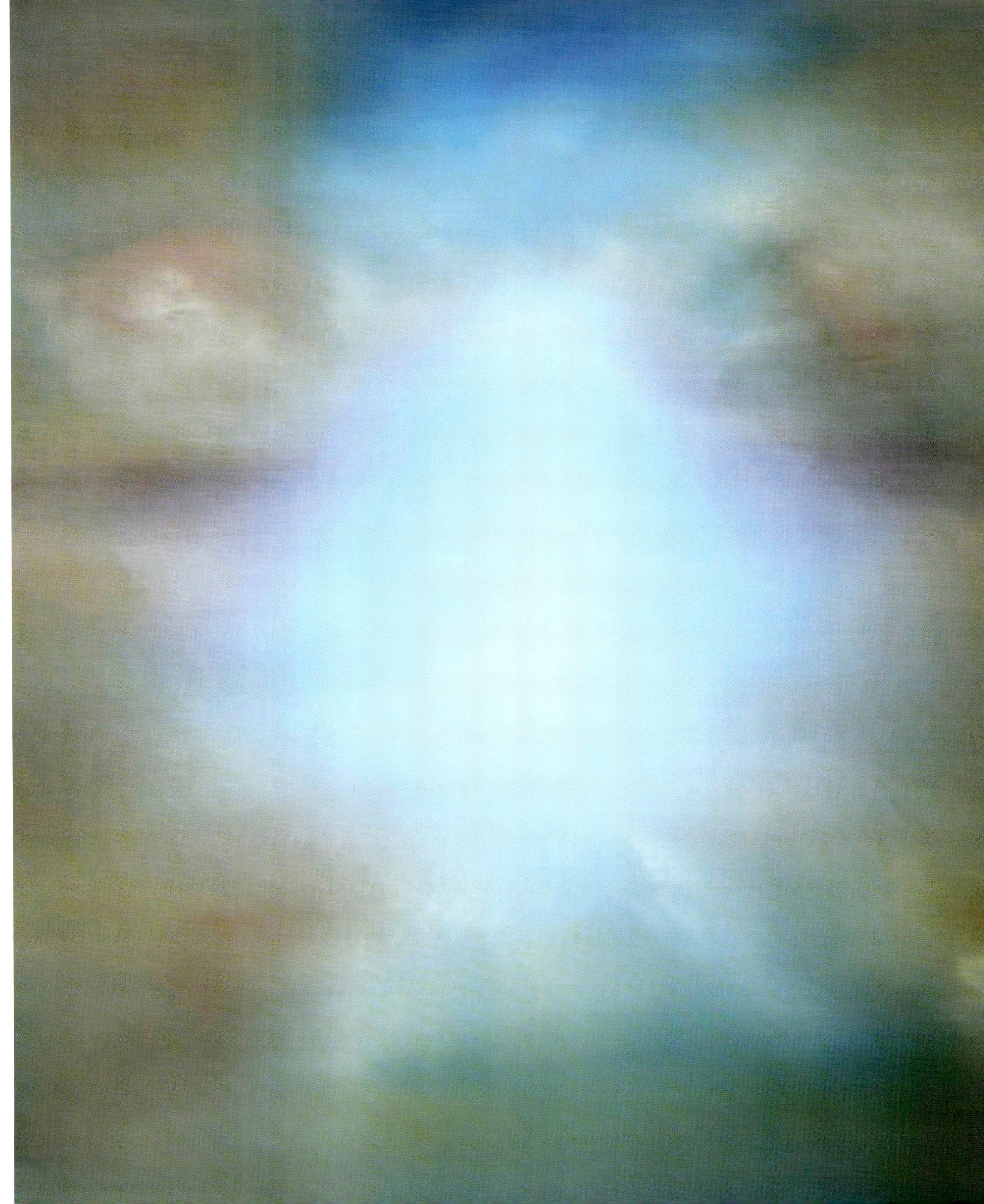

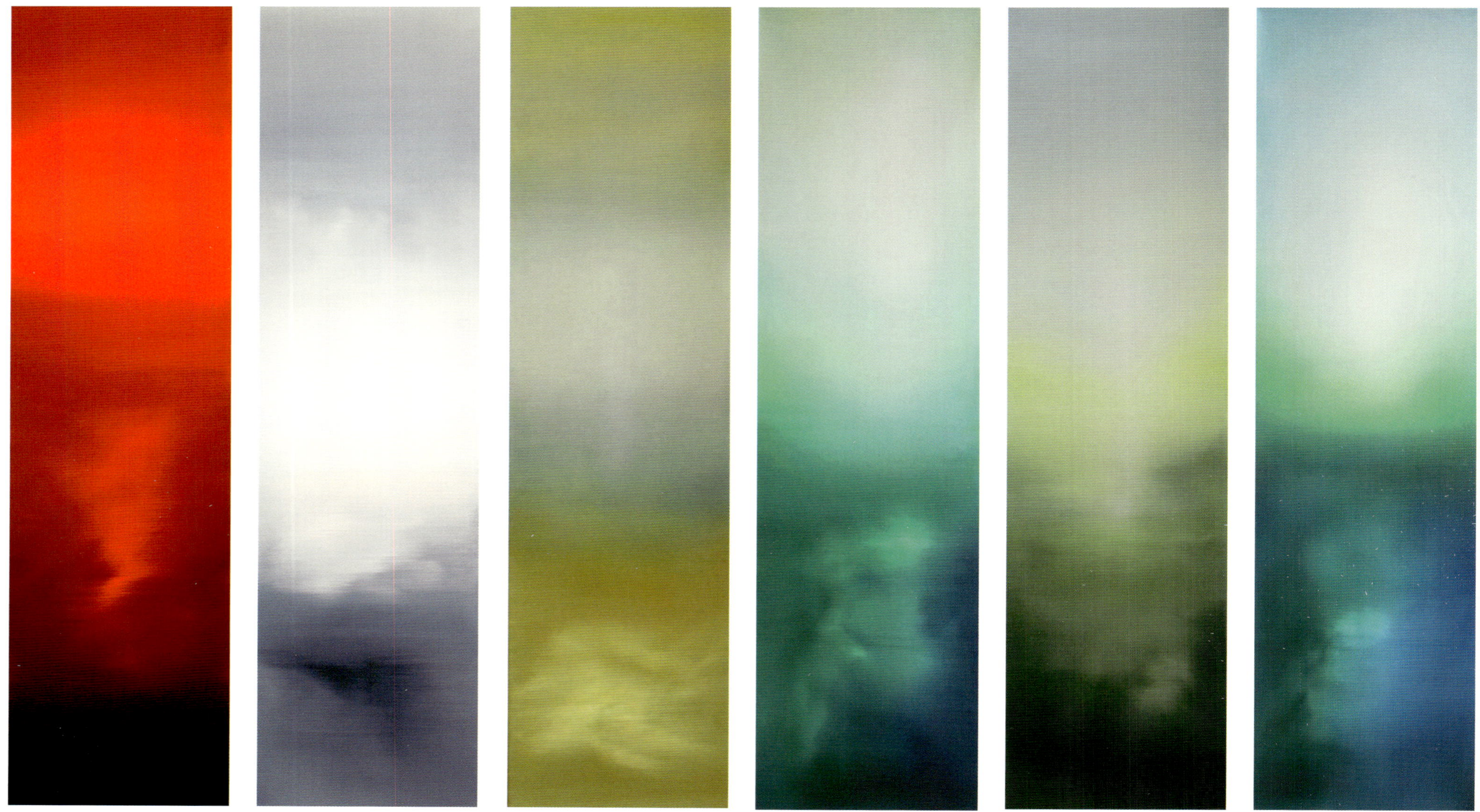

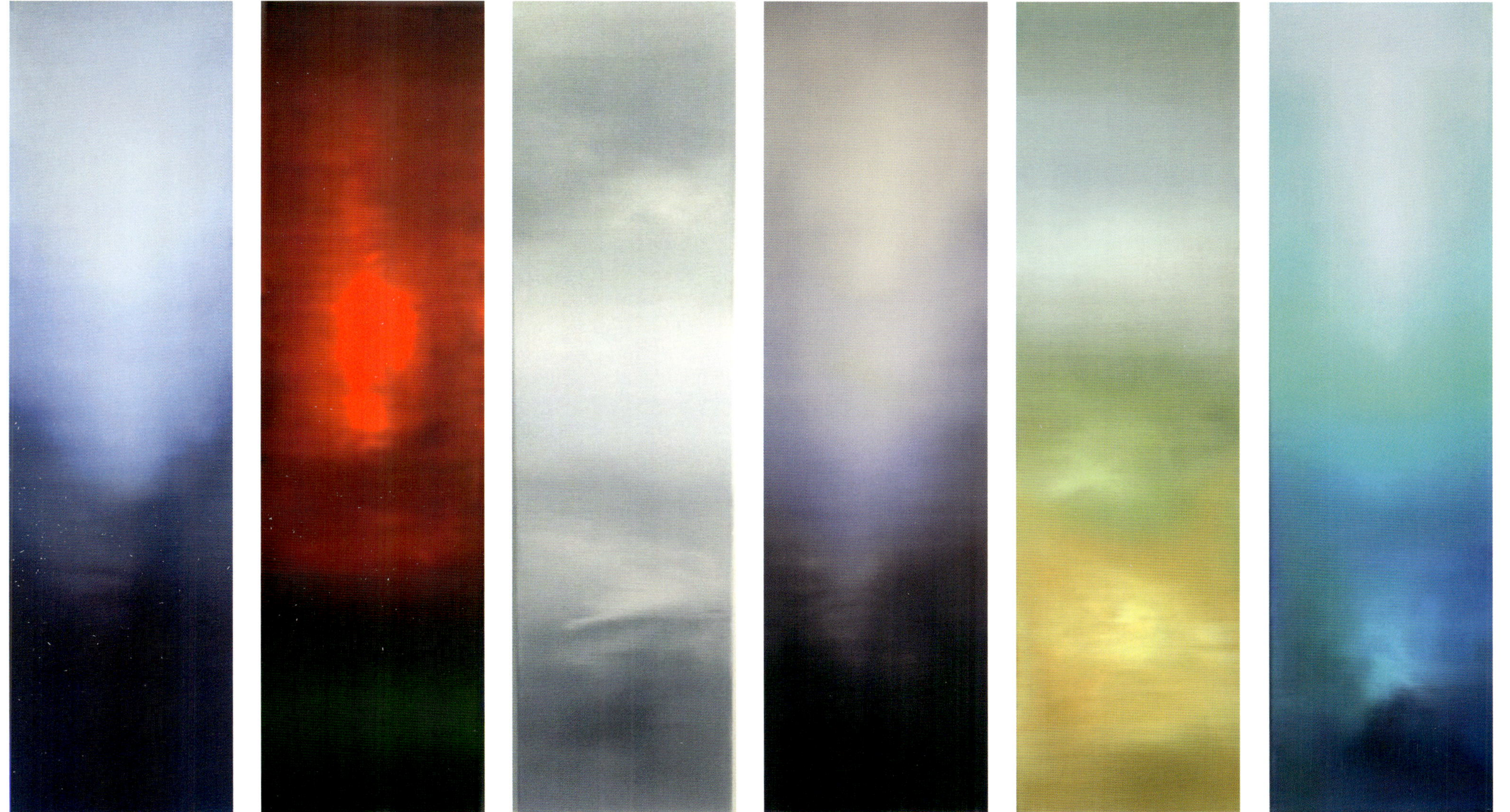

42 *Colour Pianoforte / Farbenklavier*, 2010–2015

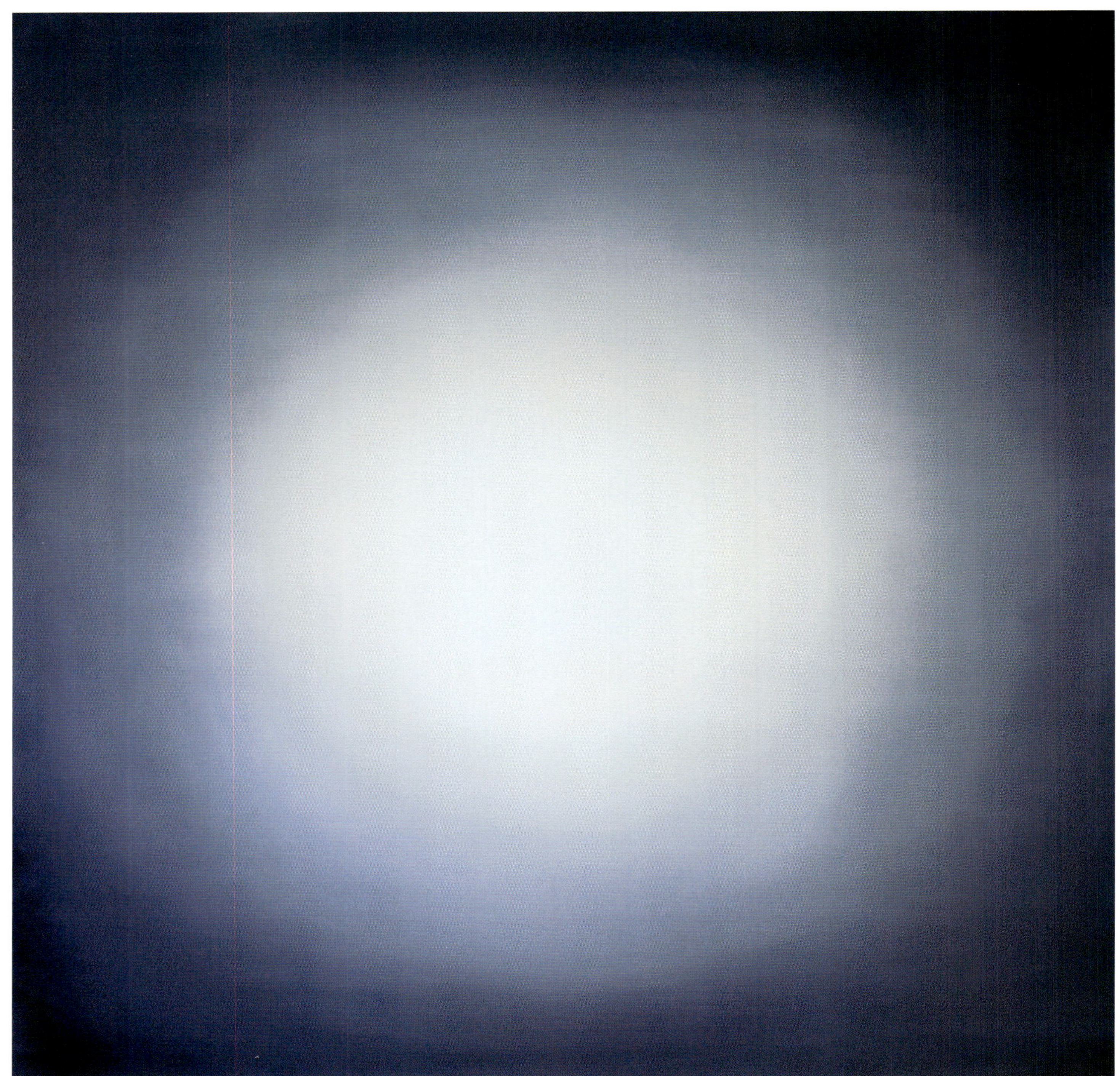

43 *Light I / Licht I*, 2014

44 *Blue / Blau*, 2014

45 *Poetry of Light V / Poesie des Lichts V*, 2015

46 *Poetry of Light VI* / *Poesie des Lichts VI*, 2015

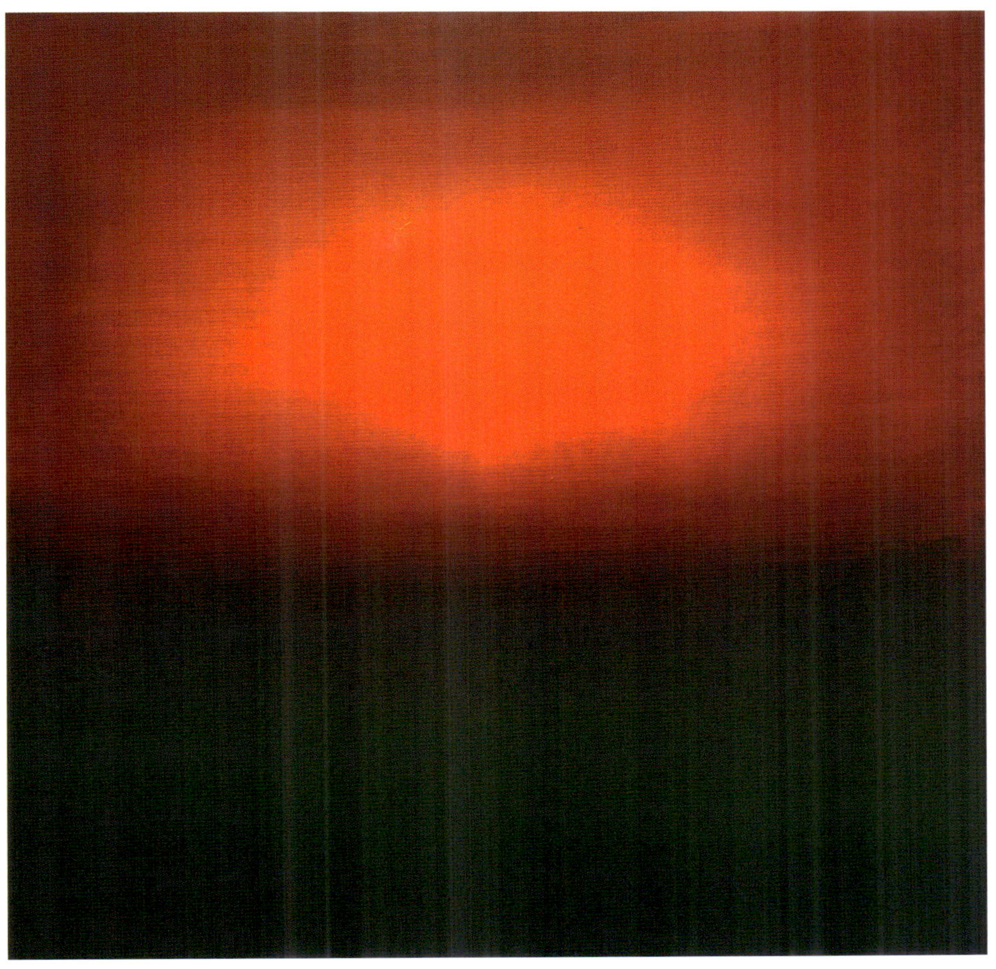

47 *Poetry of Light VII* / *Poesie des Lichts VII*, 2015
48 *XXVI-IV-10*, 2010

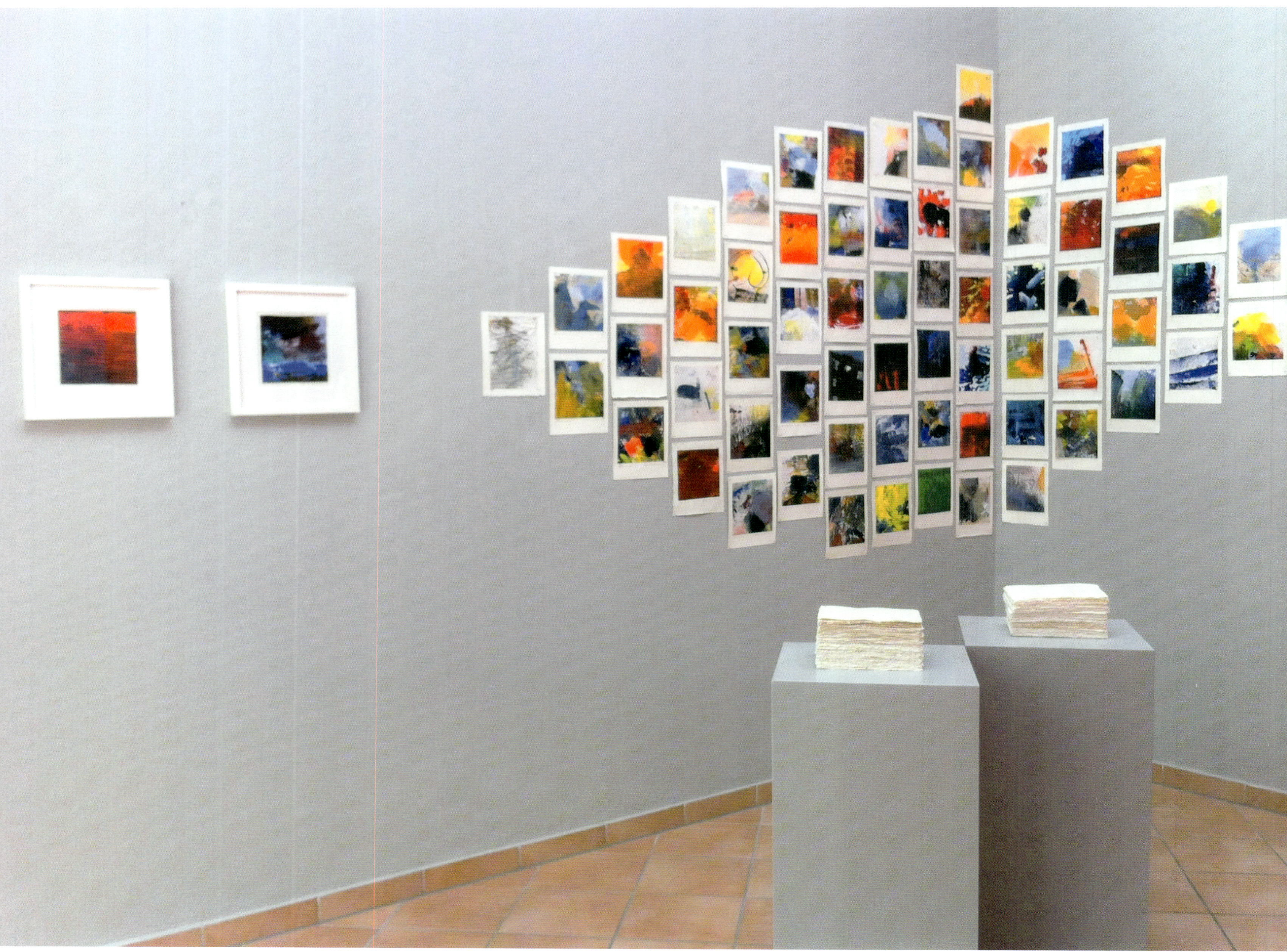

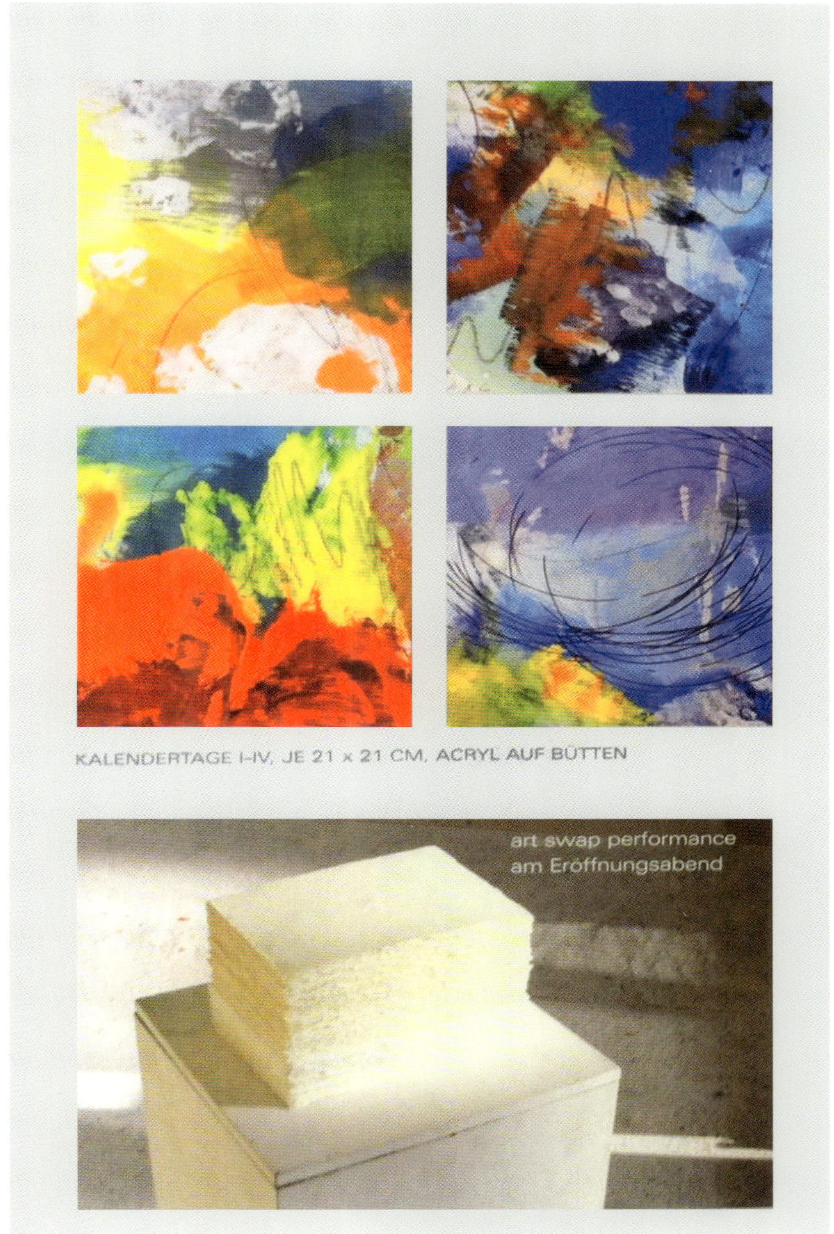

KALENDERTAGE I–IV, JE 21 × 21 CM, ACRYL AUF BÜTTEN

Art Swap Performance in Basel and Dresden
Art Swap Performance in Basel und Dresden

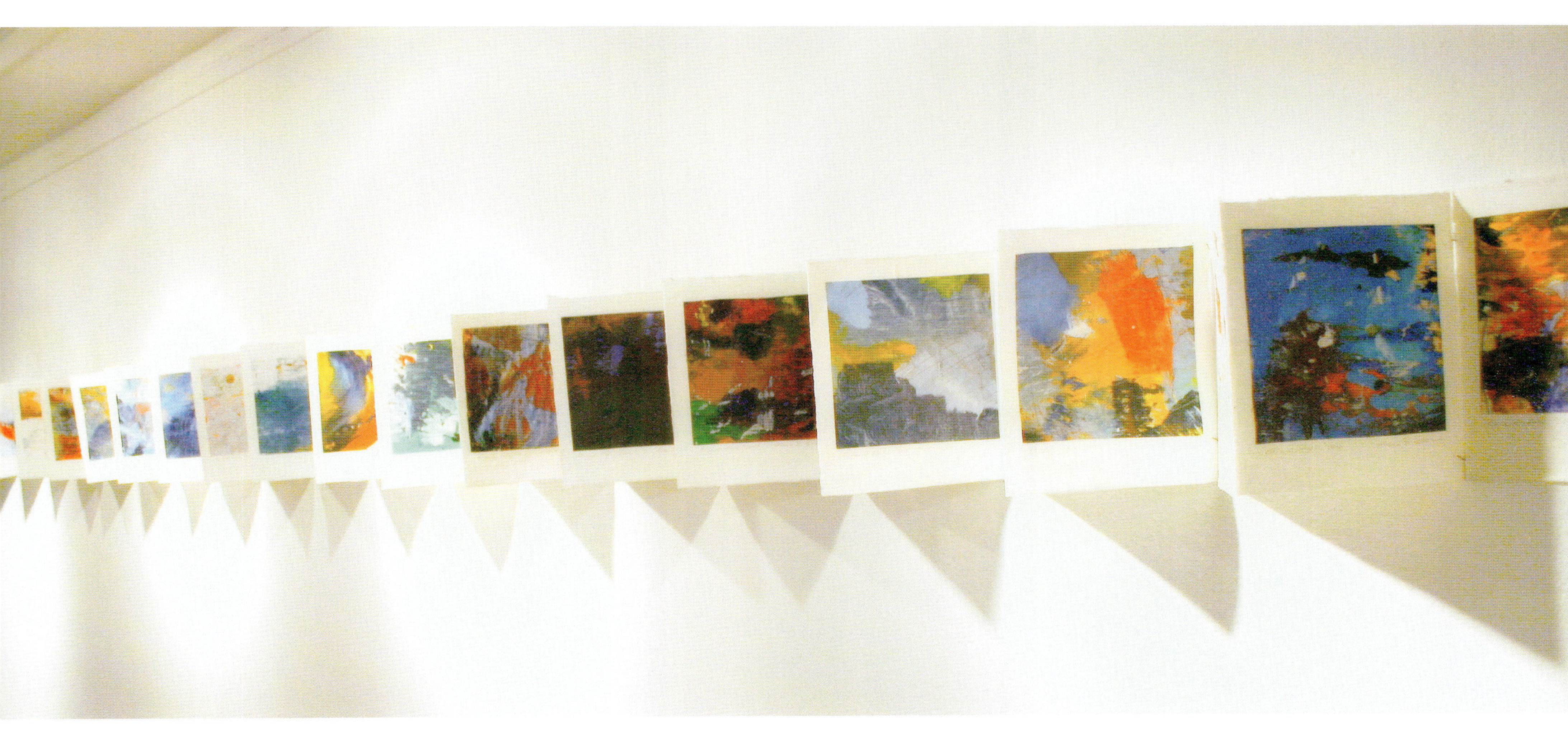

49 *VIII-II-10*, 2010
50 *Leporello*

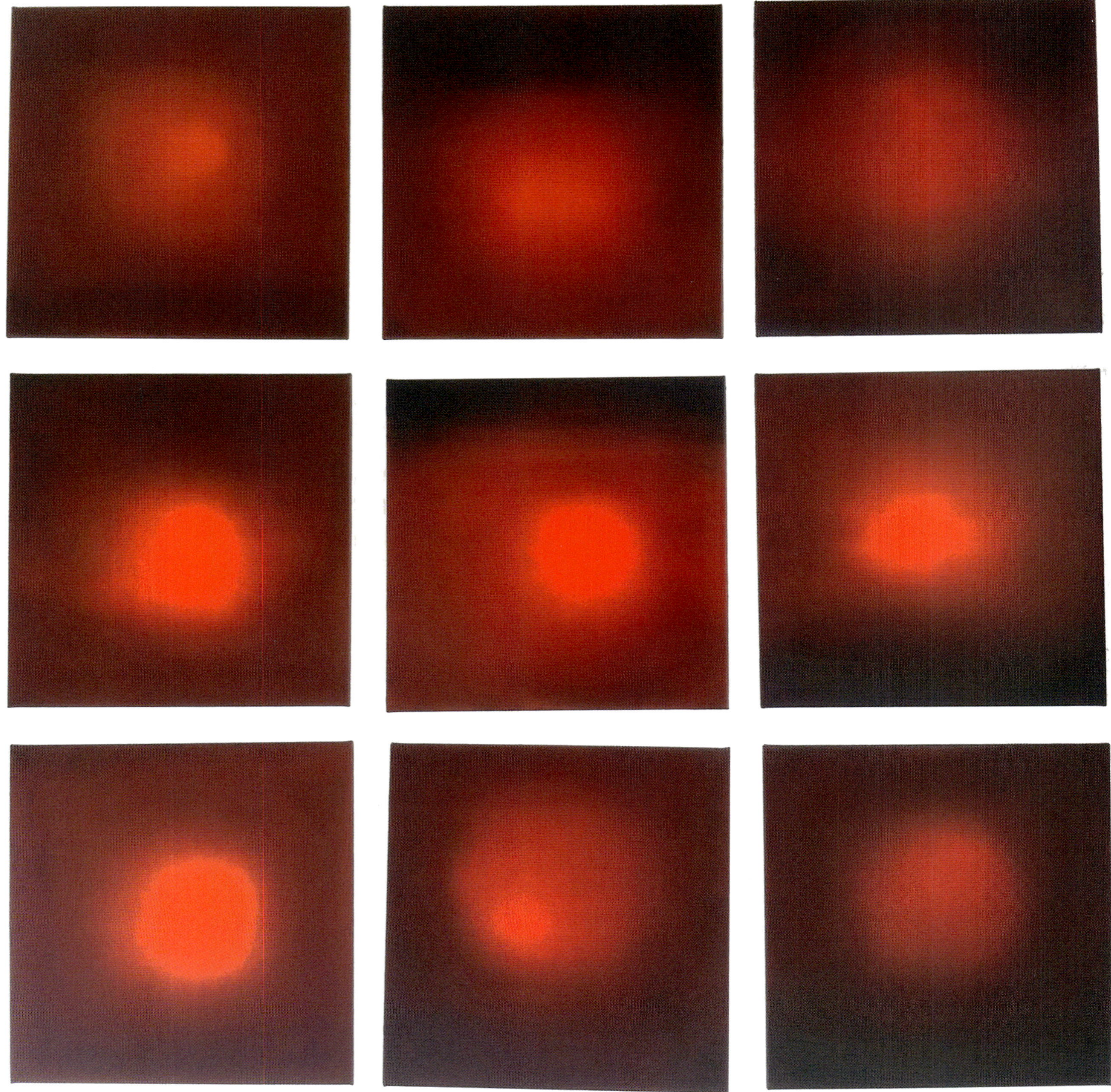

51 *Leonids / Leoniden*, 2013/14

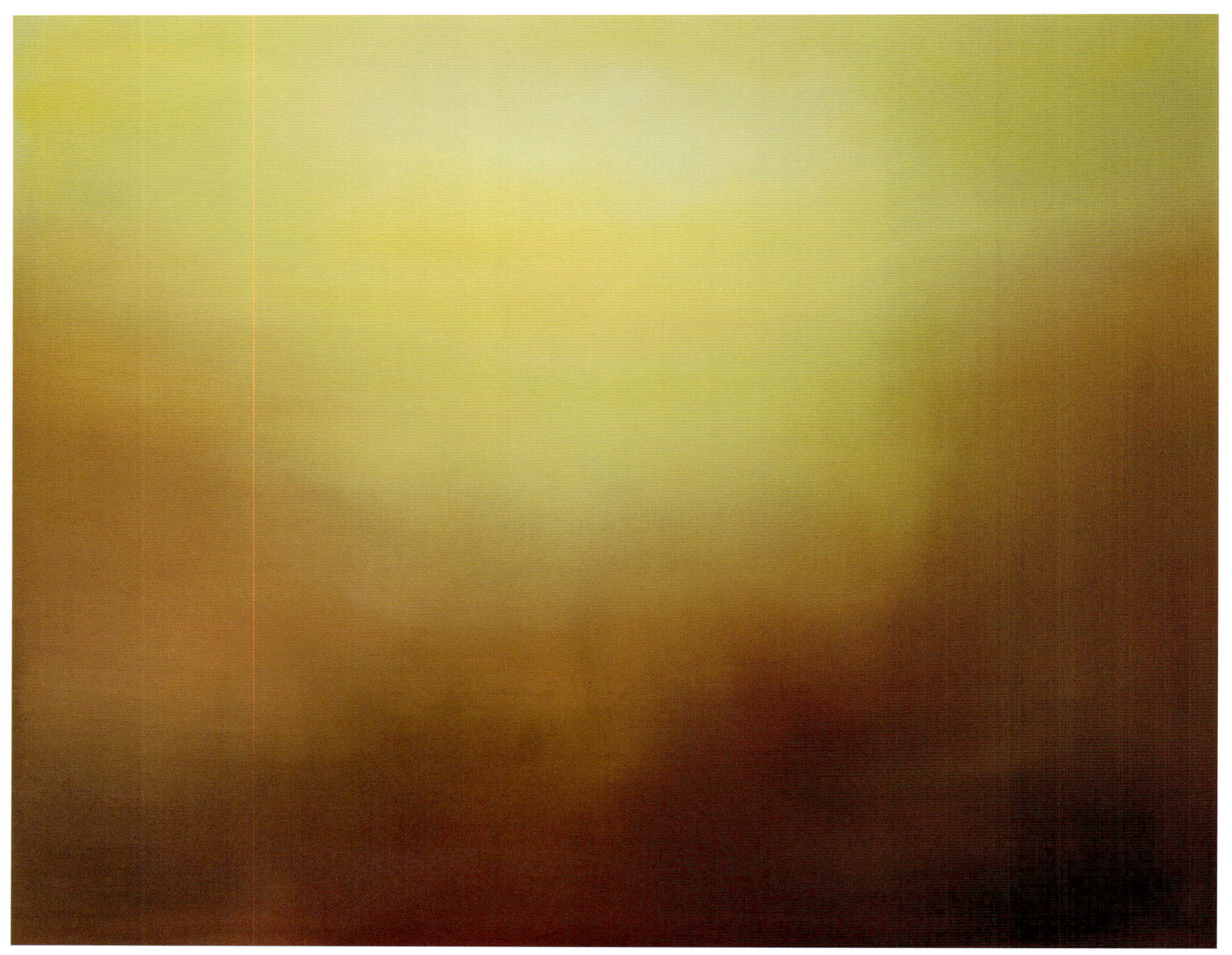

53 *VI-IV-12*, 2012

54 *Spring / Frühling*, 2016

55 *XIX-IV-11*, 2011

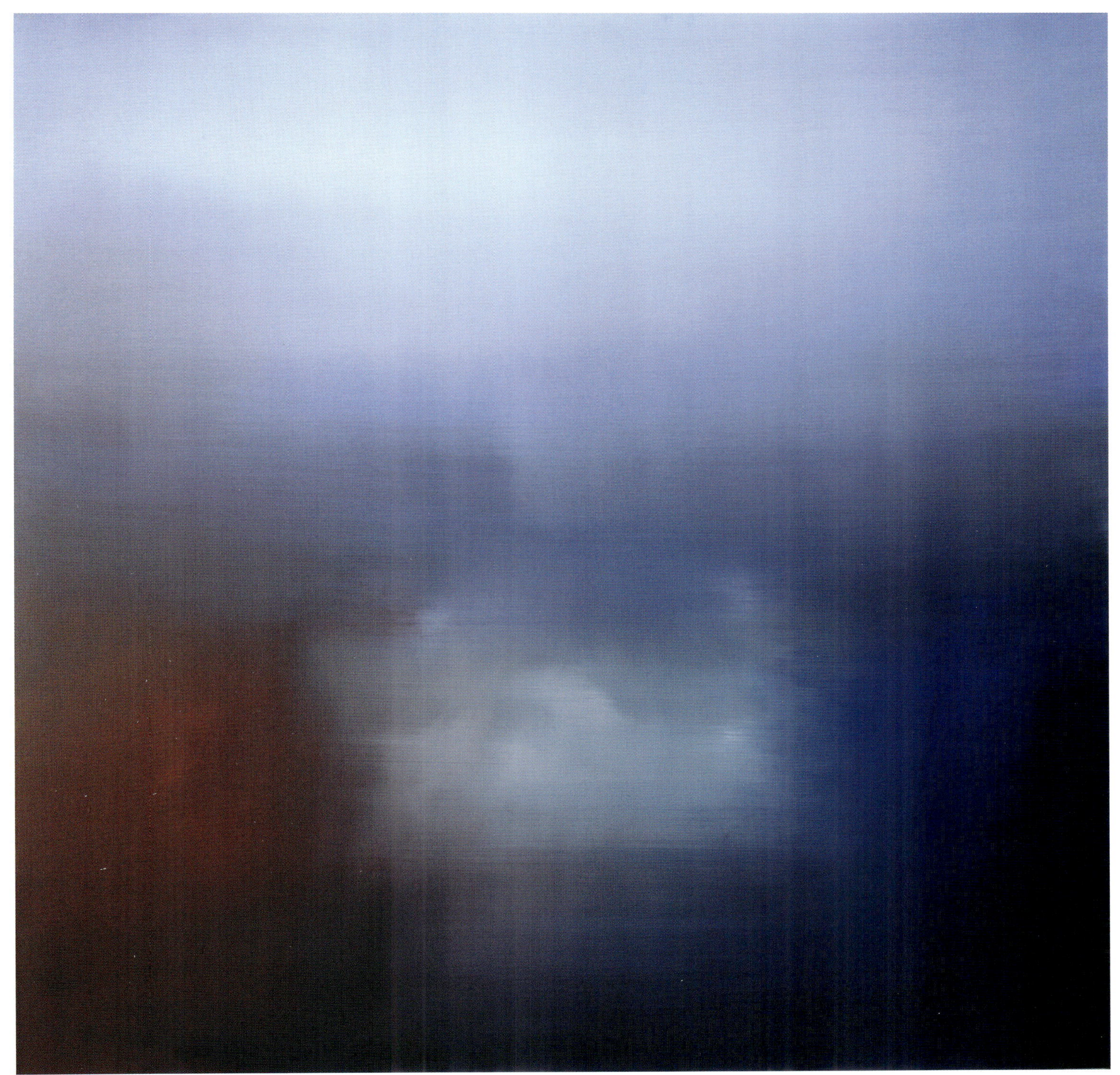

56 *III-V-12*, 2012

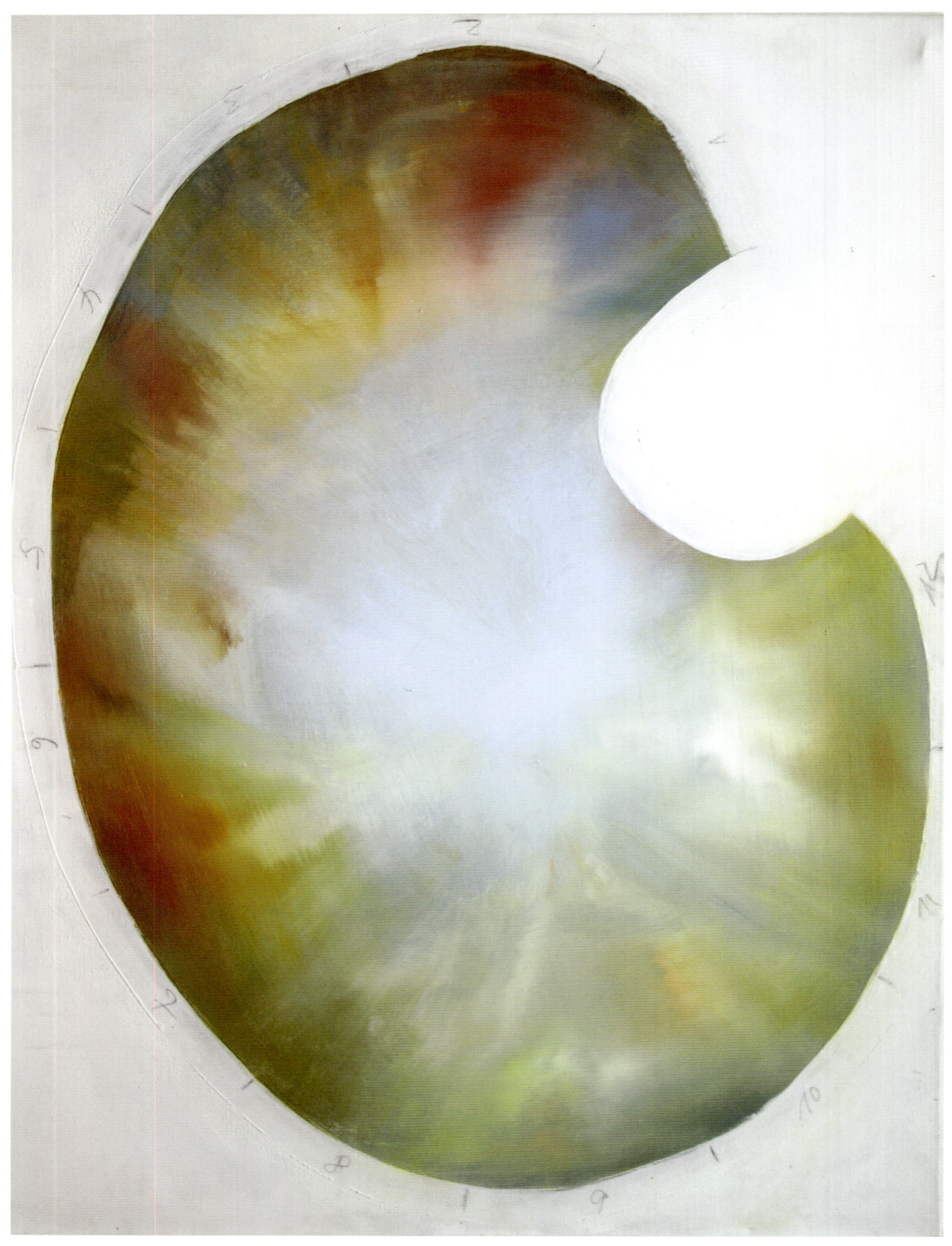

Sketch for a 35 m² ceiling fresco in Munich
Entwurf für ein 35 m² Deckenfresko in München

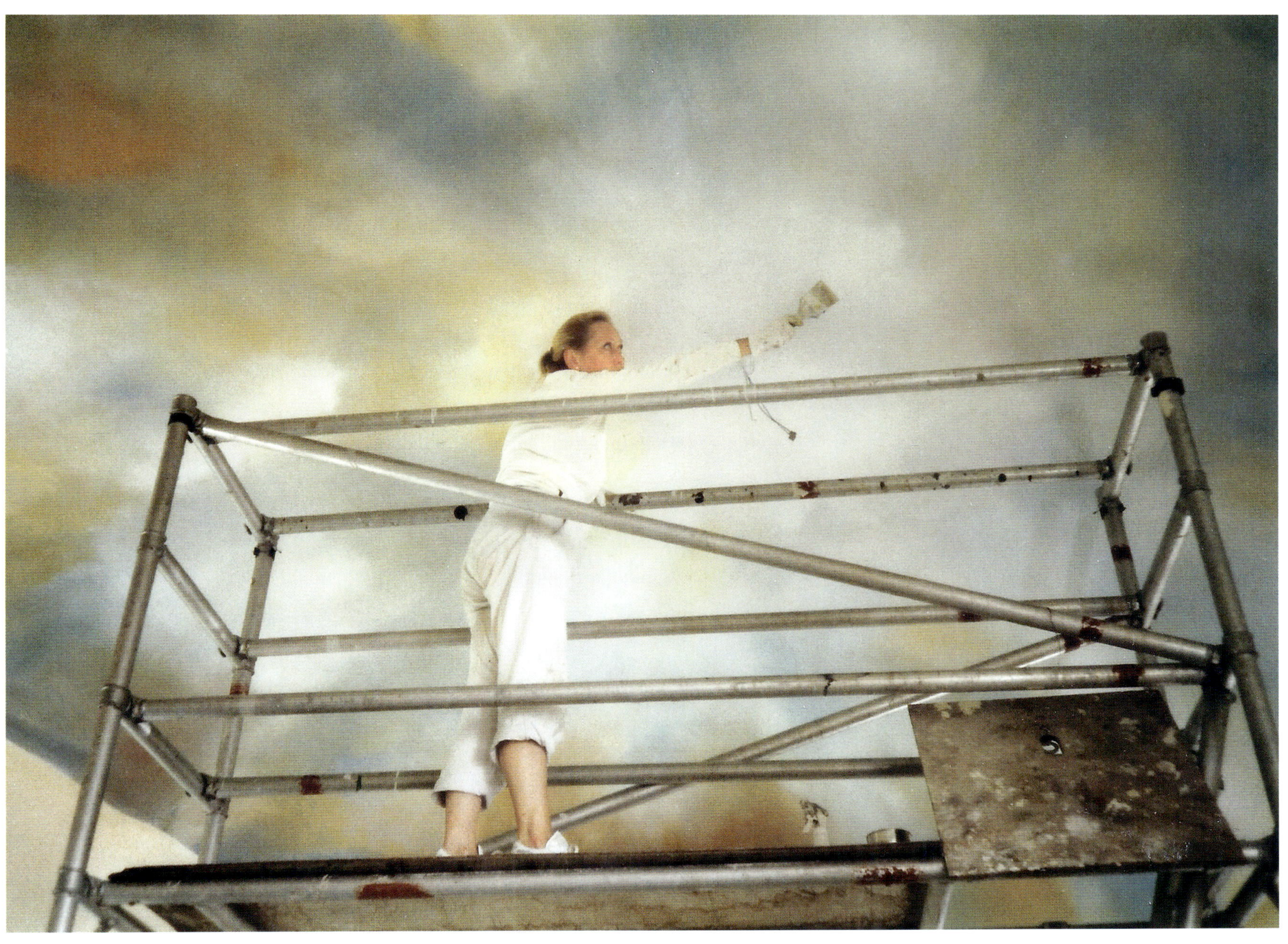

Helene B. Grossmann working on the ceiling fresco in Munich
Helene B. Grossmann am Deckenfresko in München arbeitend

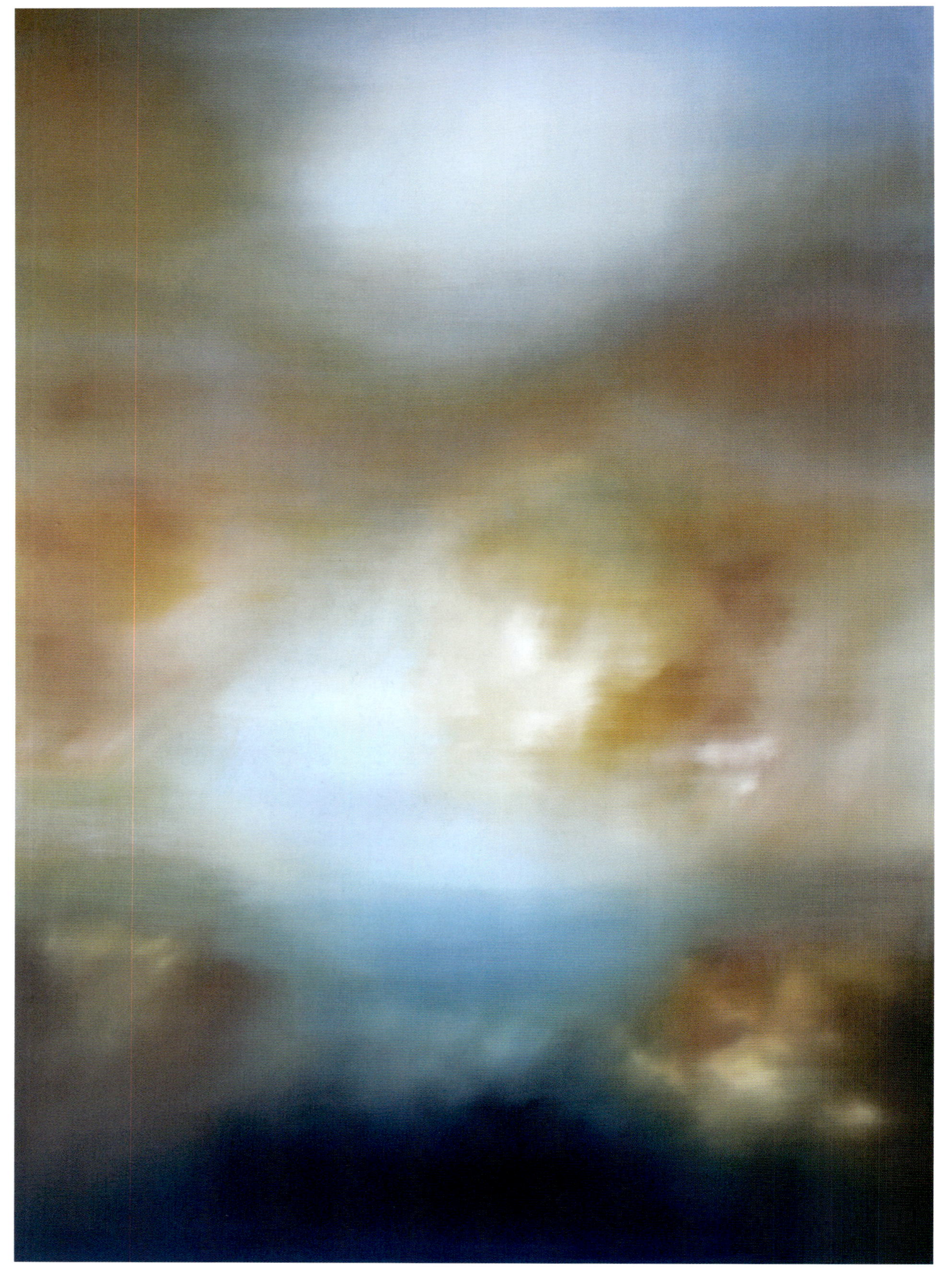

57 *X-X-07*, 2007

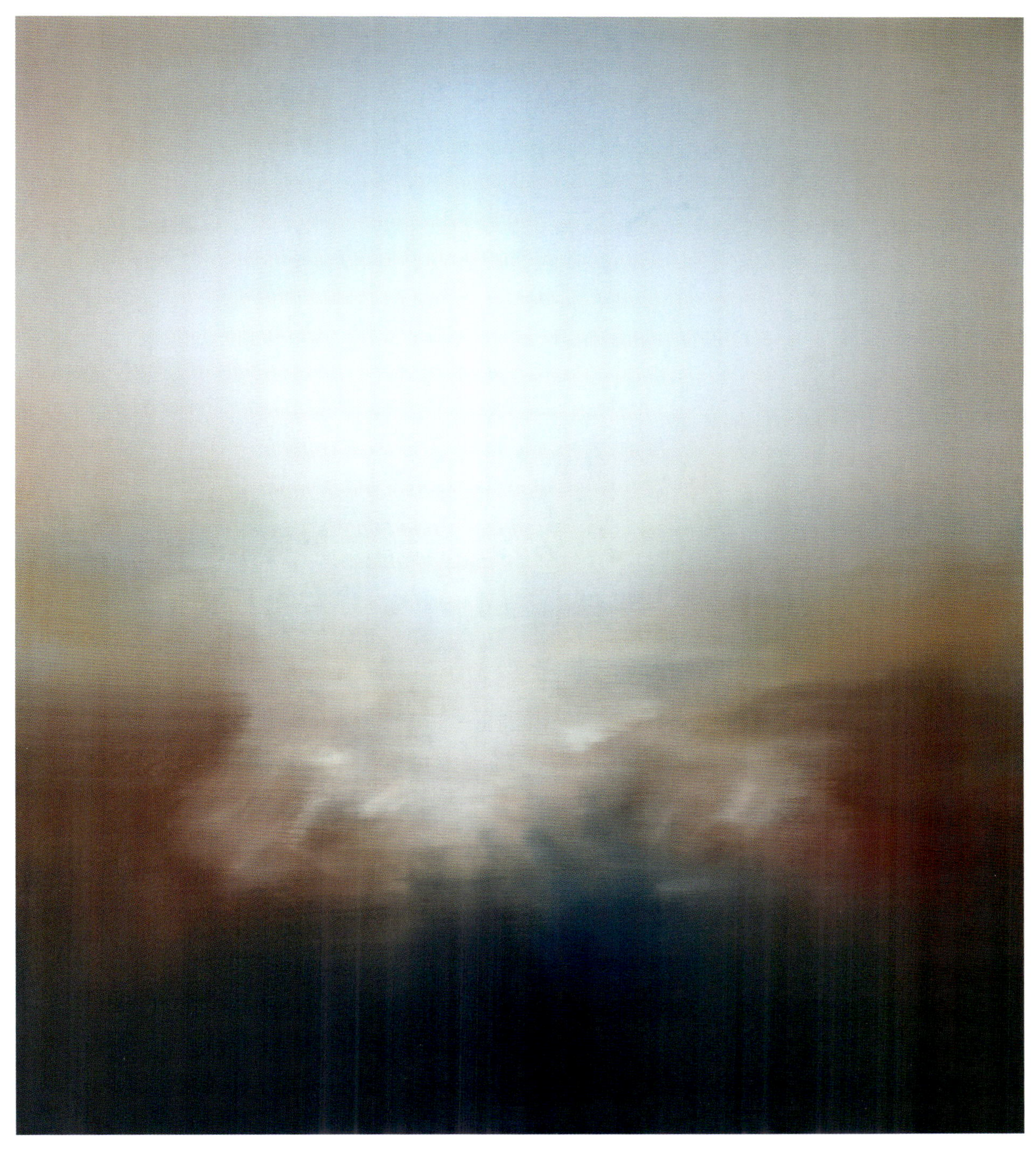

58 *XV-III-06*, 2006

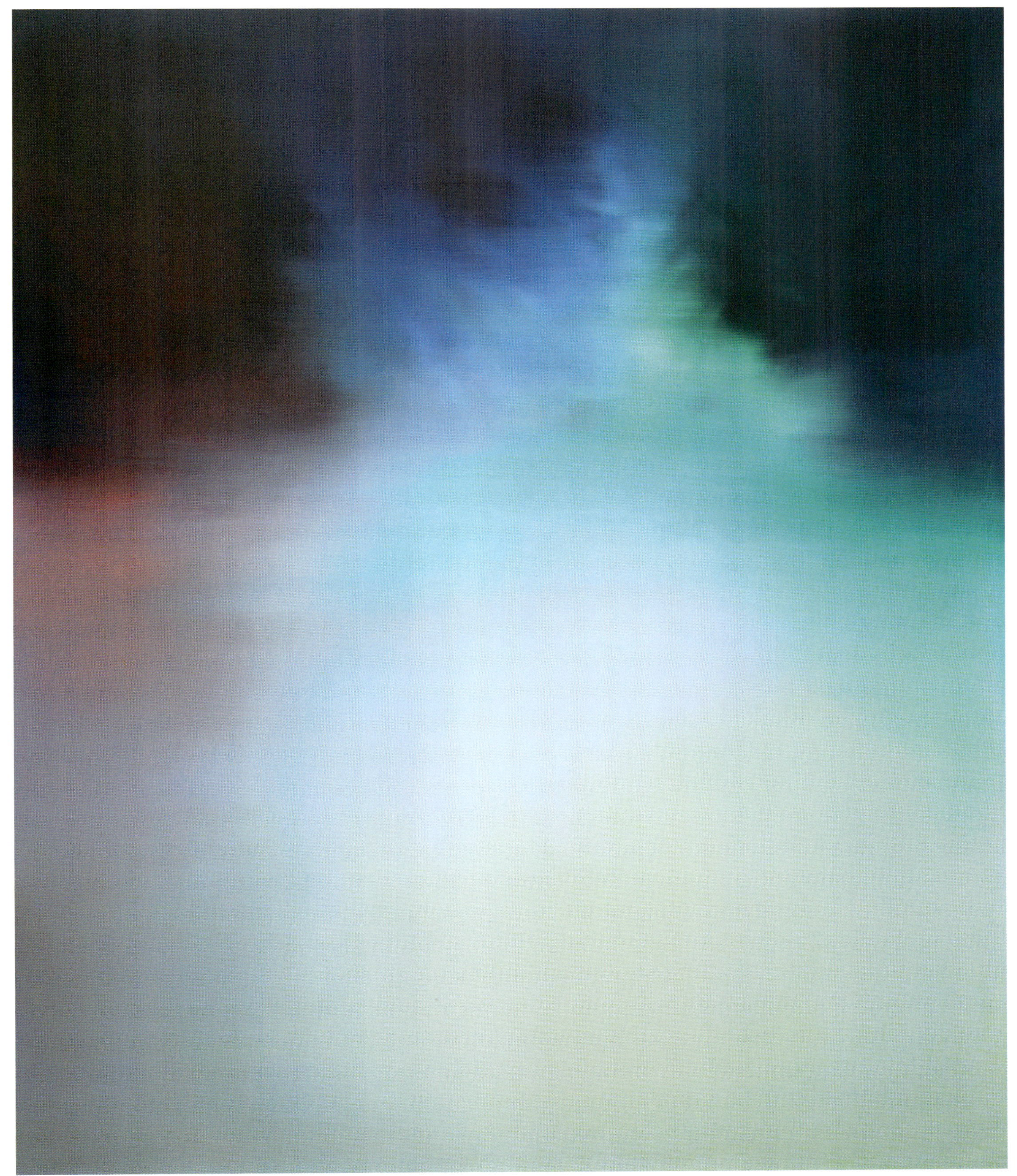

59 *XXIII-VIII-12*, 2012
60 *VII-II-12*, 2012

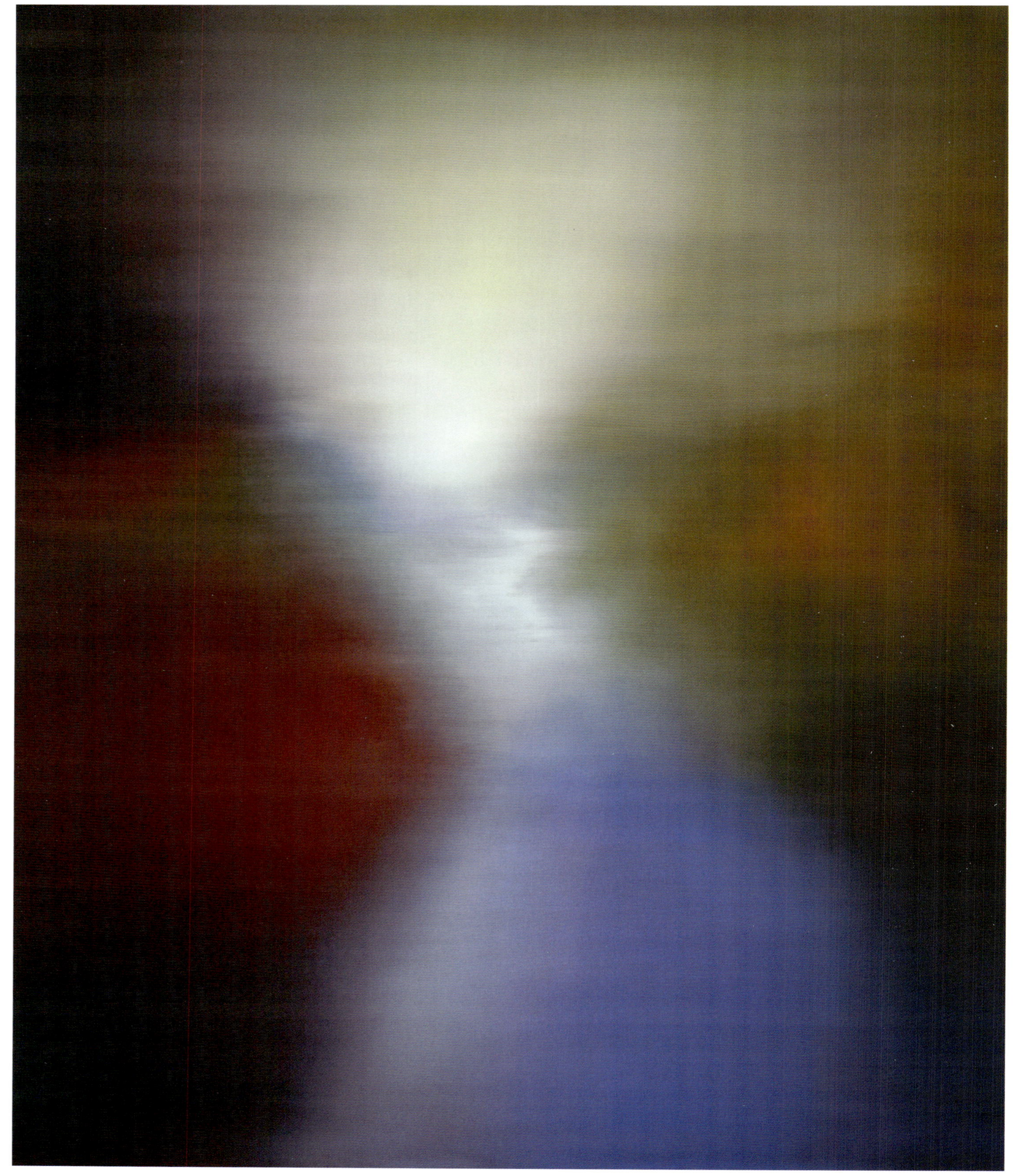

61 *XIV-III-10*, 2010

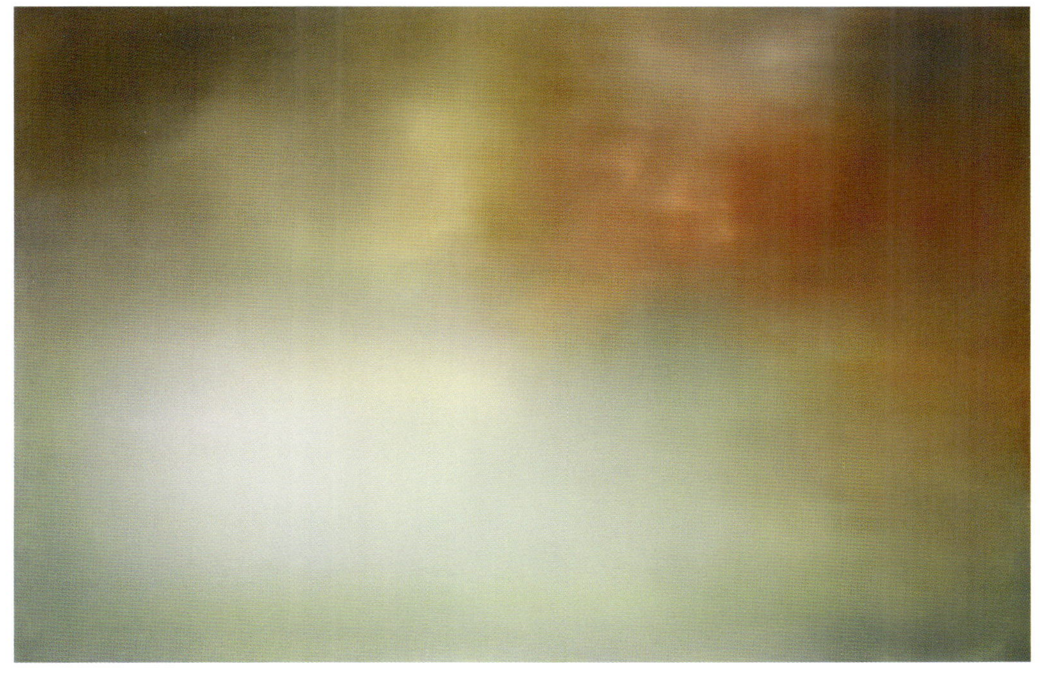

62 *Danae*, 2015

63 *XXIX-I-12*, 2012
64 *XXIV-III-12*, 2012

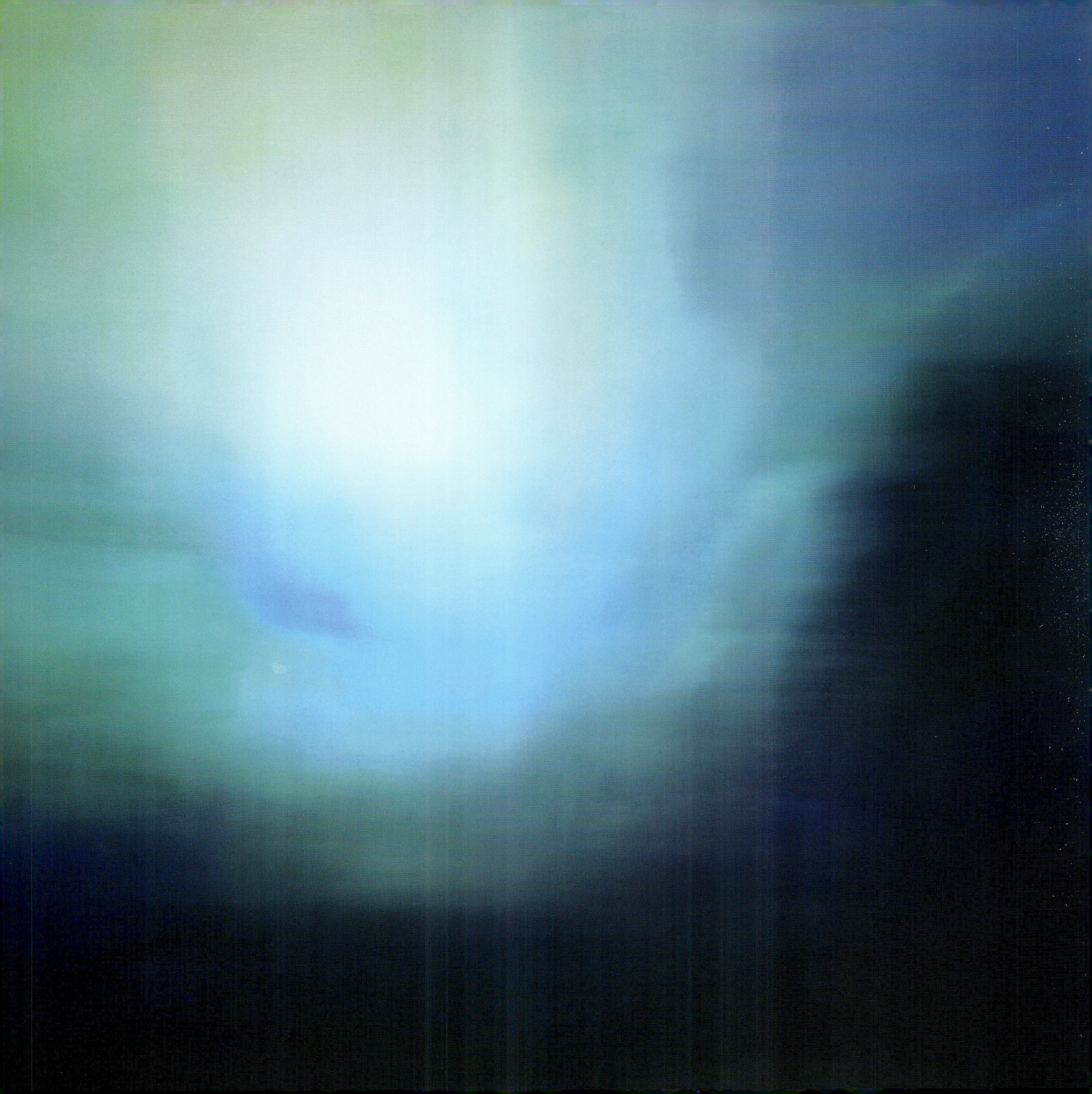

65 *XV-IV-14*, 2014

66 *XVI-IV-14*, 2014

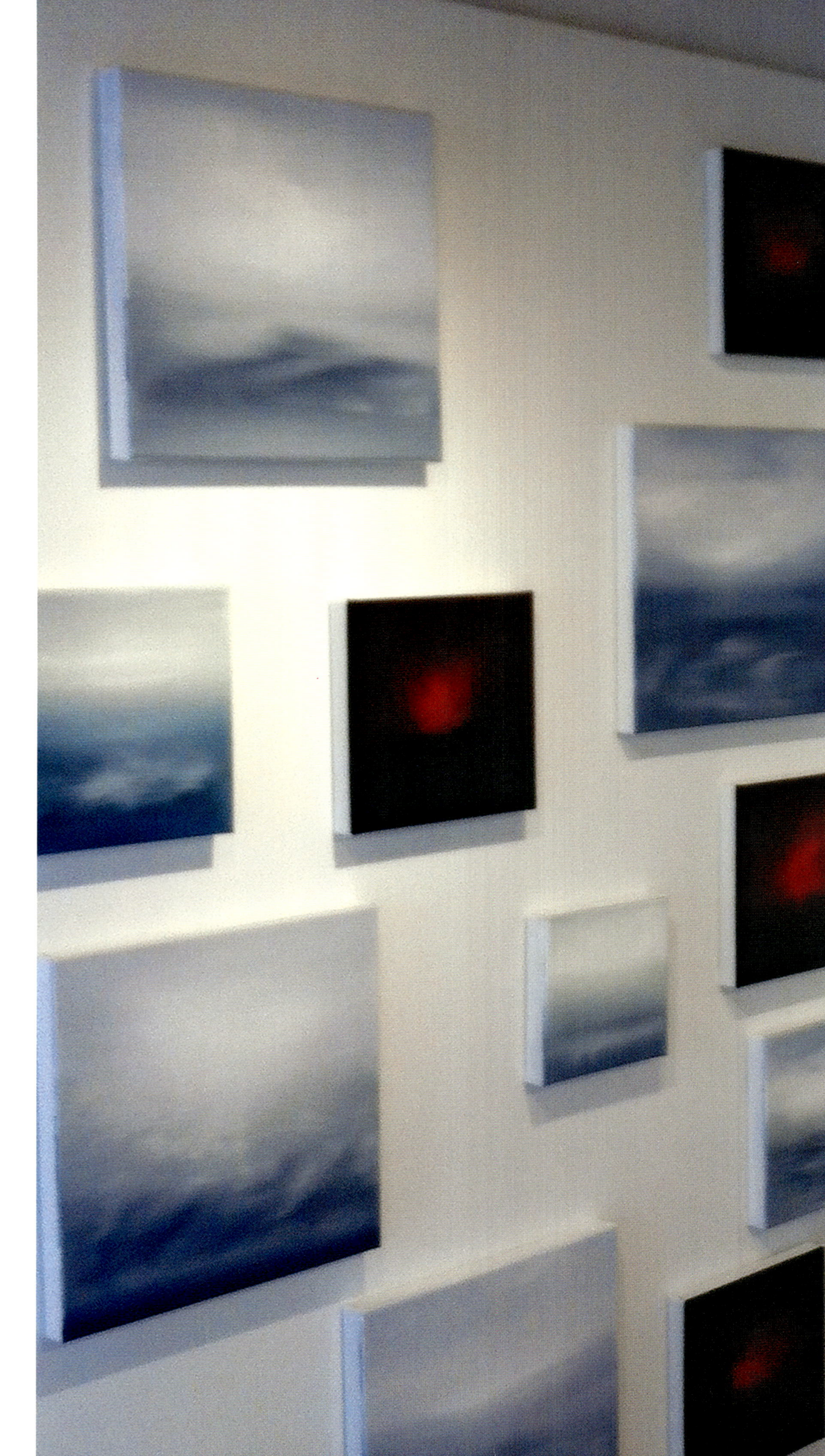

Paperback Installation, 2014
Taschenbuch Installation, 2014

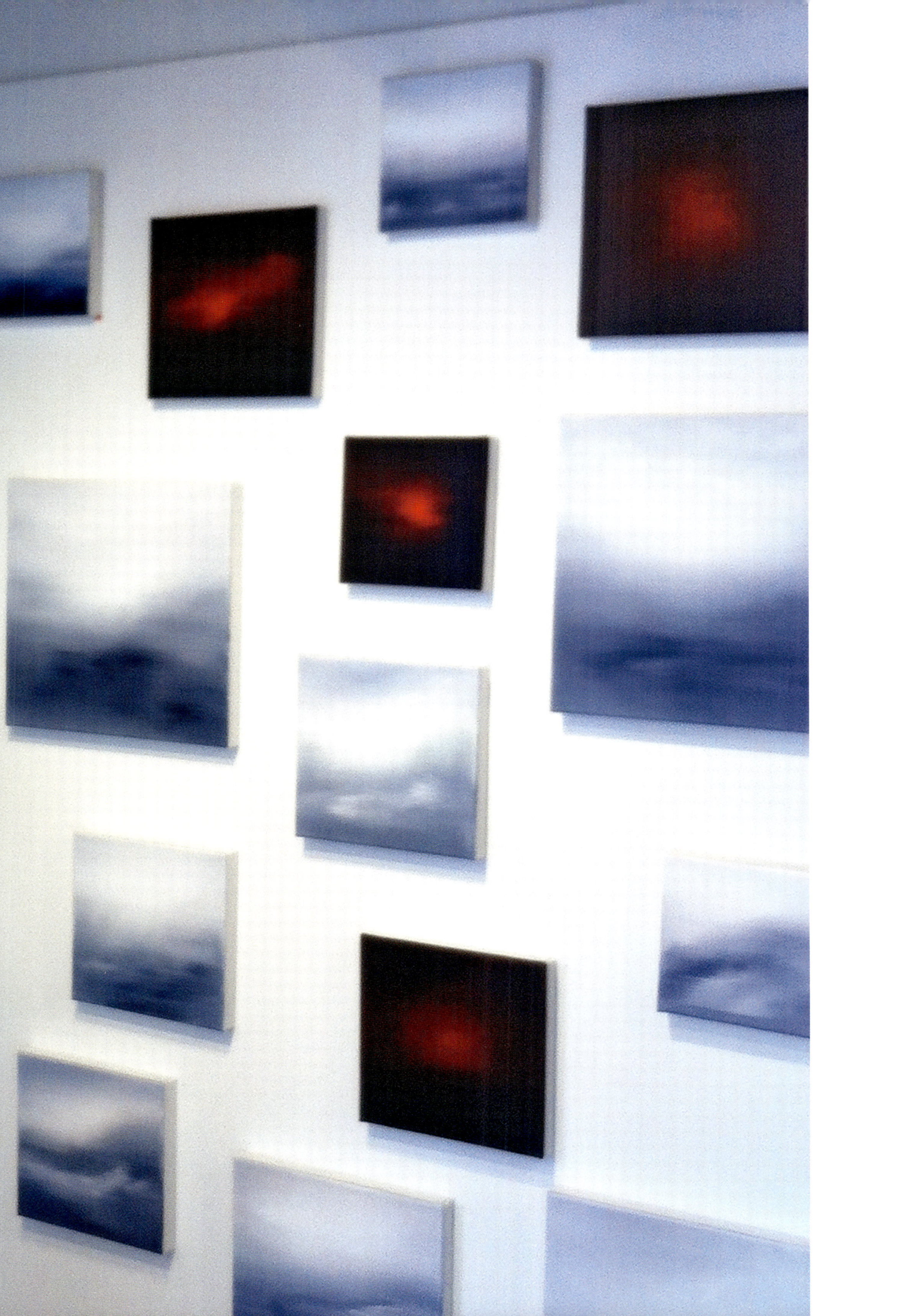

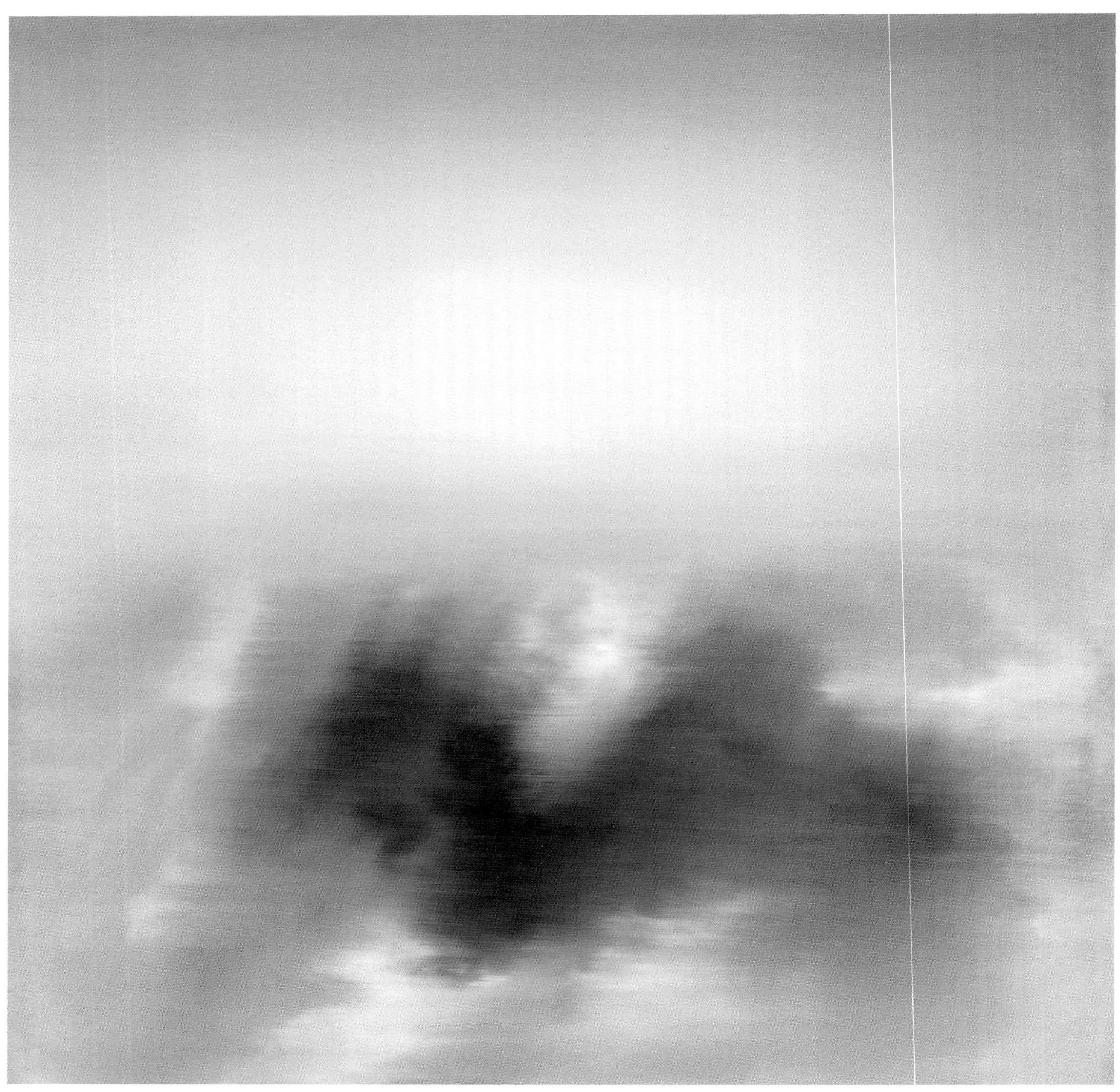

67 *Poetry of Light VIII* / *Poesie des Lichts VIII*, 2015

68 *Poetry of Light IX / Poesie des Lichts IX*, 2015

69 *XII-XII-98*, 1998

70 *Night Painting / Nachtbild*, 2016

71 *XVII-XI-16*, 2016

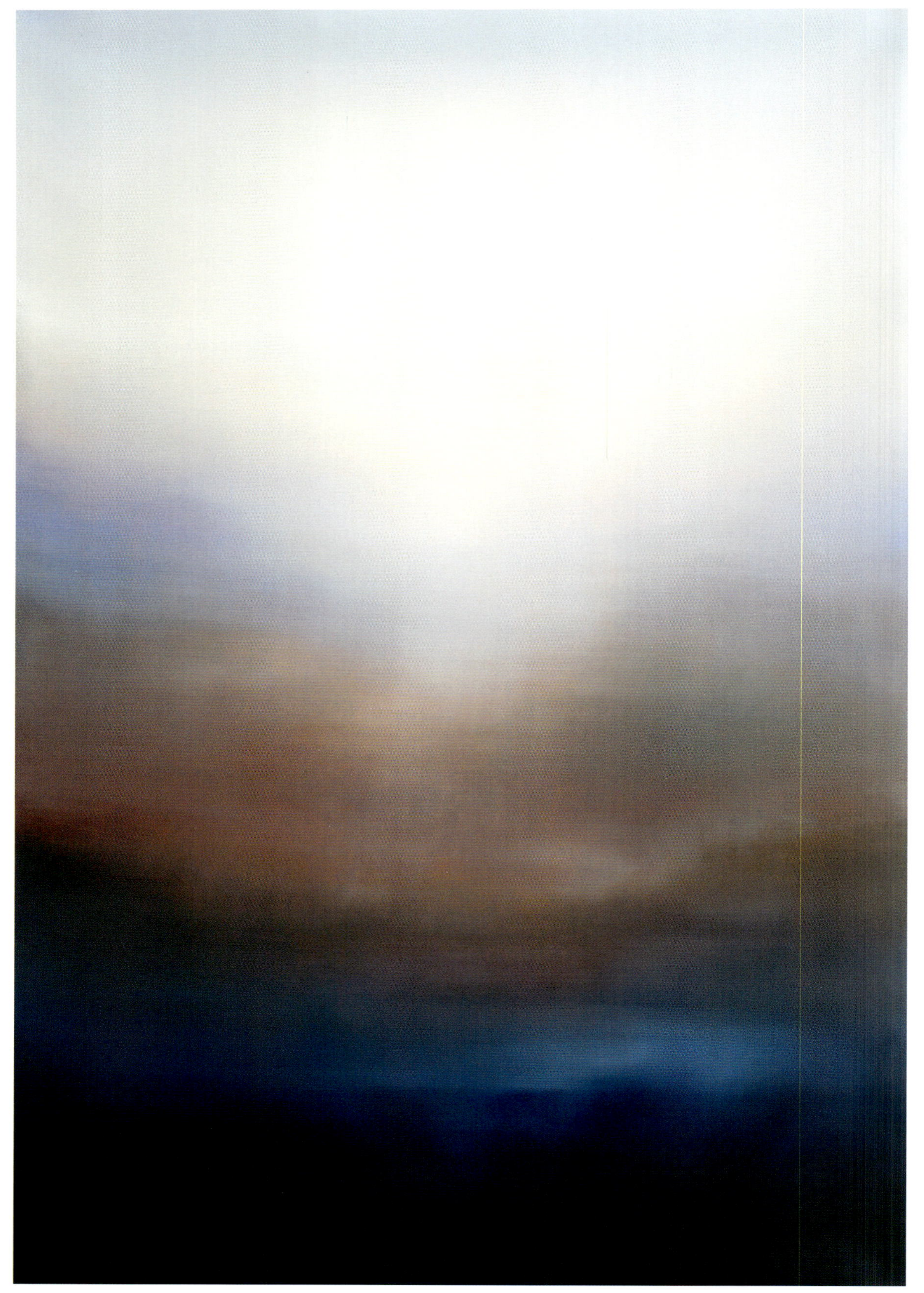

72 *III-II-11*, 2011

73 *XI-III-11*, 2011

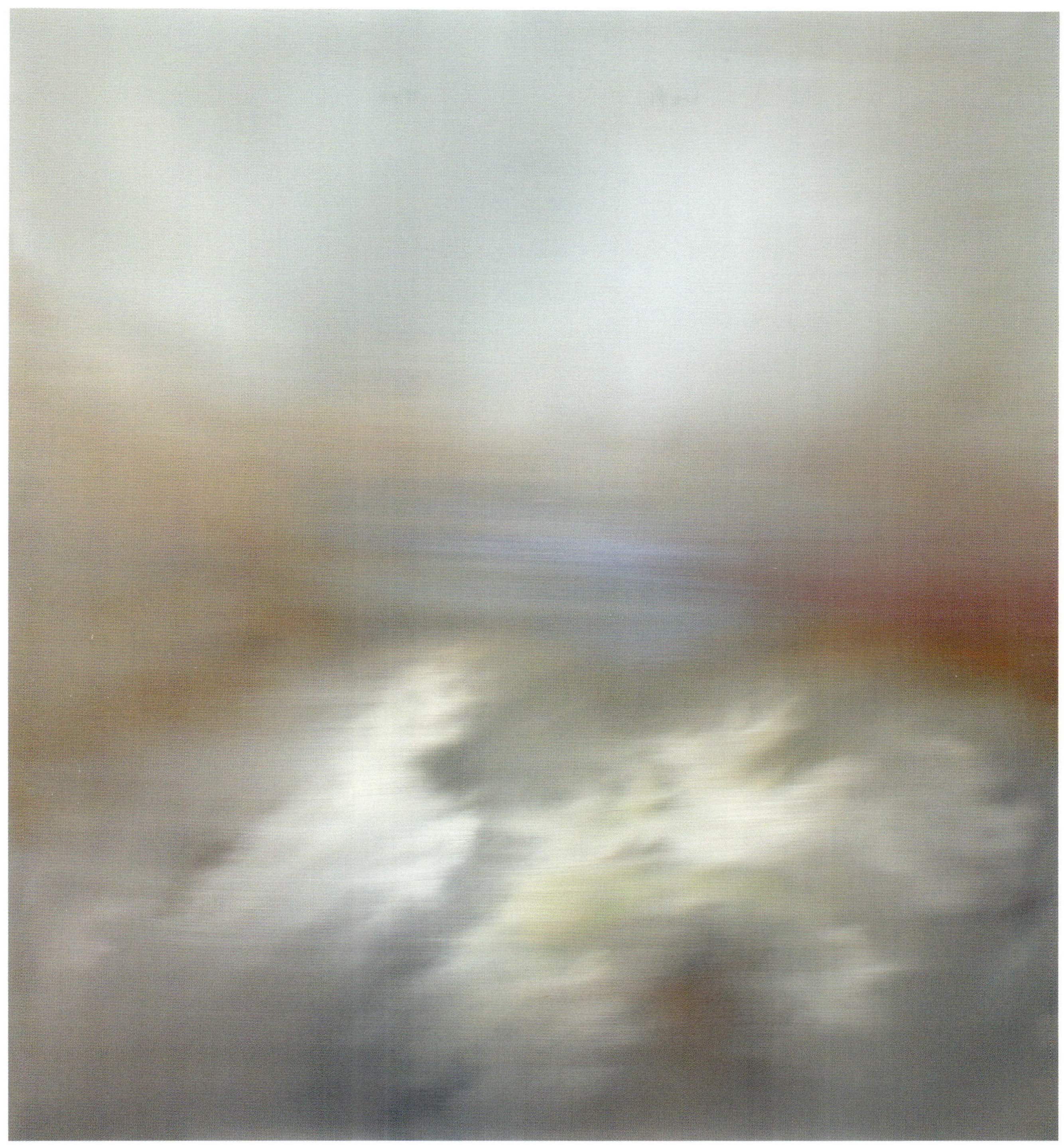

74 *Venus Flycatcher / Venusfliegenfalle*, 2015
75 *XIX-I-15*, 2015

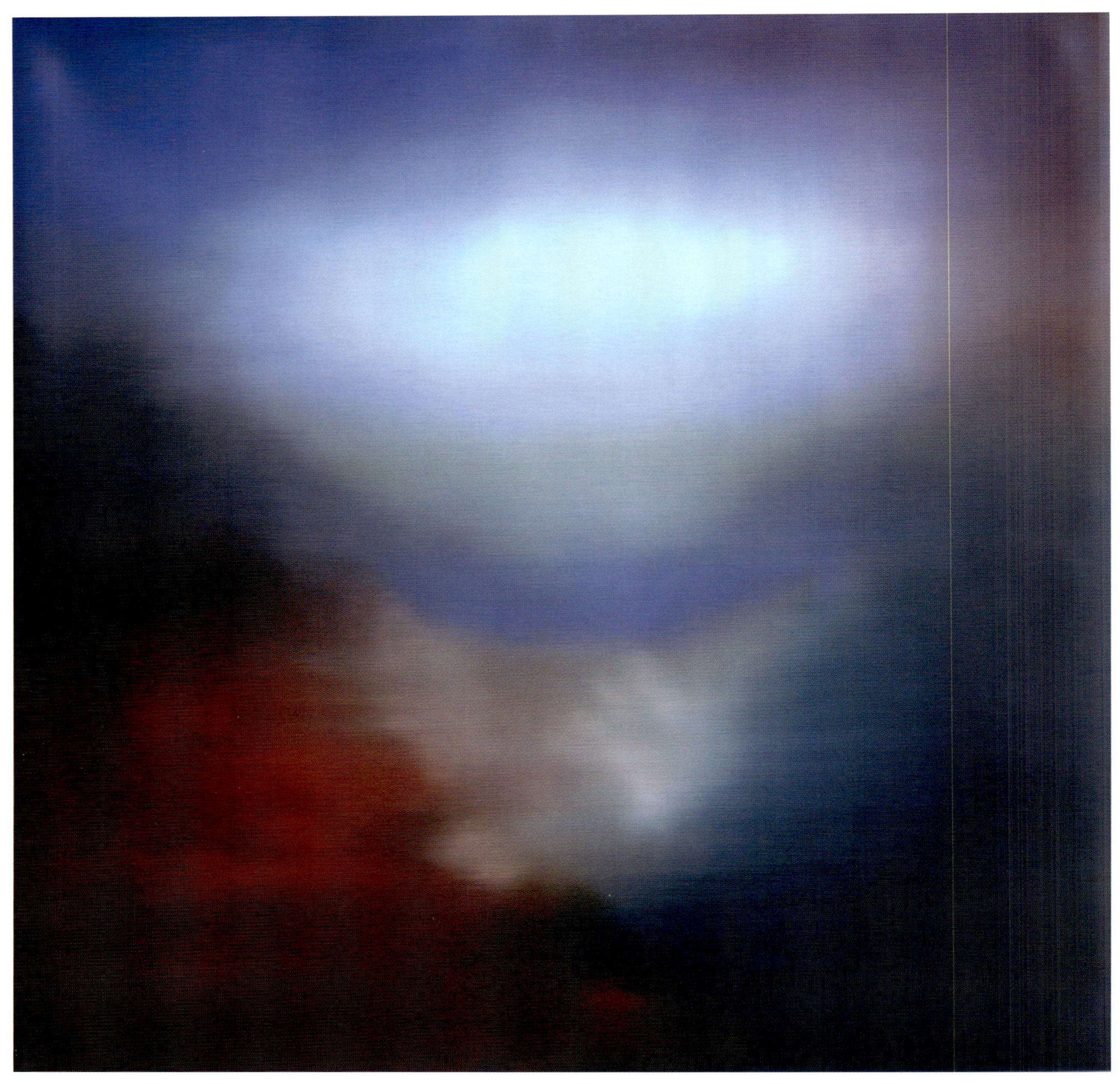

76 *XXV-III-11*, 2011

77 *II-V-11*, 2011

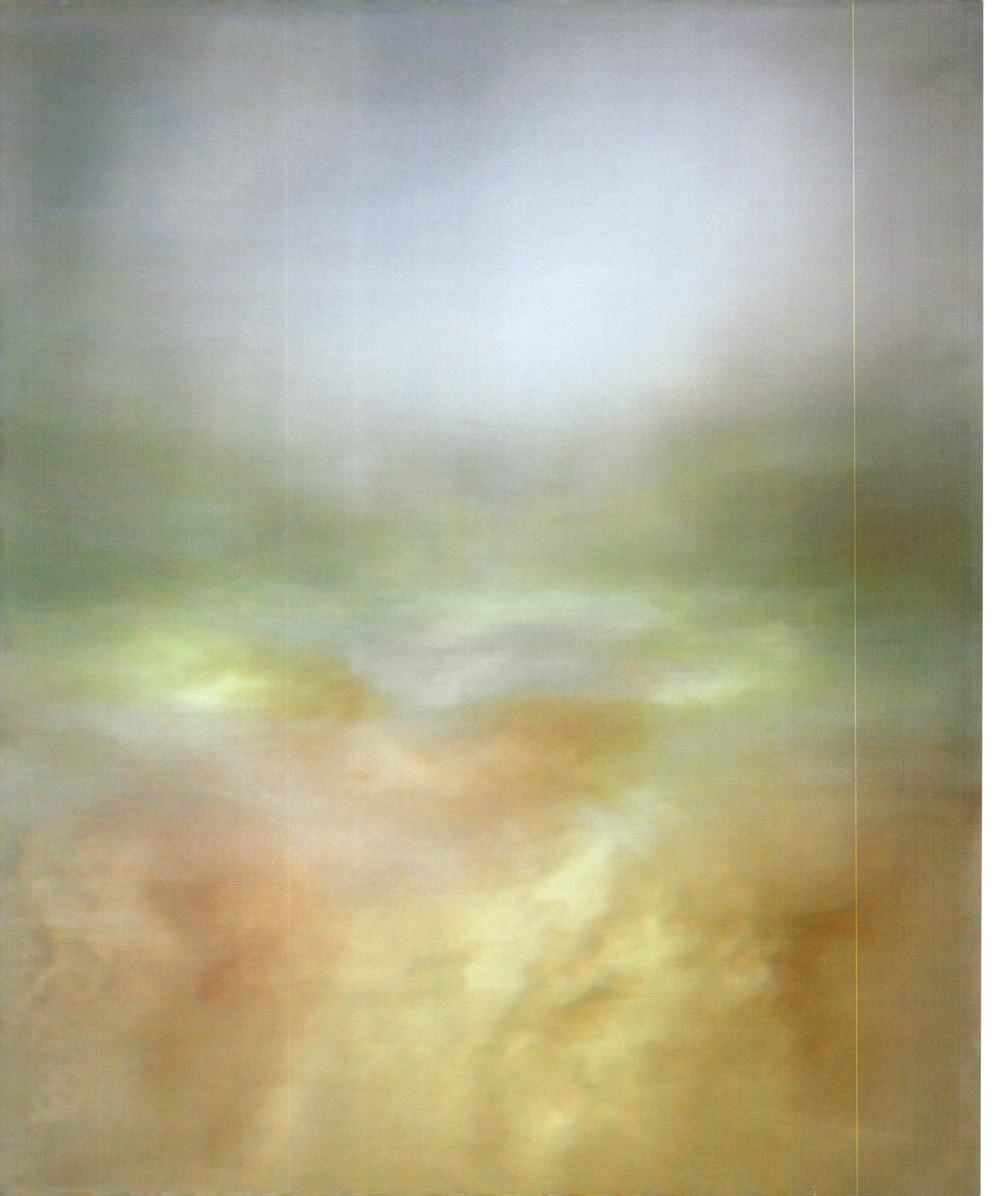

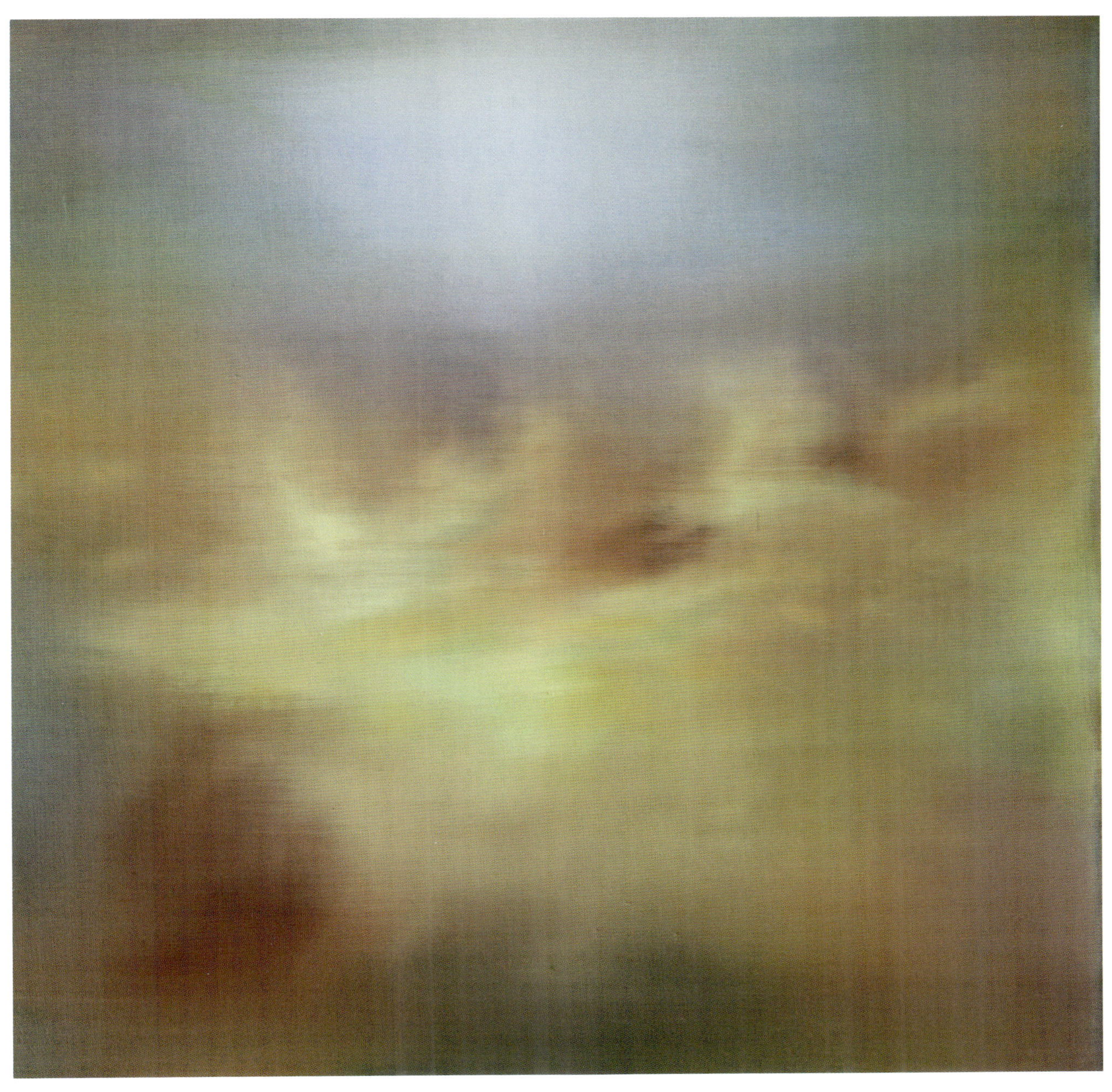

78 *XIV-X-15*, 2015
79 *XXVII-II-07*, 2007

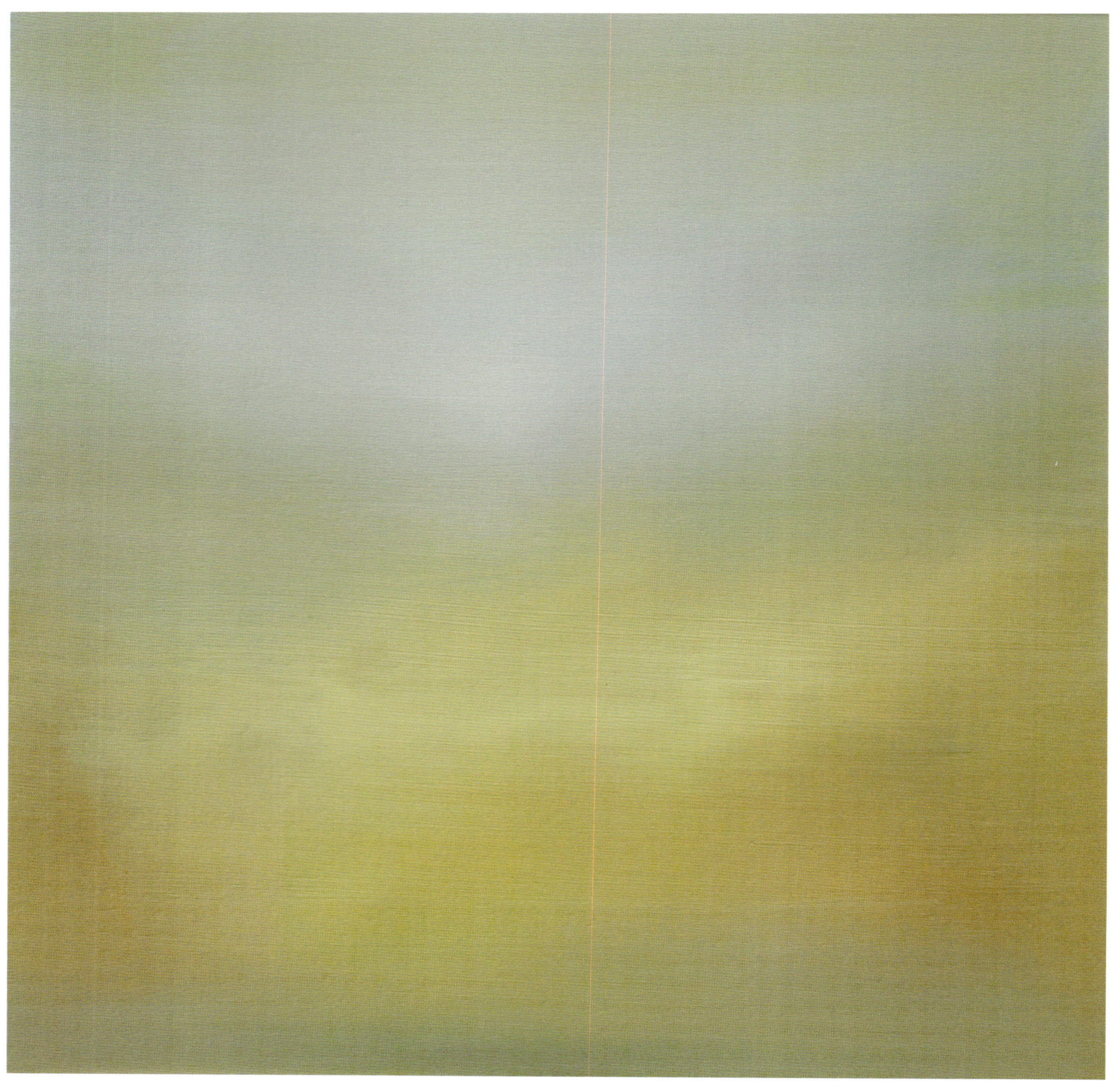

80 *XI-X-11*, 2011

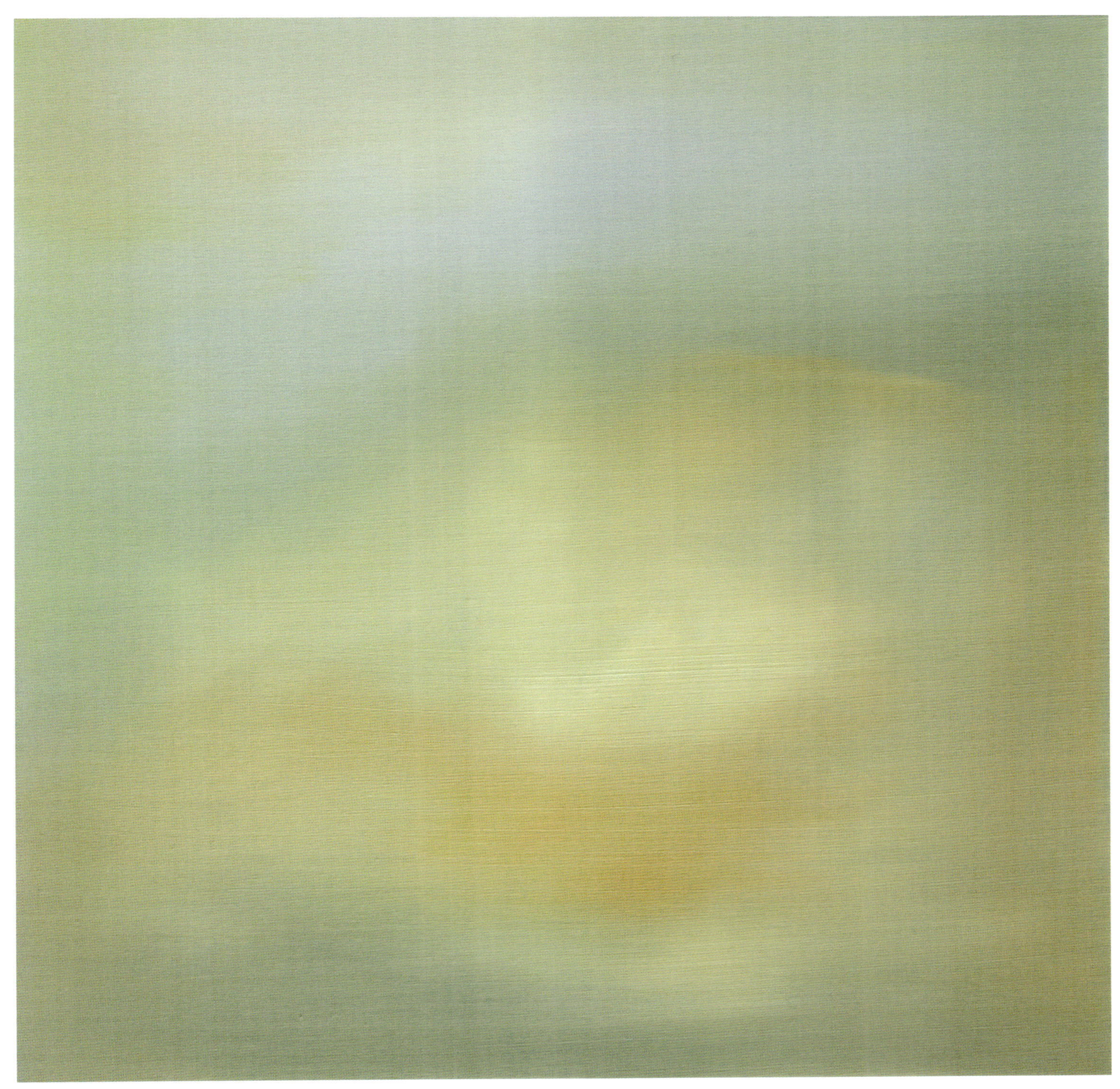

81 *X-X-11*, 2011

83 *Sun / Sonne*, 2015

84 *II-IV-10*, 2010

85 *III-IV-10*, 2010
86 *I-IV-10*, 2010

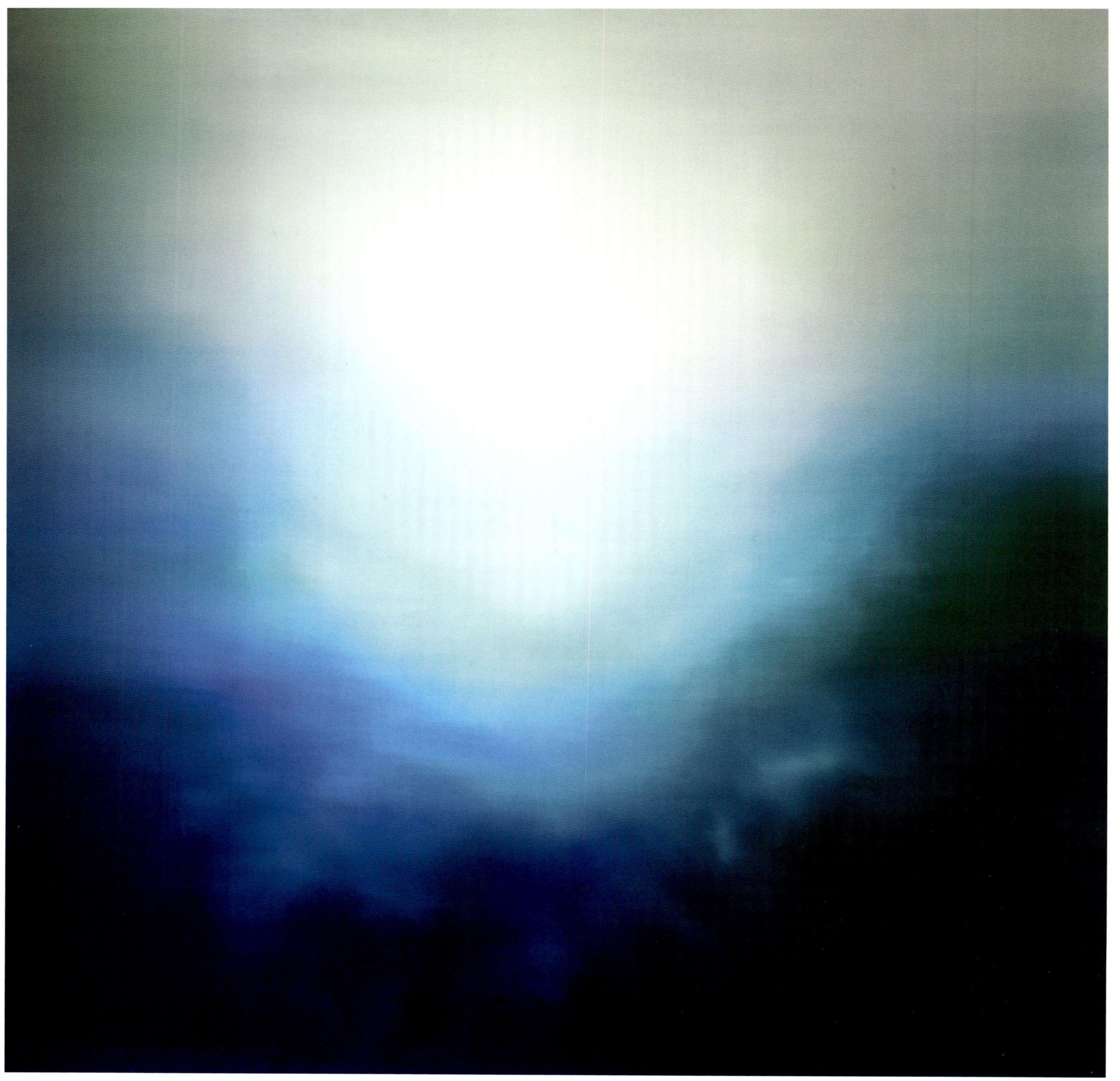

87 *XV-VI-08/09*, 2009

88 *XXX-VIII-08*, 2008
89 *XXV-VIII-08*, 2008

90 *For H. H. / Für H. H.*, V-IV-14, 2014

91 For G. H. / *Für G. H.*, 2016

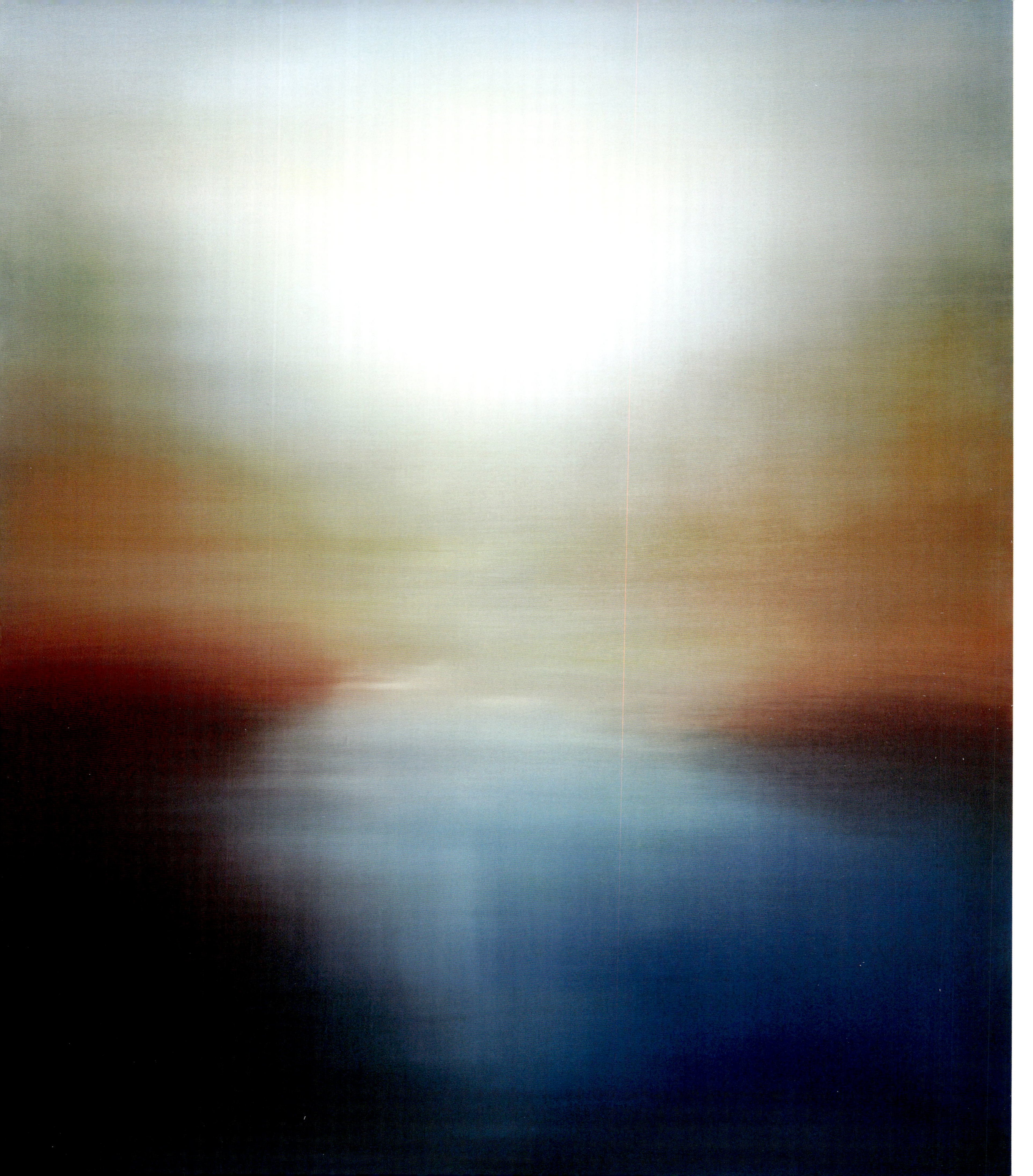

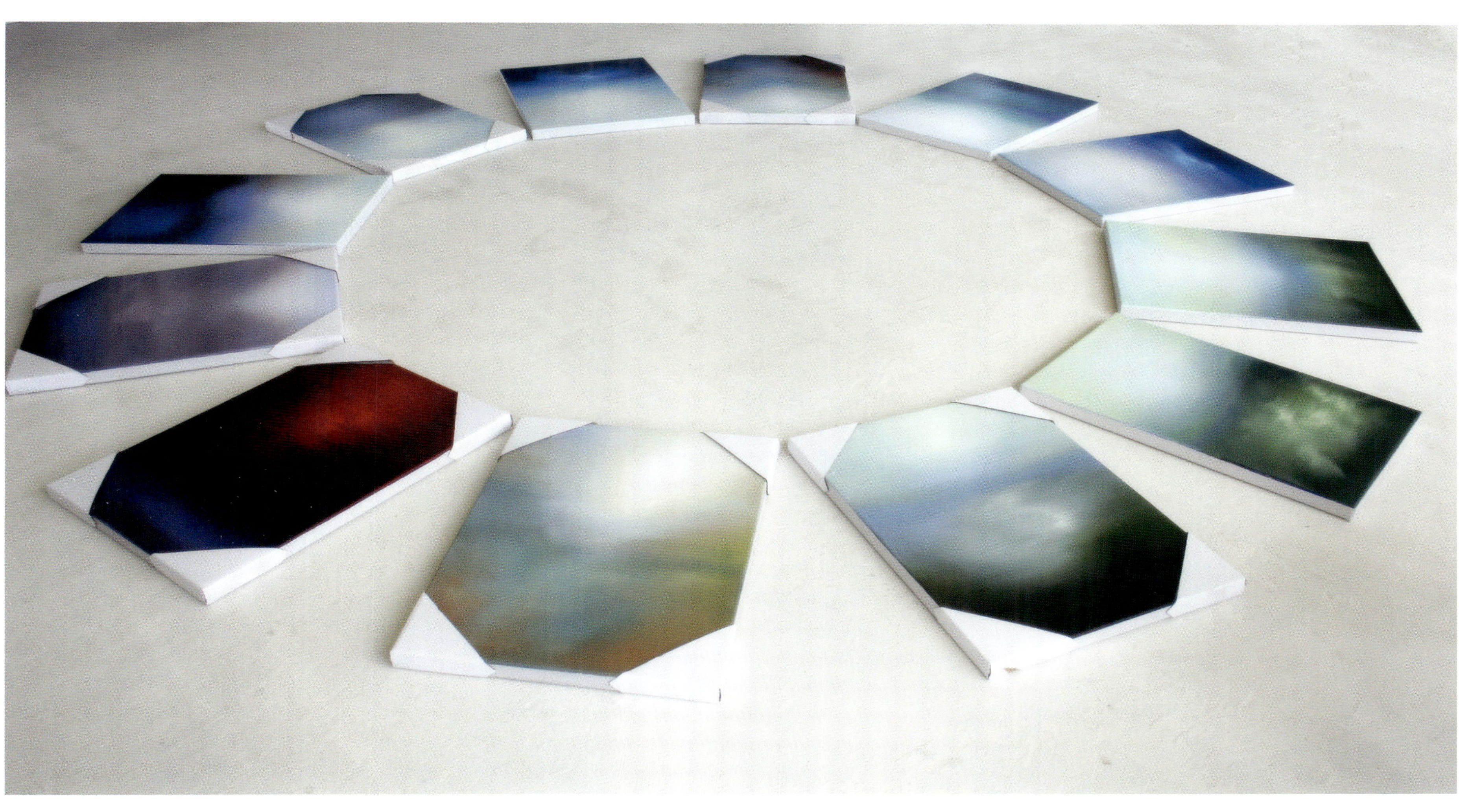

92 *XVI-VII-10*, 2010
93 *Circle / Kreis*, 2013

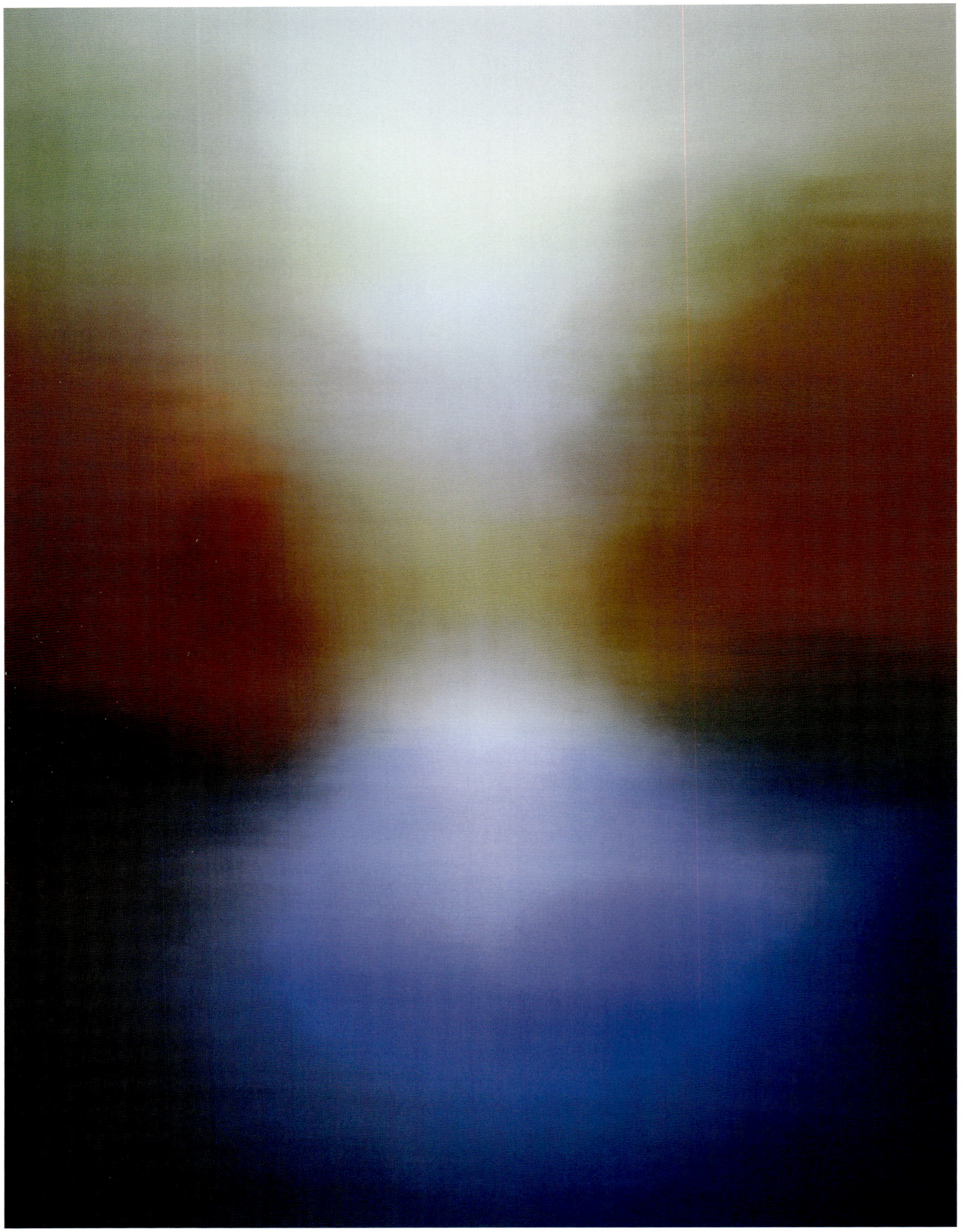

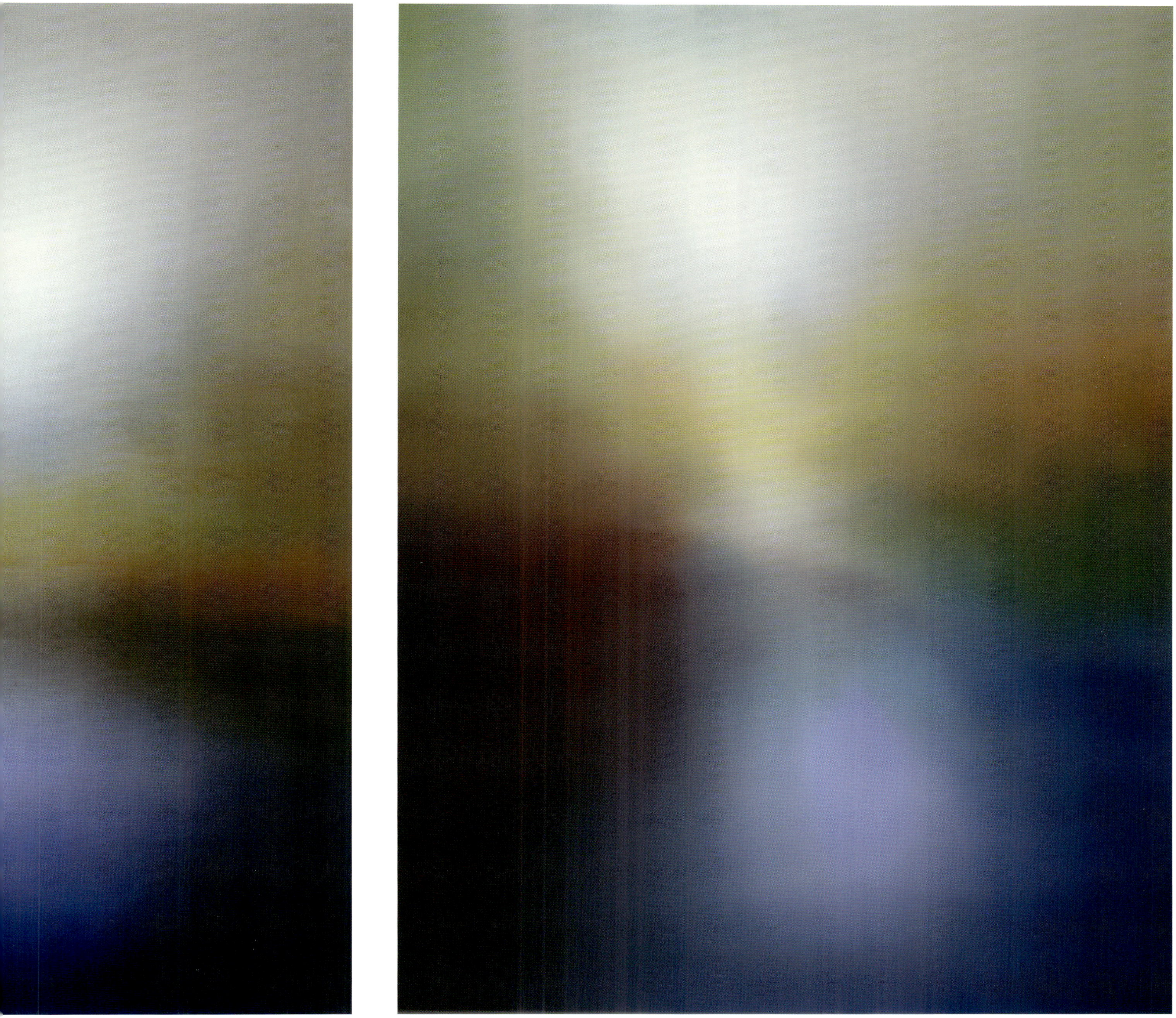

94 *VIII-IV-11*, 2011

95 *I-III-11*, 2011

96 *XXII-IX-10*, 2010

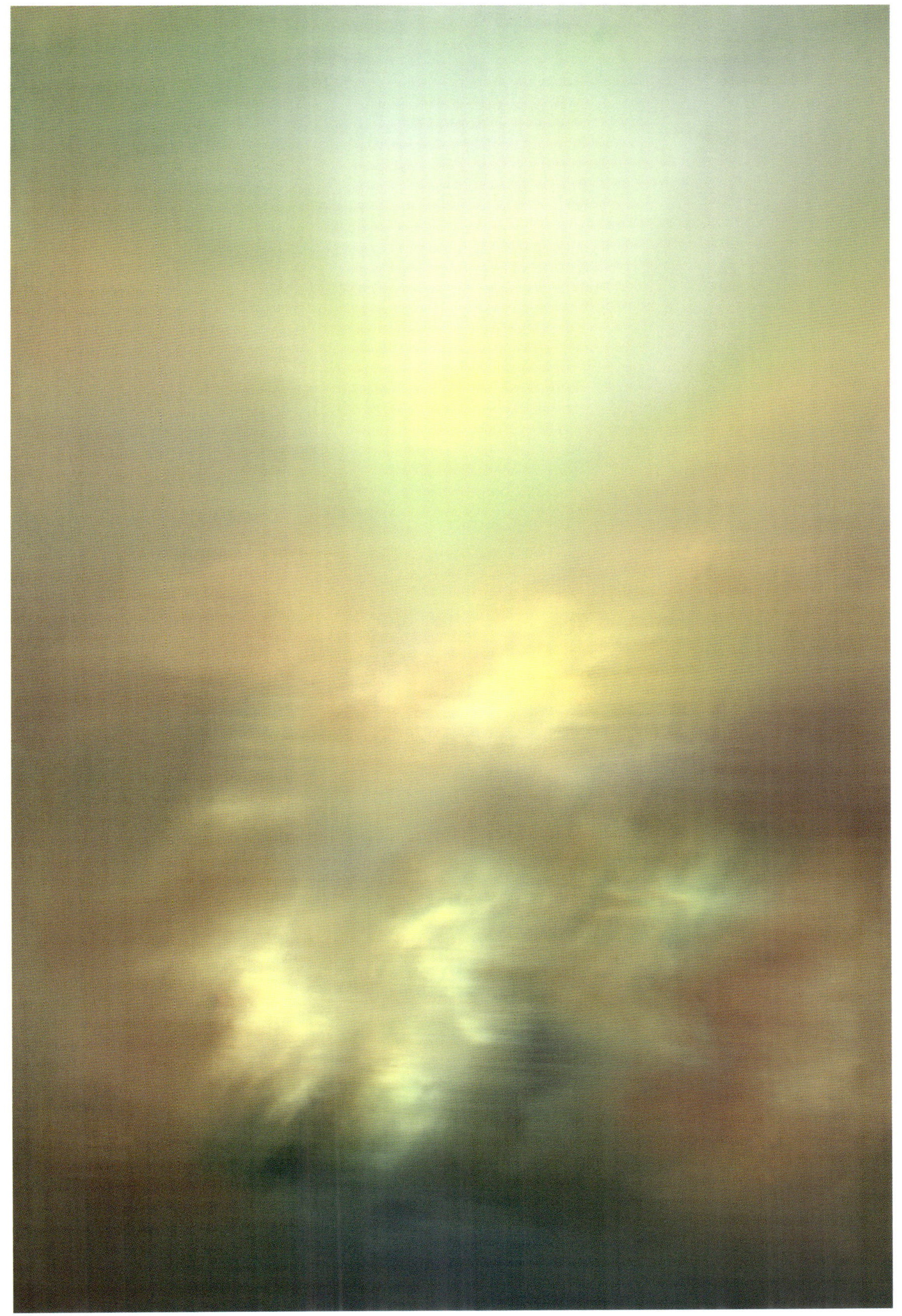

97 *jan-2000*, 2000

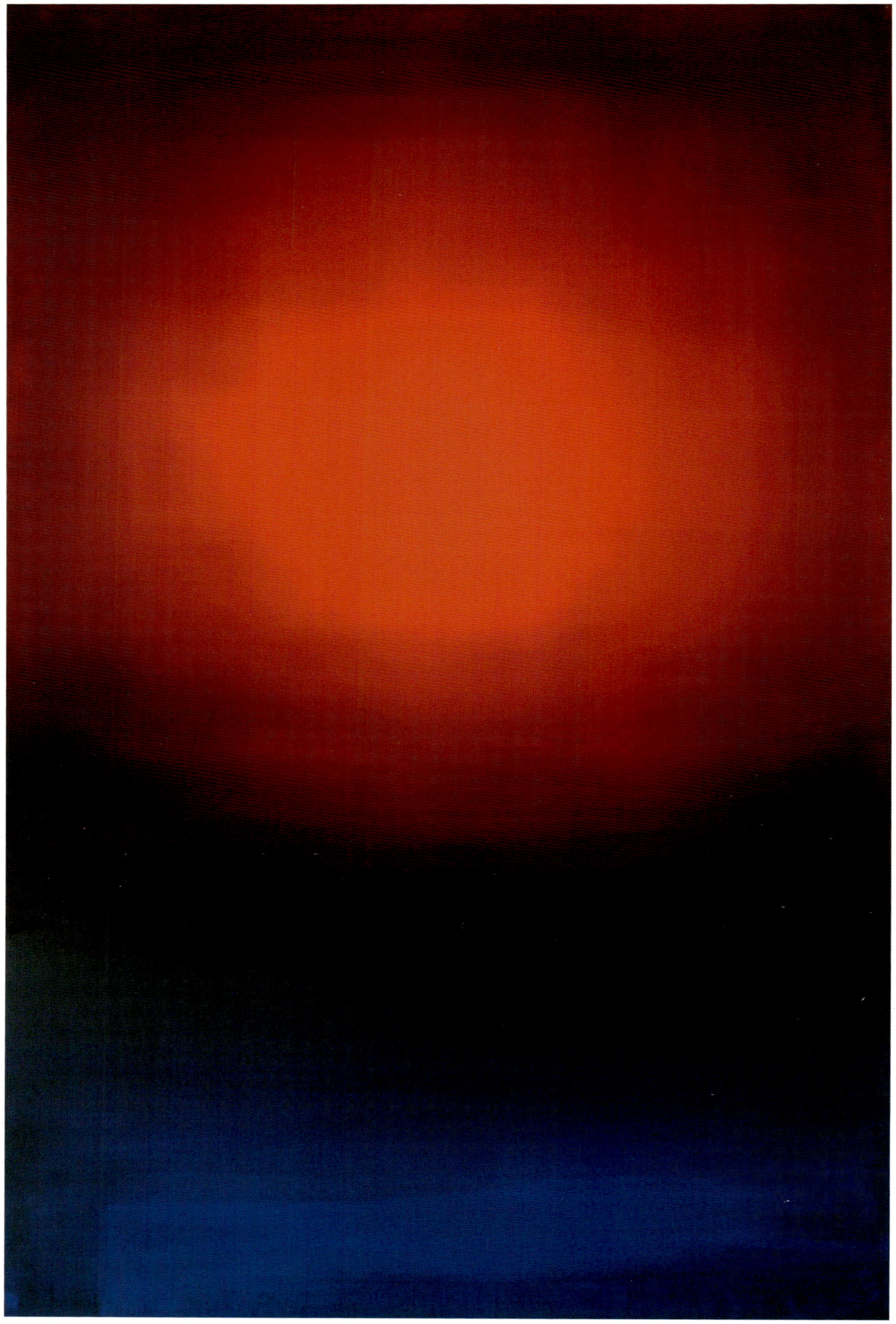

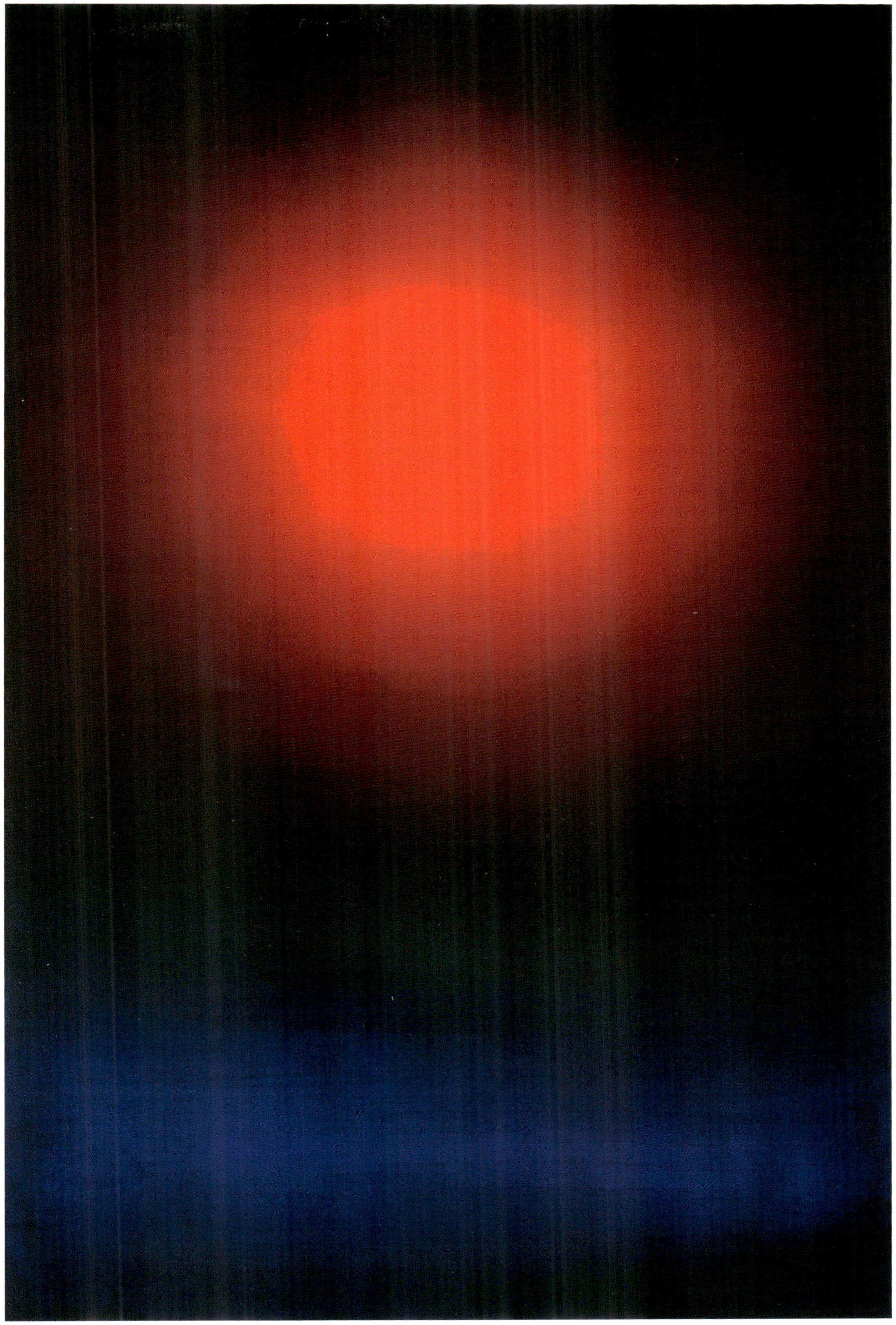

98 *Alpha I, Alpha II, Alpha III*, 2016

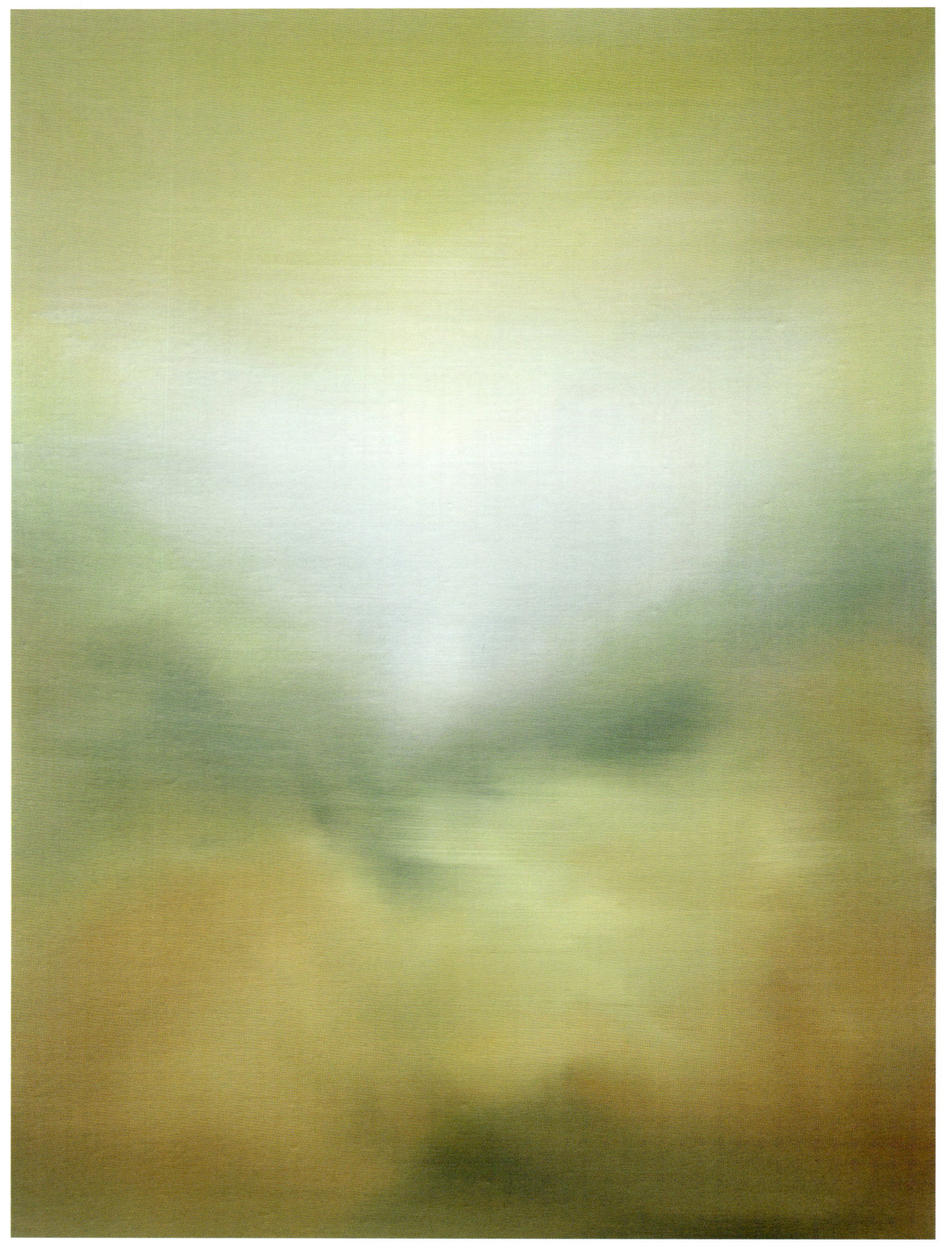

99 *VIII-X-11*, 2011

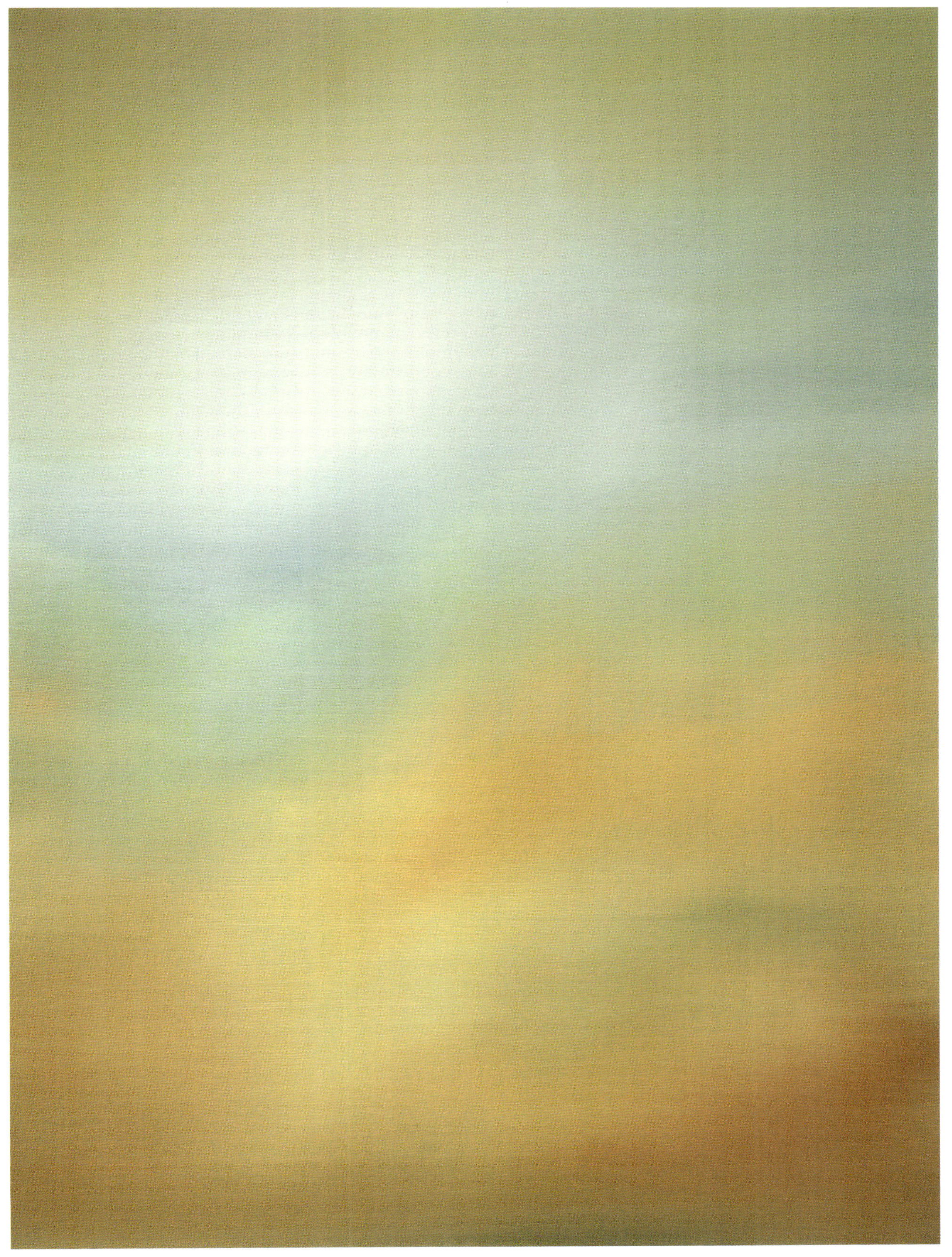

100 *VII-X-11*, 2011

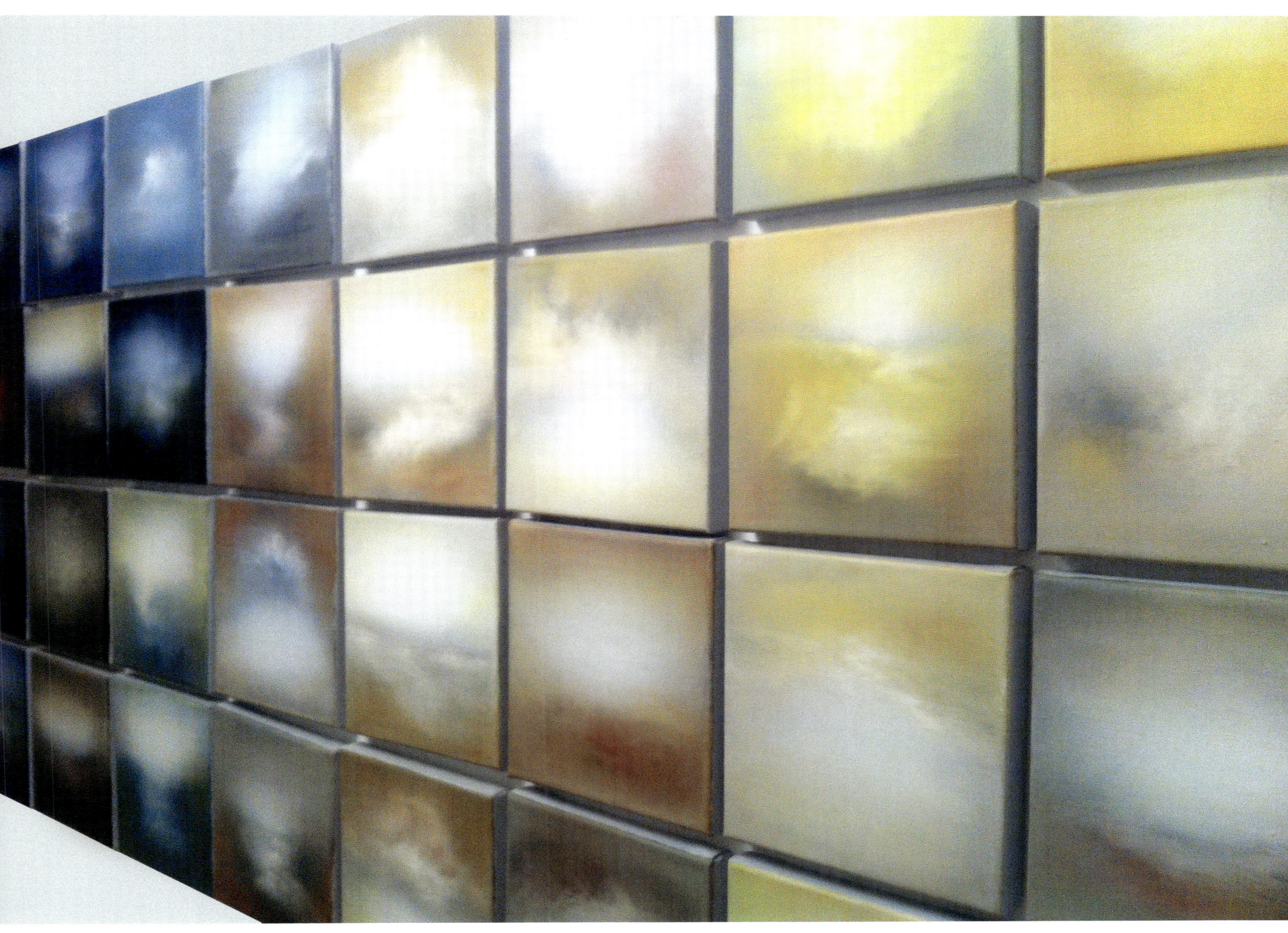

101 *Light and Darkness / Licht und Dunkelheit*, 2016

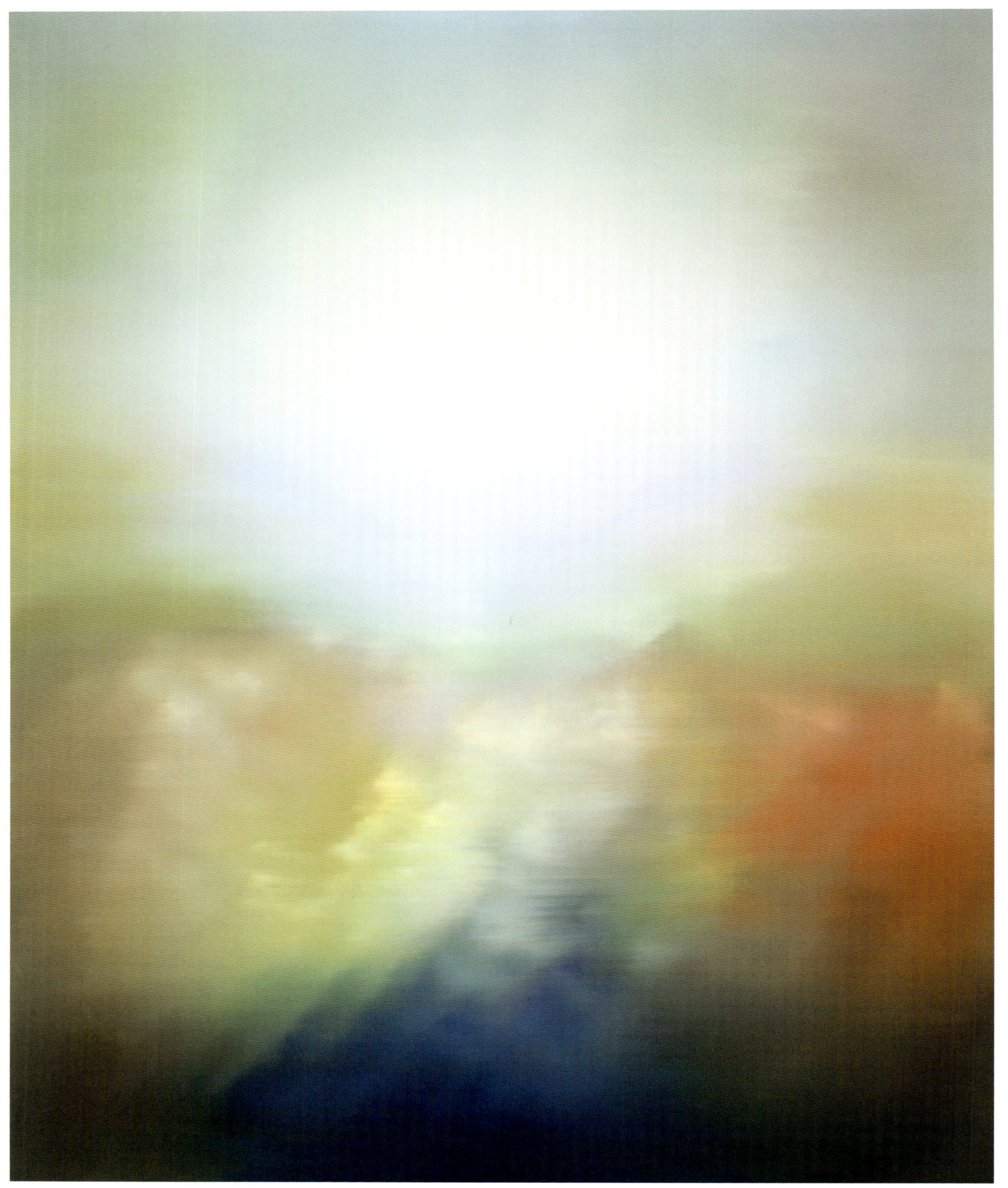

102 *XXIX-VIII-09*, 2009

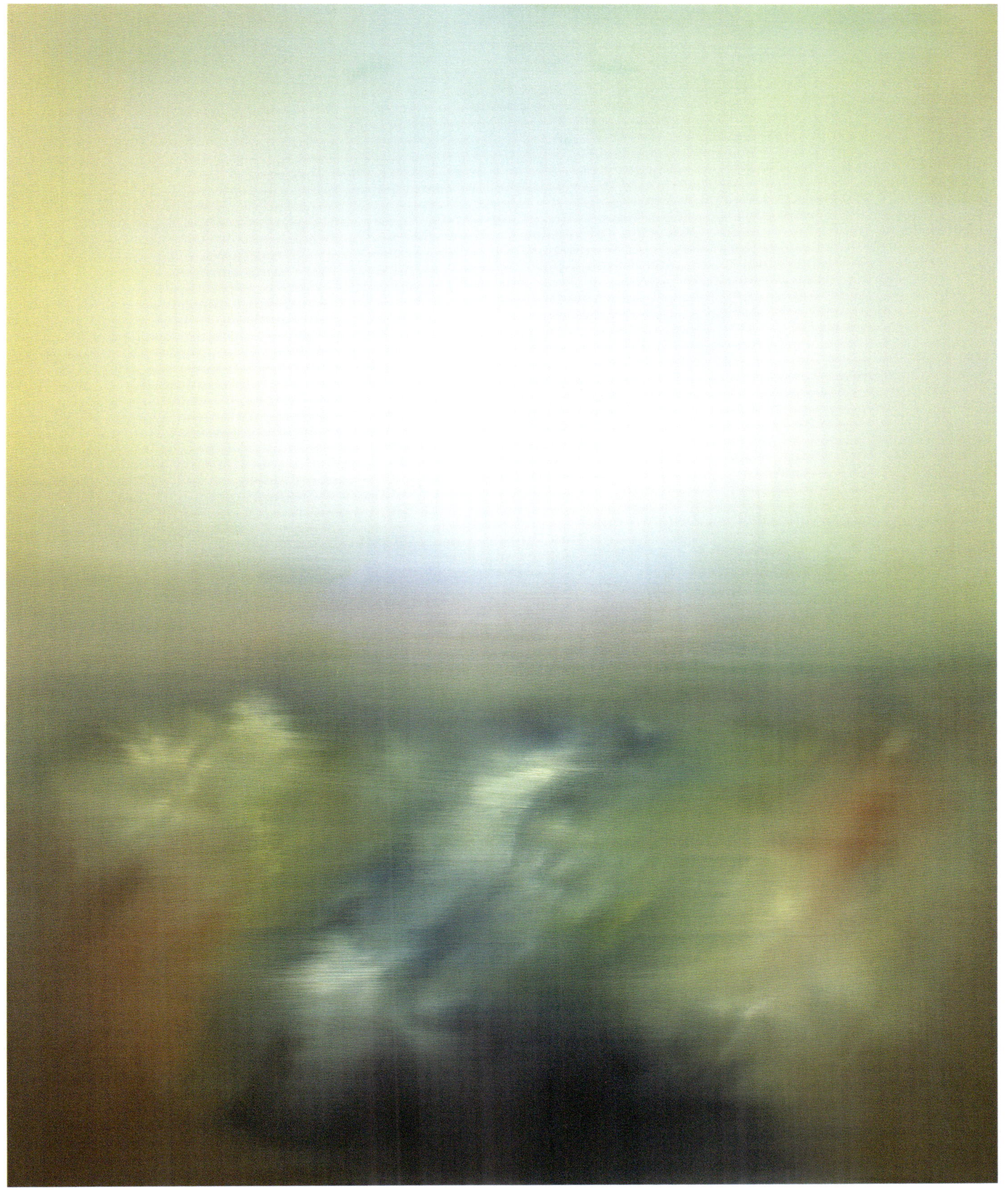

103 *I-IV-09*, 2009

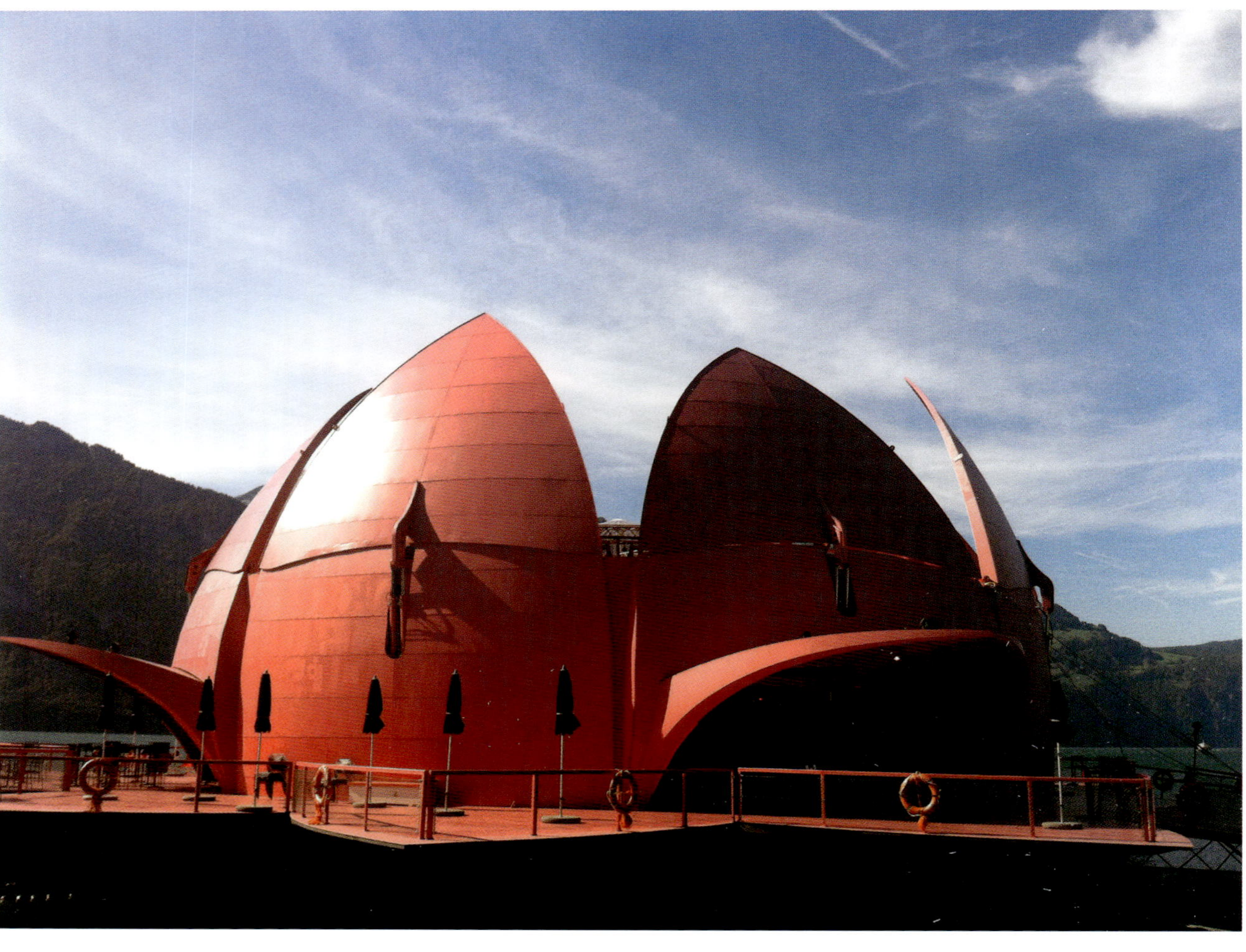

Gästival 2015, Vierwaldstättersee, Switzerland
Gästival 2015, Vierwaldstättersee, Schweiz

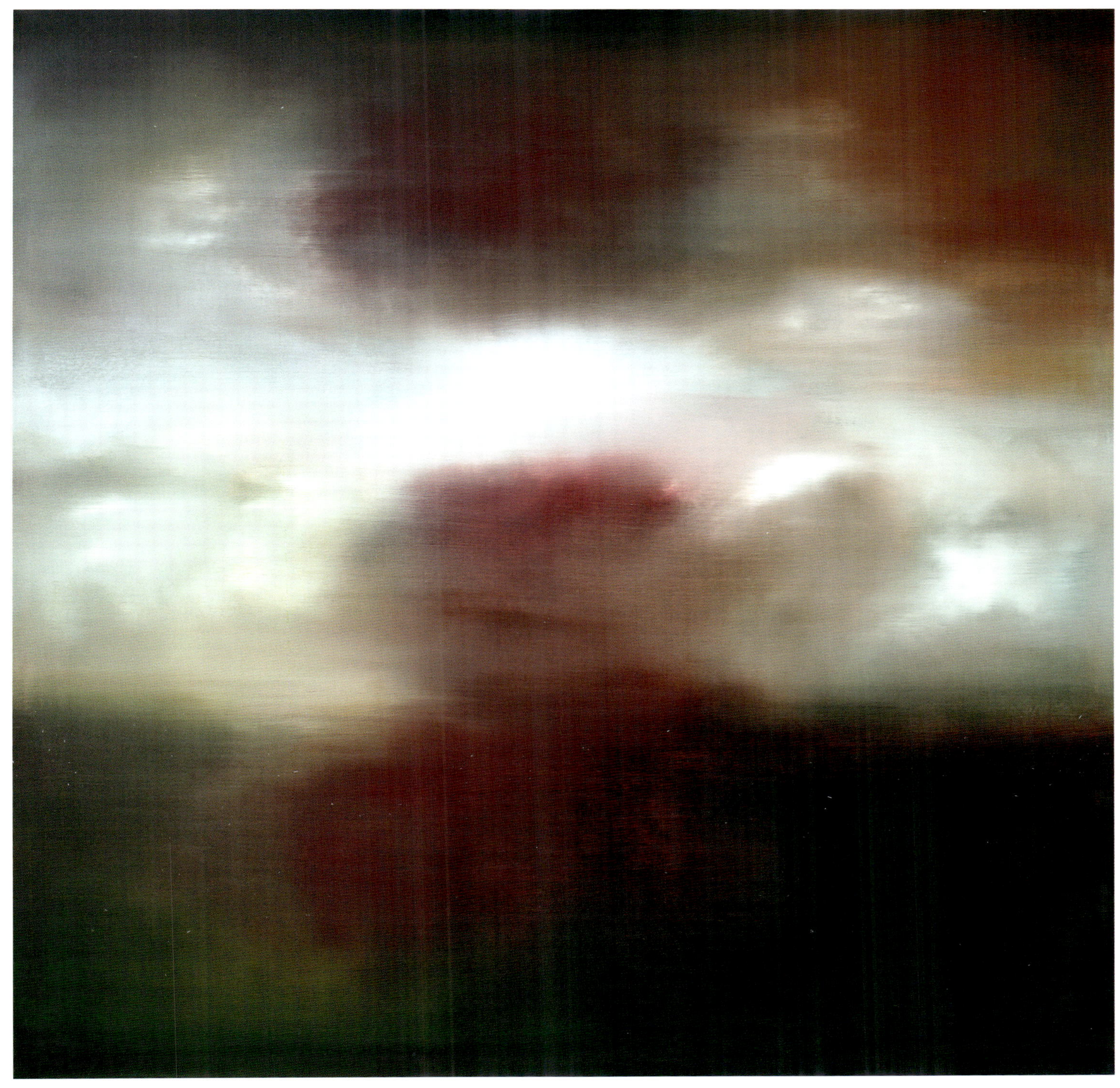

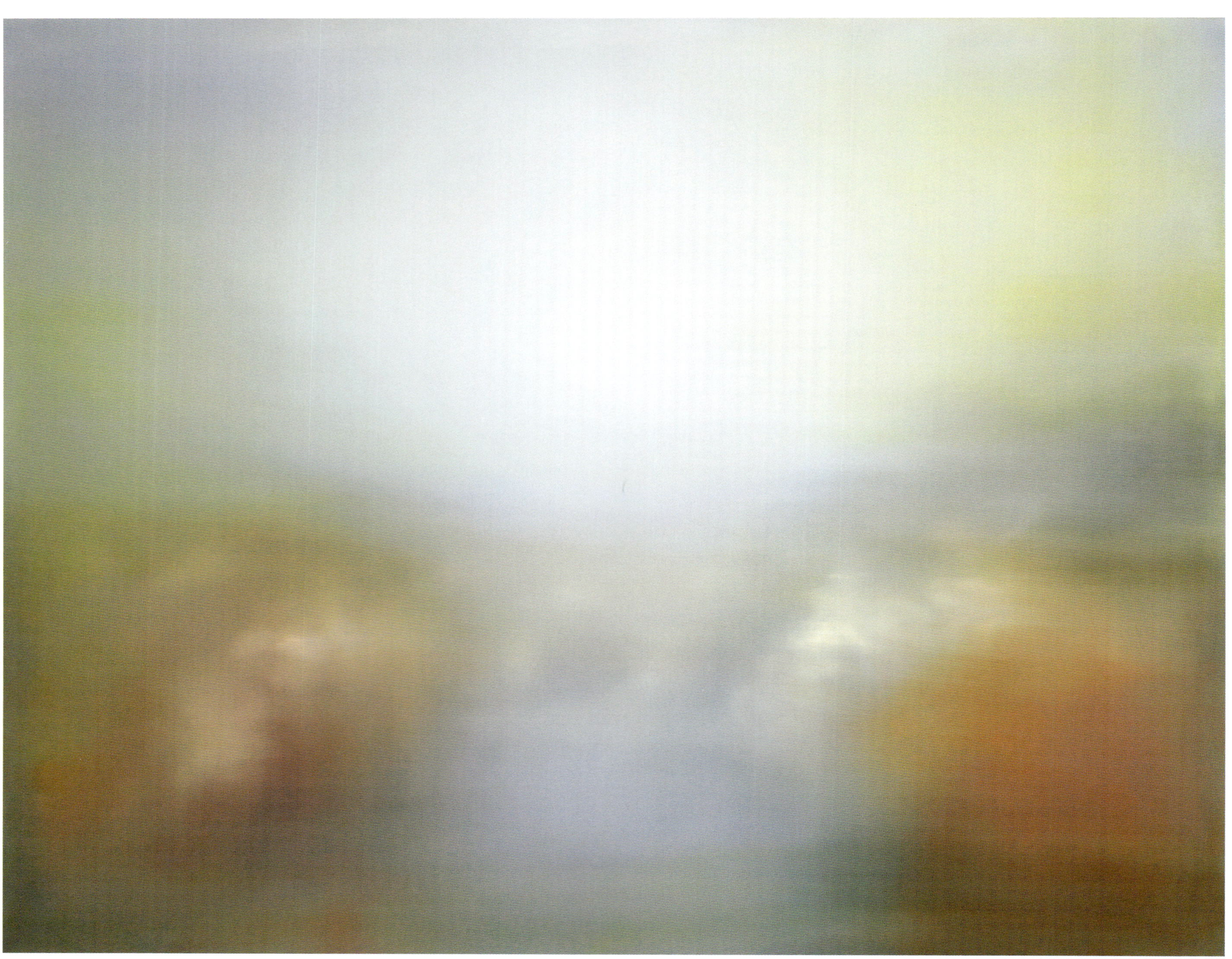

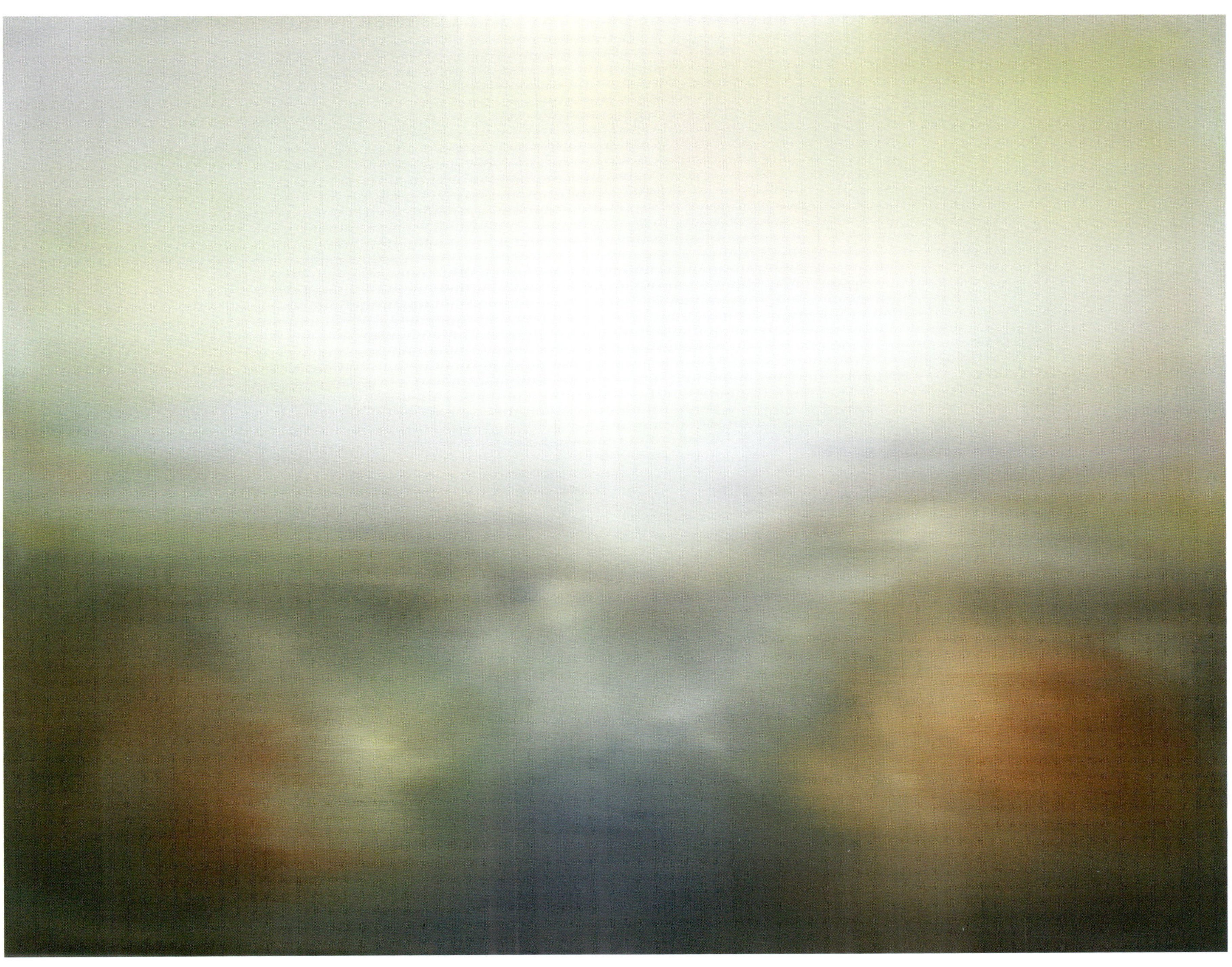

106 *In the Footsteps of M. W. Turner III* / *Auf den Spuren von M. W. Turner III*, 2015

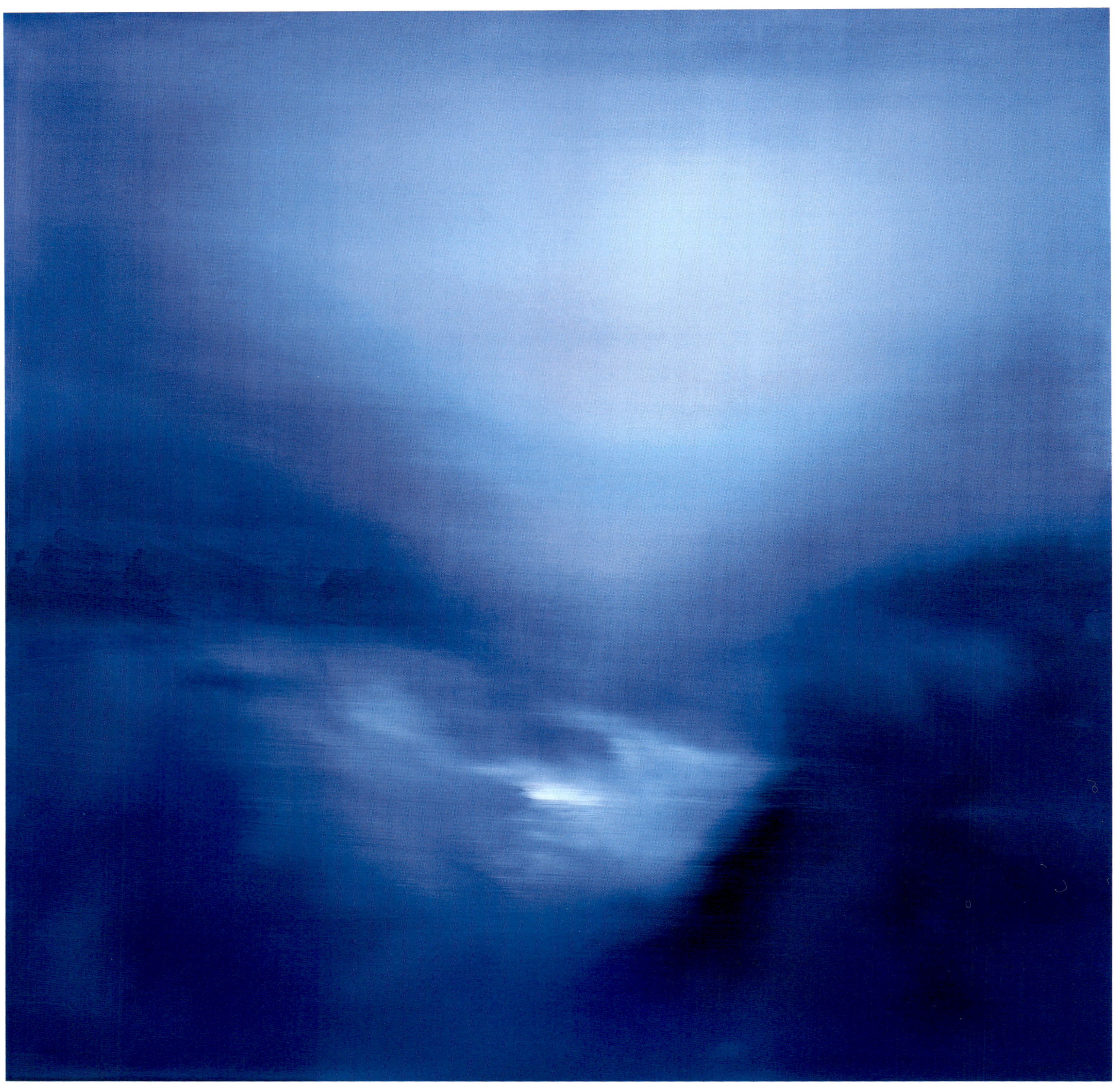

107 *Blue Rigi by Moonlight* / *Blaue Rigi bei Mondschein*, 2015

108 *XXVII-V-14*, 2014

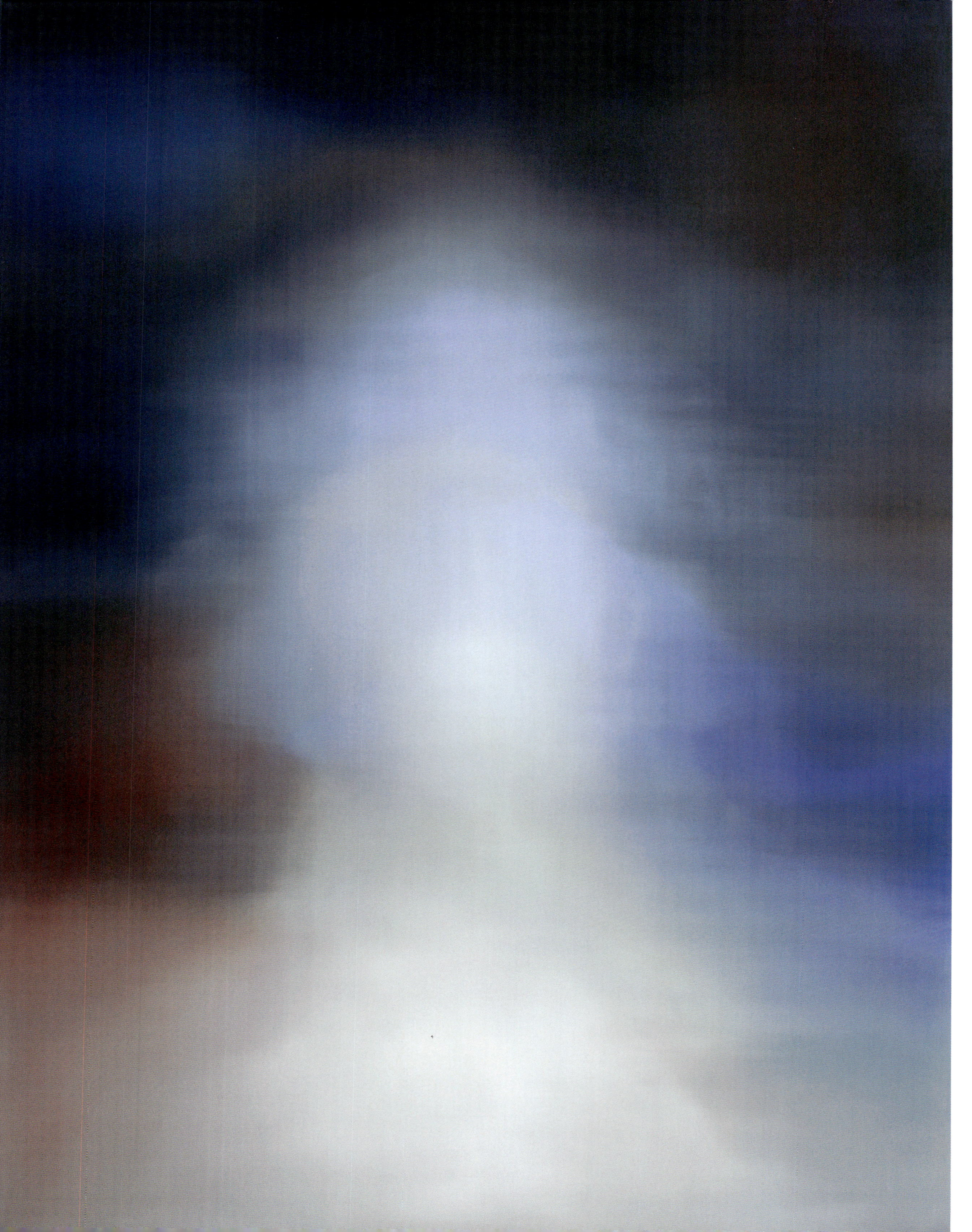

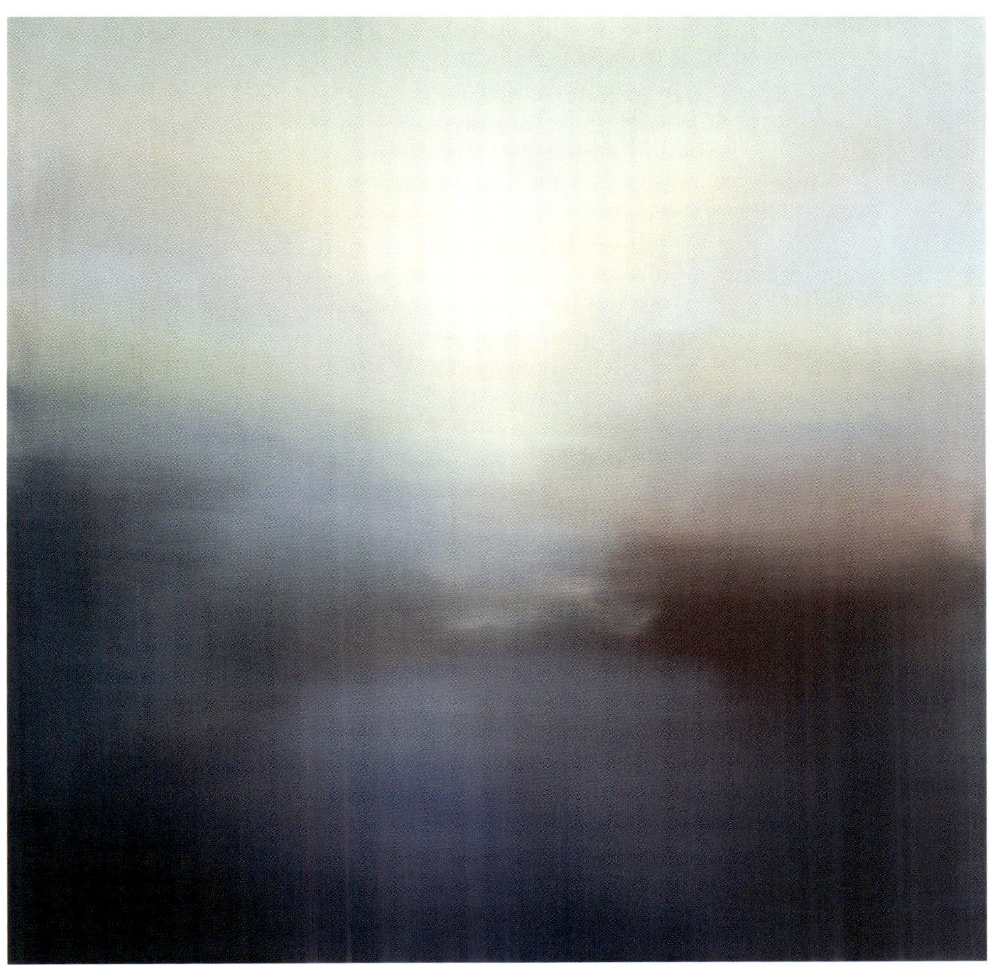

109 *Chameleon* / *Chamäleon*, 2014
110 *VII-III-13*, 2013

111 *I-VI-15*, 2015

112 *Light III / Licht III*, 2015

113 *X-I-13*, 2013

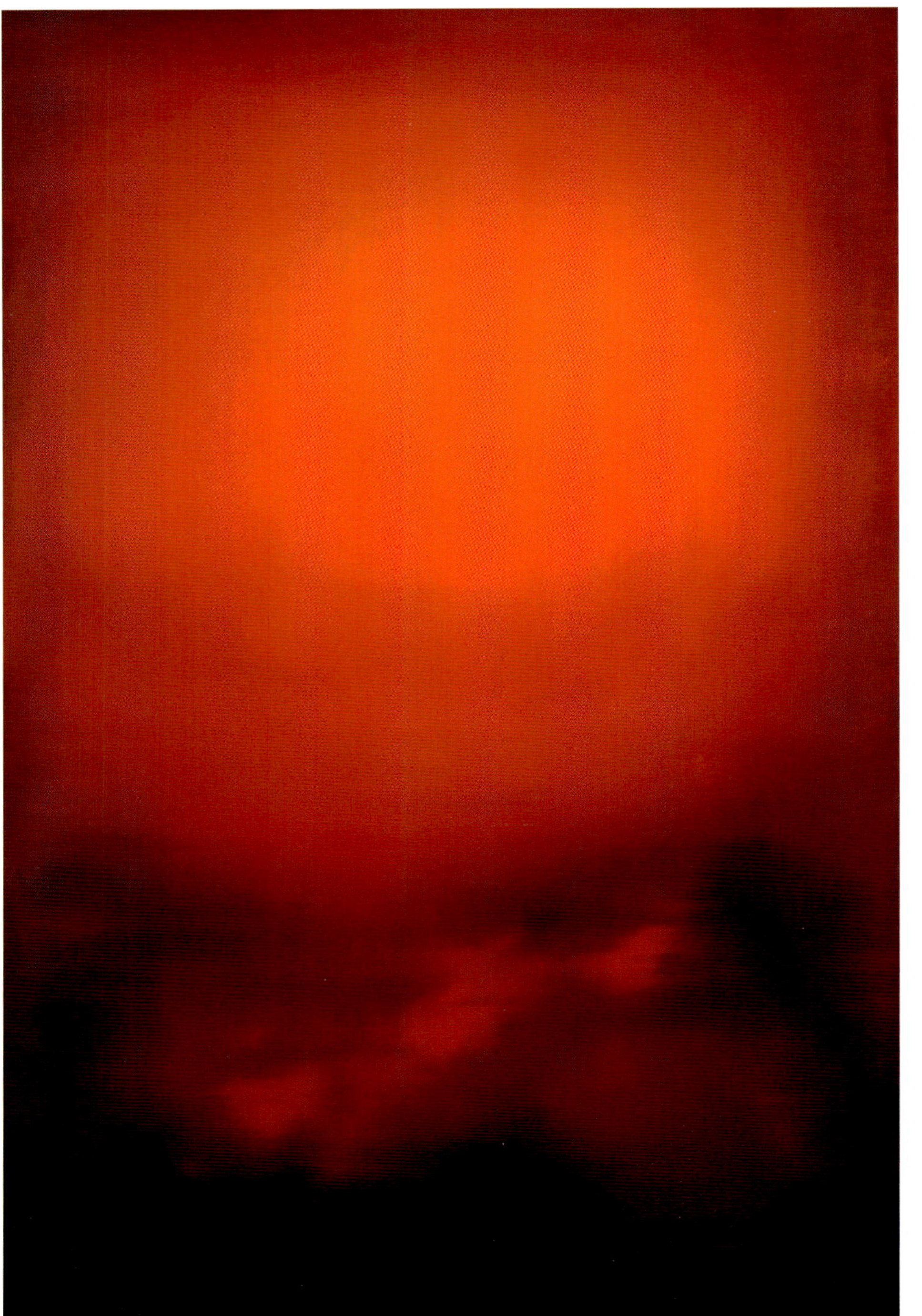

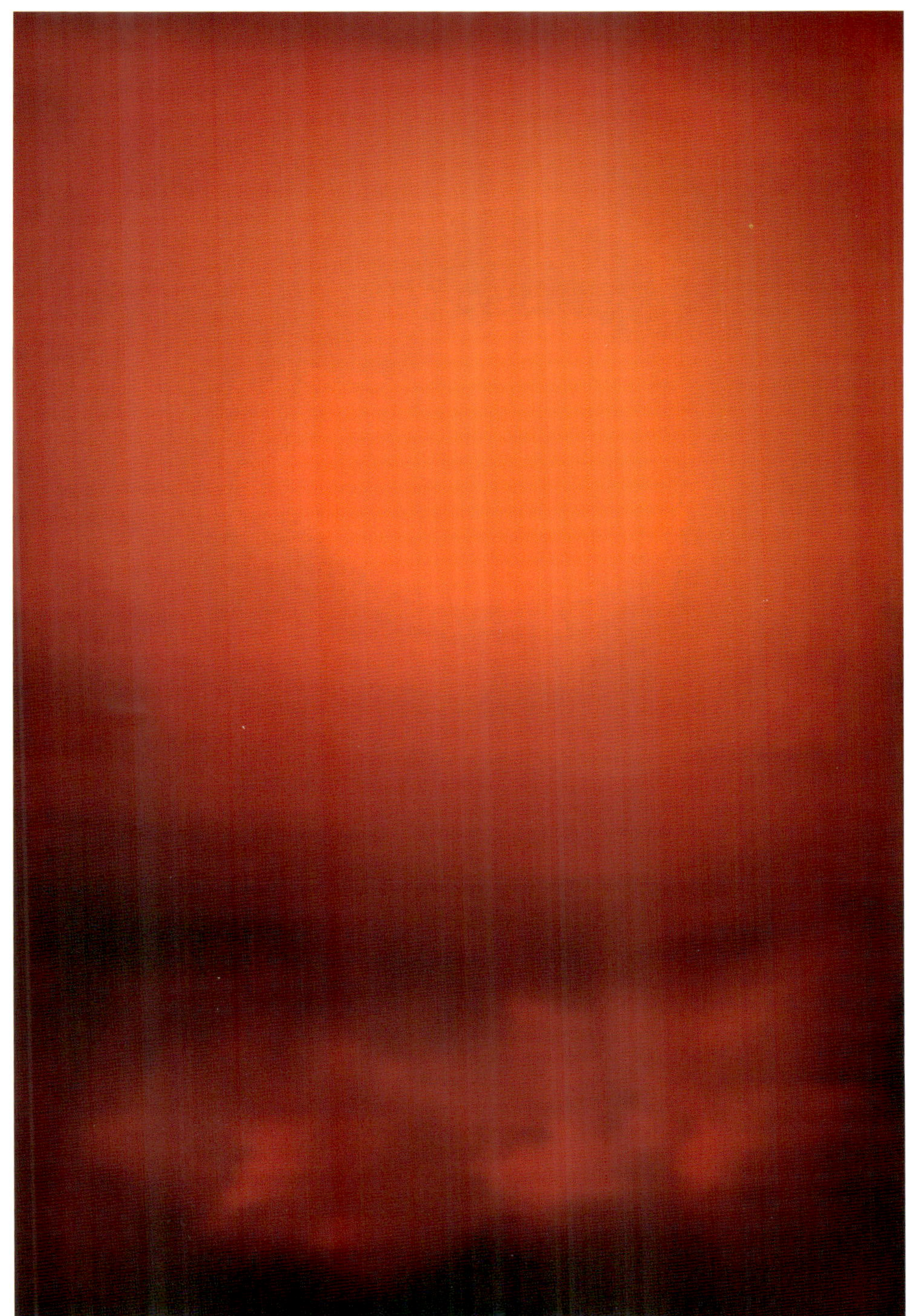

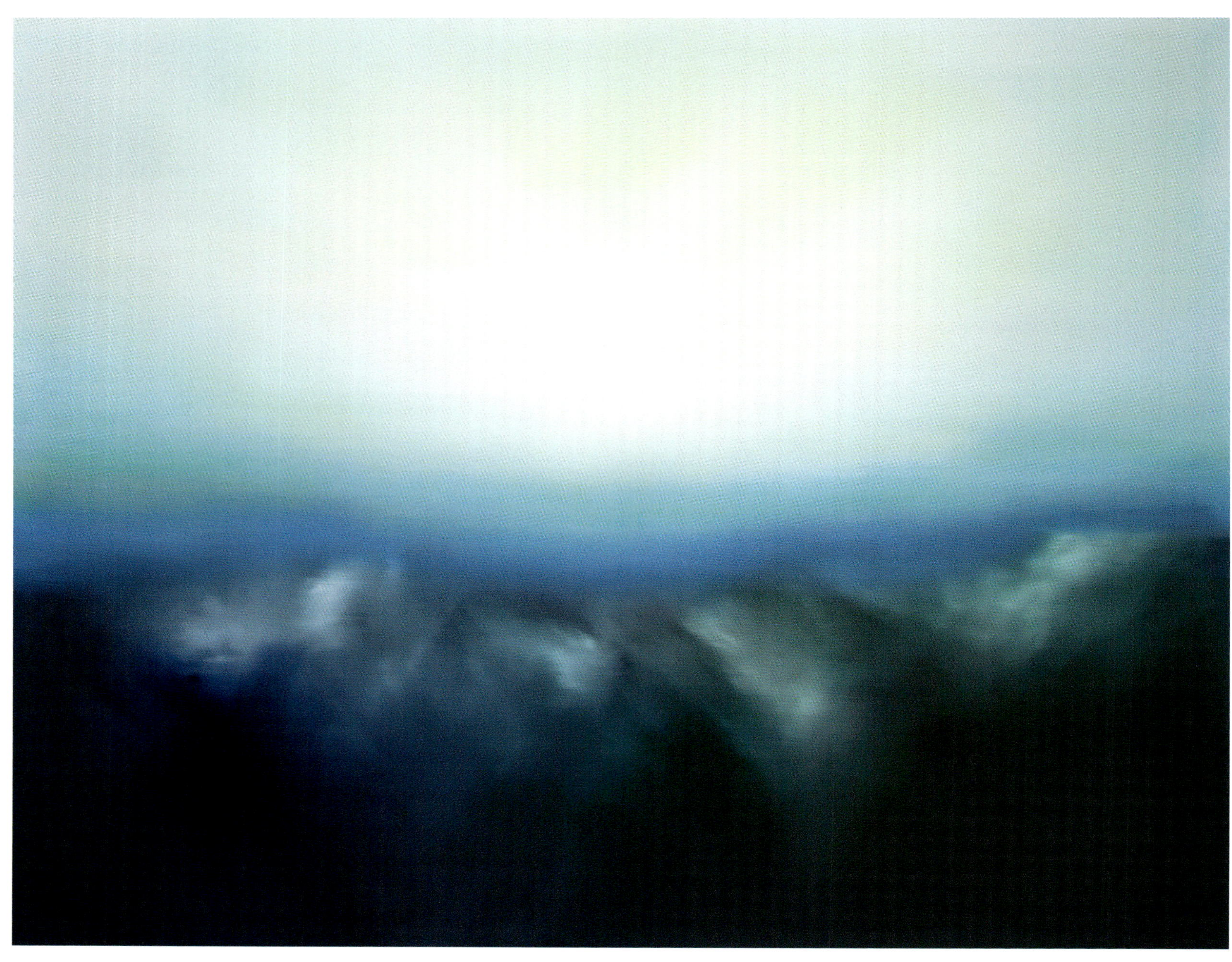

115 *Swiss Impressions I* / *Schweizer Impressionen I, XX-II-10*, 2010
116 *Swiss Impressions III* / *Schweizer Impressionen III*, 2015

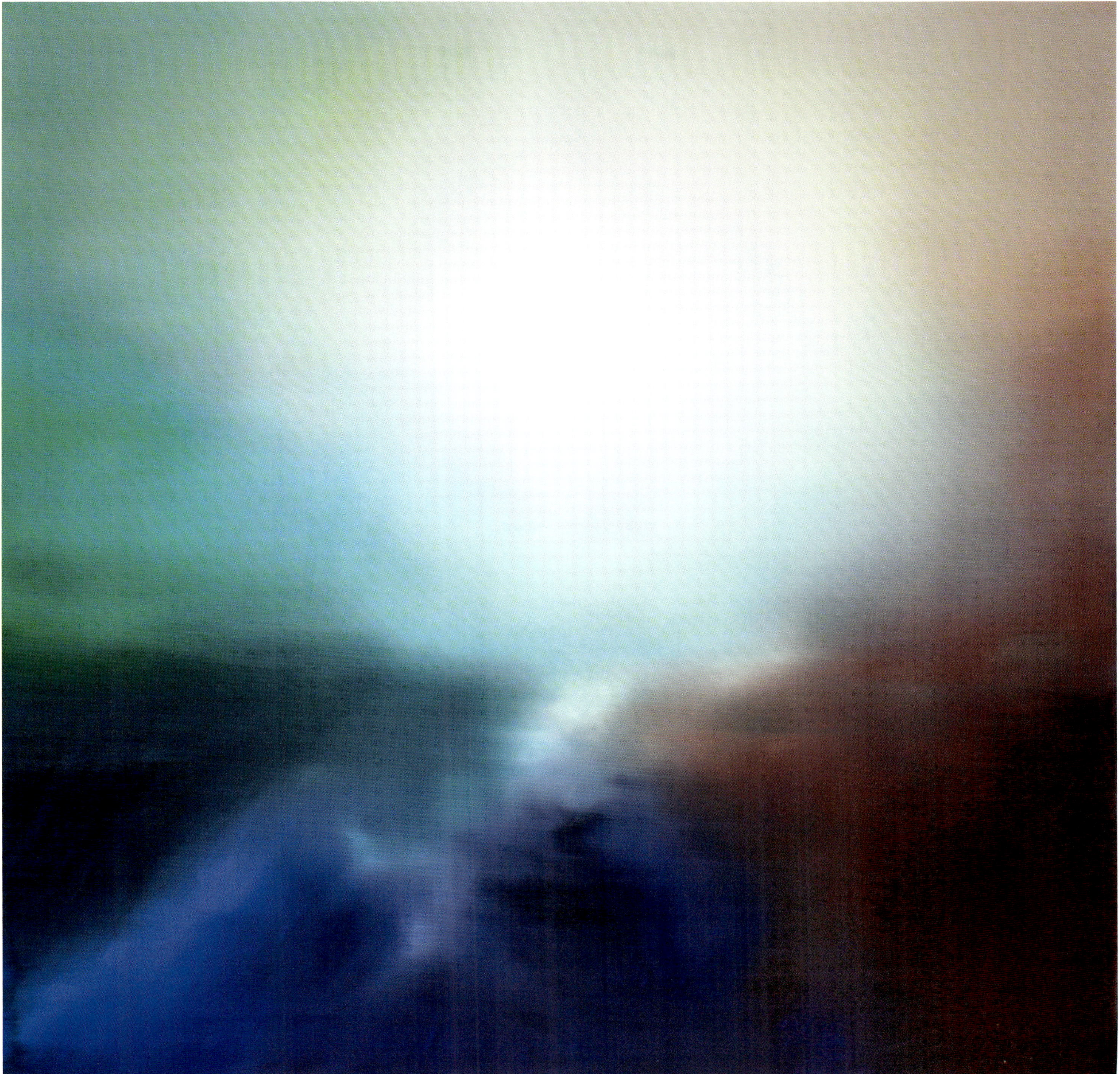

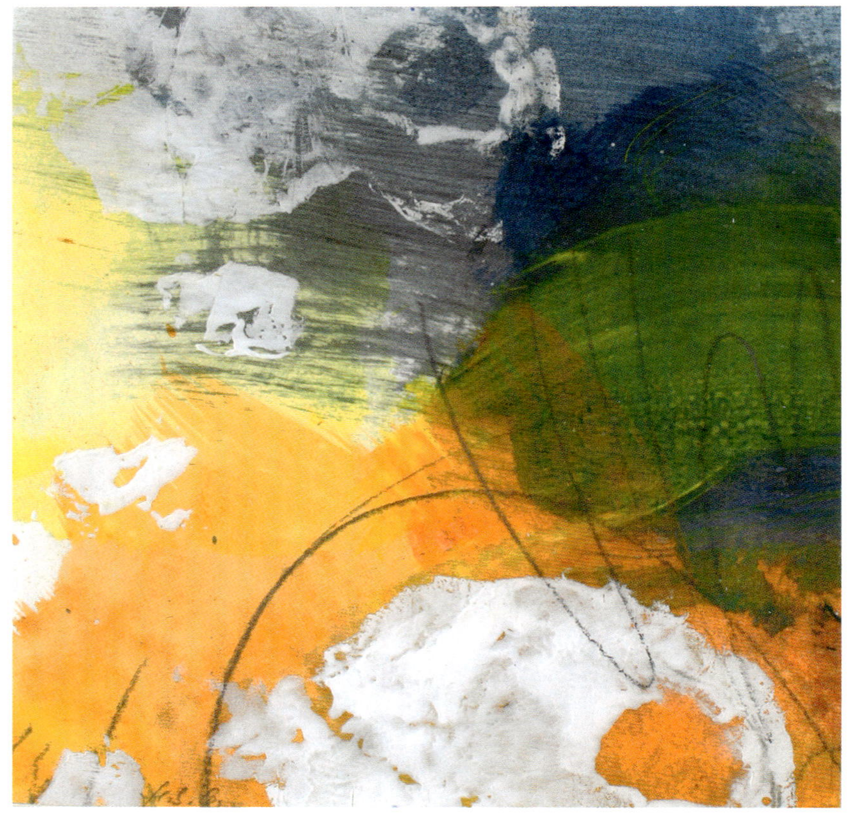

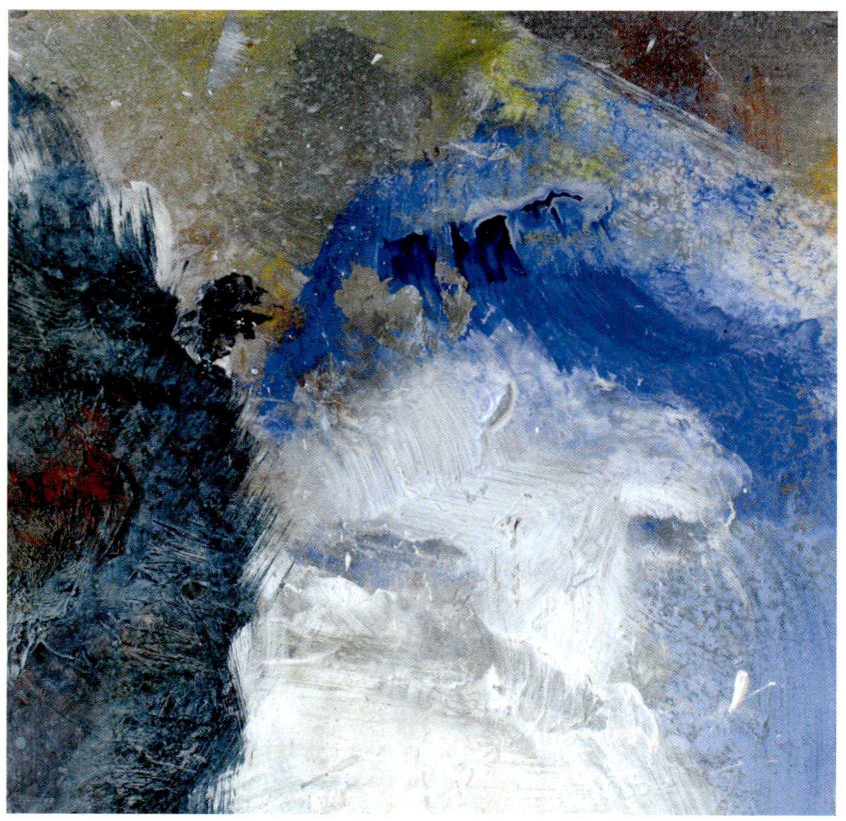

Details from the sketchbook *Calendar Days*, acrylic on paper
Details aus dem Skizzenbuch *Kalendertage*, Acryl auf Bütten

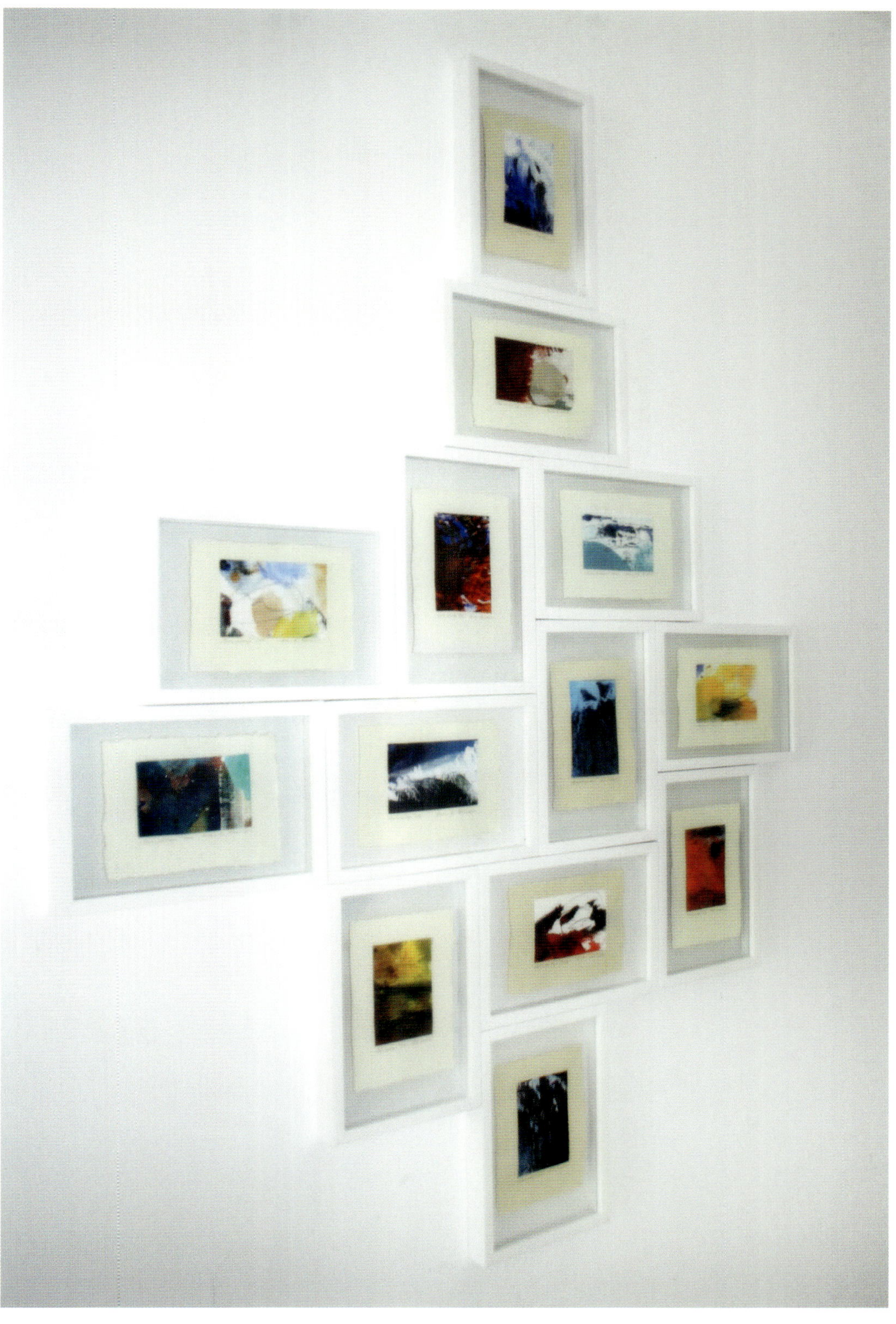

Installation *Calendar Days*
Installation *Kalendertage*

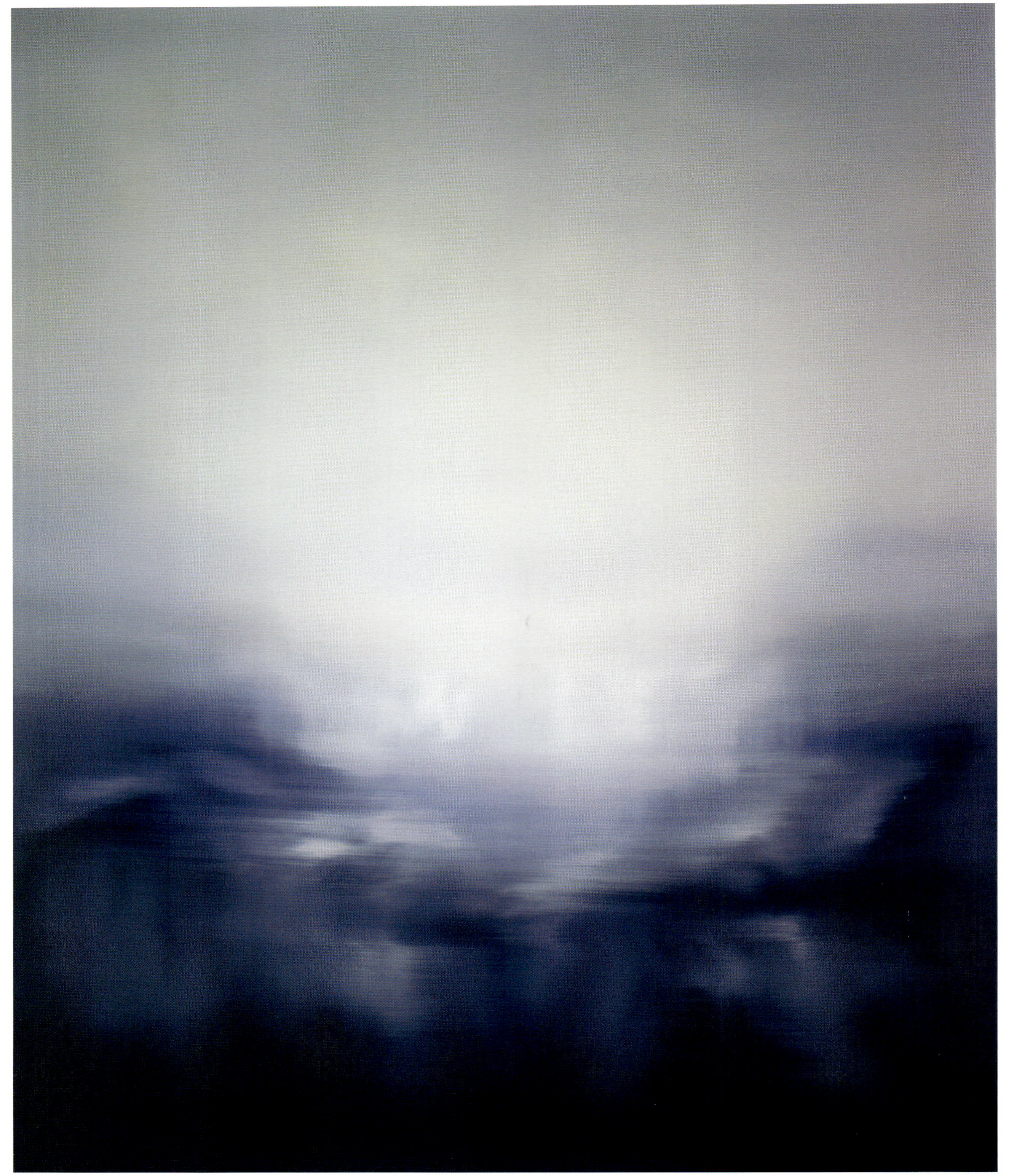

117 *Dual III*, 2015

118 *Dual IV*, 2015

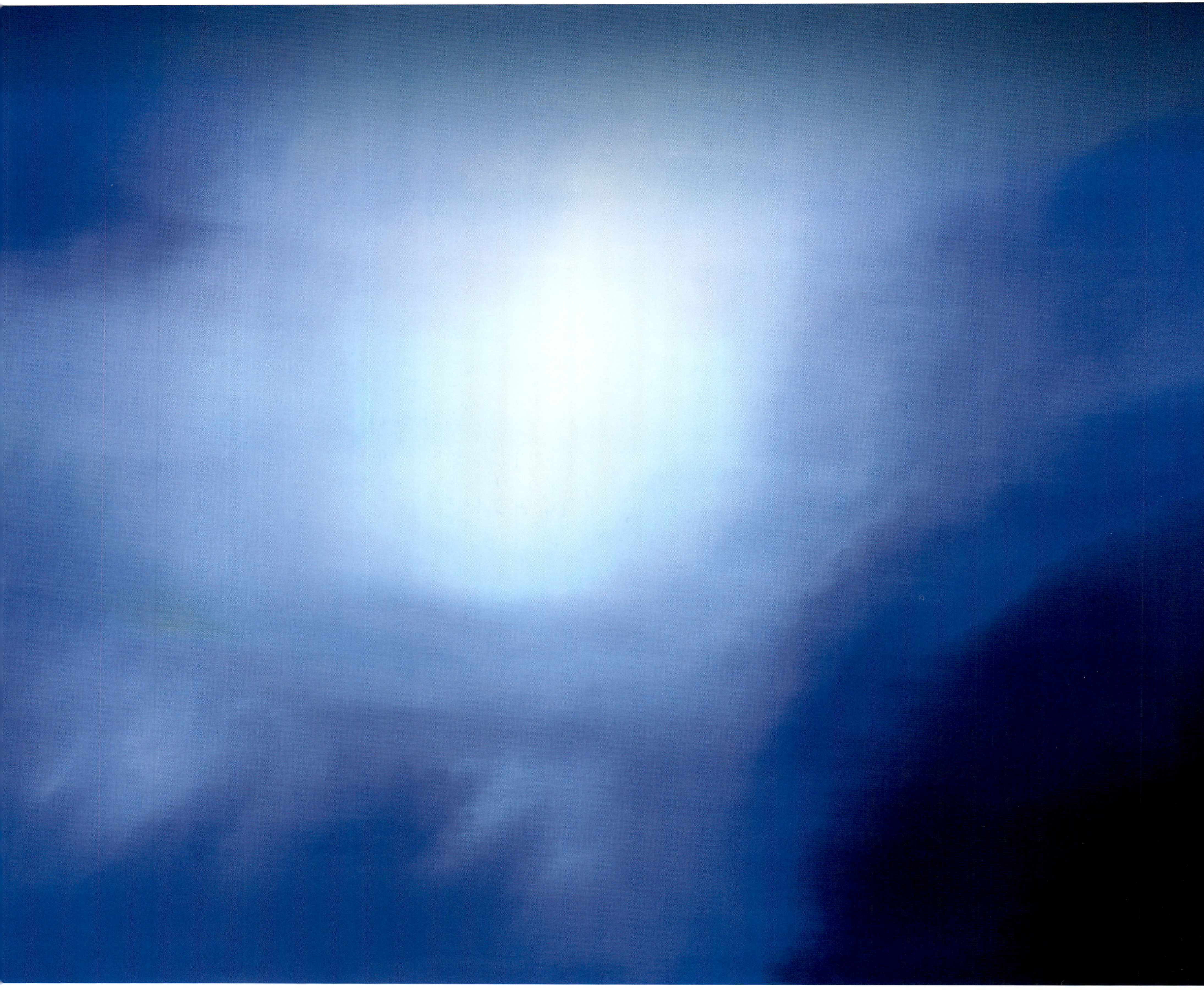

119 *XXIV-VI-08/12*, 2012

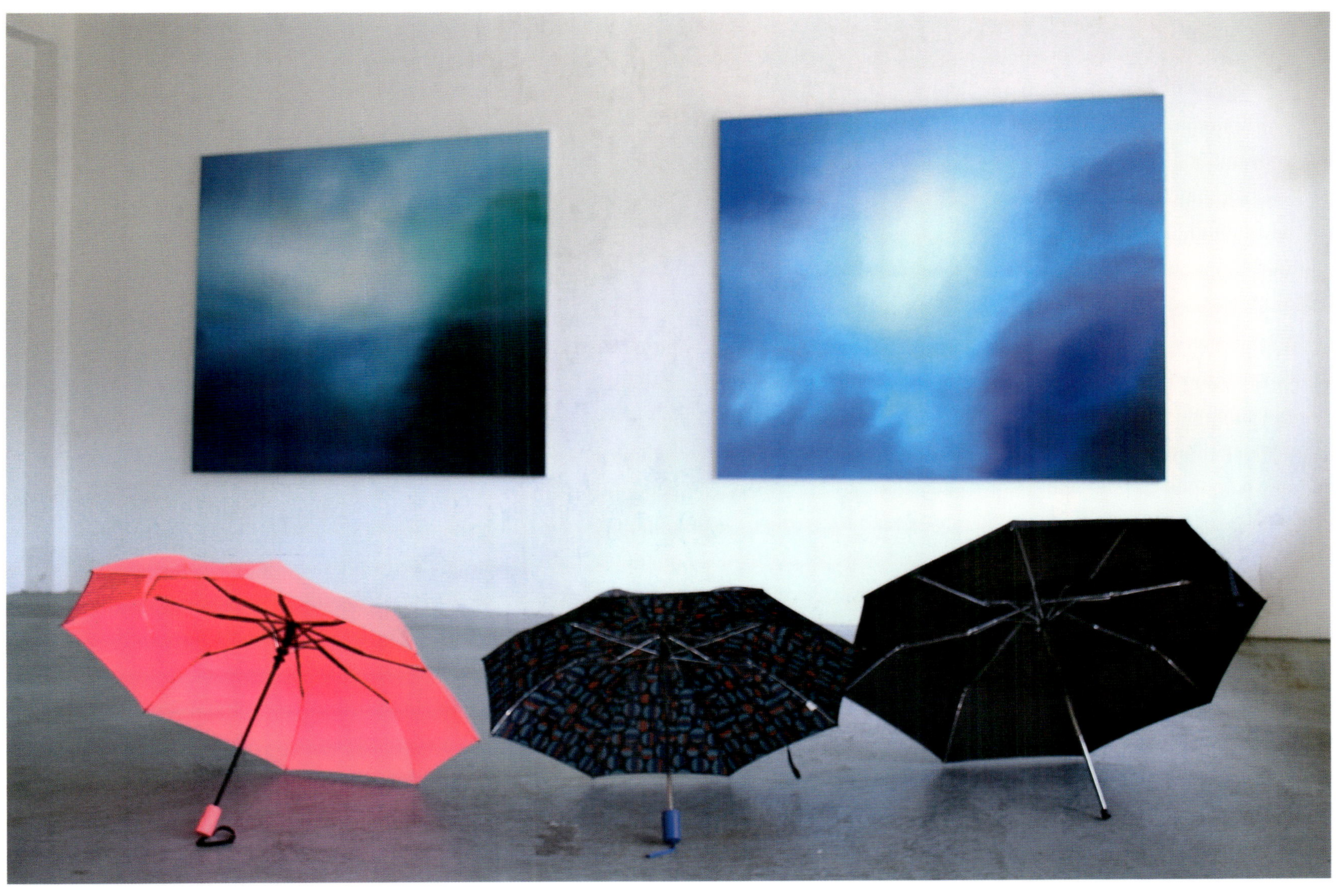

A rainy day in the studio in Switzerland
Ein Regentag im Schweizer Atelier

Helene B. Grossmann
Nur Licht

Gern möchte ich Ihnen etwas über meine Arbeitsweise und Ziele vermitteln. Themen sind das Licht und der Farbraum. Das Ziel ist, Bilder voller pulsierenden Lebens im Detail und Ruhe im Ganzen zu schaffen. Der Betrachter soll nicht festgezurrt auf etwas hingewiesen werden, sondern freien Geistes sich den natürlichen Prozessen seiner Betrachtungsweise öffnen können.

So haben meine Arbeiten etwas mit dem Wesen des Malens zu tun, dem Licht und der Farbe. Seit meinem Studium versuche ich das Licht maltechnisch zu materialisieren. Ich habe mich lange mit der Lichtbrechung der Farben und damit mit Veränderlichkeit im Bild beschäftigt. Meist ist es so, dass man auf den ersten Blick weniger sieht und sich die Farbigkeit der Bilder erst später entfaltet. Diese Veränderlichkeit ist auch den Tageszeiten und Lichtverhältnissen unterworfen. Man entdeckt immer wieder etwas anderes bei wechselnder Stimmung.

Es ist eine Gratwanderung zwischen Abstraktion und Gegenständlichkeit. Für alles Gegenständliche gibt es eine Vorlage. Für die Abstraktion gibt es keine Vorlage. Es ist die Wirklichkeit selbst.

Ich versuche, elementare menschliche Gefühle auszudrücken, indem ich den Raum zwischen Betrachter und Bild zu aktivieren suche. Mit Hilfe des Lichts erleben die Betrachter einen Tiefenraum, der jenseits der realen Räumlichkeit liegt.

Das Konzept der meisten Bilder entsteht so komplex, dass ich es selbst schwer in Worte fassen kann.

Grundlage für jedes Bild ist mein Skizzenbuch. Einen Teil können Sie unter »Grafik« sehen. Ich habe dieses Skizzenbuch *Kalendertage* genannt. Es sind sehr abstrakte Vorarbeiten und das Festschreiben von Erlebnissen. Diese Art von Skizzenbuch habe ich 1993 begonnen. Die Vorgehensweise besteht darin, in farbigen Flecken und breit hingeworfenen Strichen die charakteristische Anlage im Bild zu suchen und das Weitere einer Überarbeitung in einem größeren Format zu unterwerfen.

Meine Technik bedingt einen langsamen koloristischen Malvorgang, das Auftragen von Schicht um Schicht, um die Farben auf der Leinwand steuern zu können. Matisse nannte es »Navigation«. Dieser tastende Suchweg zieht mich an. Dieser klassische Malweg birgt viele Gefahren und Schwierigkeiten, aber er konfrontiert mich immer mit unbekannten Ereignissen und mit überraschenden Wendungen. Im ungewissen Spannungsfeld versuche ich die Mitte des Farbkosmos zu finden.

Dieser Prozess, den malerischen Grundnerv zu finden, hat etwas Reinigendes. Auf dieser Suche wirft man Moden und sinnlose Spleens weg.

Mein Weg ist, etwas mit den Mitteln der Malerei ins Bild zu setzen, um dem Motiv eine Tiefe, ein Vorher und Nachher zu geben. Einen neuen Ein- und Ausblick zu schaffen und Kraft gebende Stille zu erzeugen.

Helene B. Grossmann
Only Light

I would like to tell you about my working methods and aims. My subjects are light and colour space. My aim is to create pictures full of pulsating life in detail and peace as a whole. I do not intend viewers to be pointed rigidly in a certain direction and told what to see, but rather to be able to open themselves in a spirit of freedom to the natural processes of their own ways of viewing.

Thus my work has to do with the essence of painting, of light and of colour. Ever since I was a student, I have tried to depict light in my painting as a material substance. I have spent a lot of time on the refraction of colours and thus with changeability in the picture. At first glance, we usually see less, and the colourfulness of the pictures does not reveal itself until later. This changeability is also subject to the time of day and to light conditions. We always discover something else when the mood changes.

It is a balancing act between abstraction and figuration. For everything figurative, there is a model. For abstraction, there is no model. It is reality itself.

I try to express elementary human feelings by seeking to activate the space between the viewer and the picture. Light helps viewers to experience a depth of space beyond real spatiality.

The concept of most of the pictures comes about in such a complex way that even I can hardly put it into words.

The basis of every picture is my sketchbook. You can see part of it under "Graphics". I call this sketchbook "Calendar Days". It contains very abstract groundwork and records of experiences.

I started this kind of sketchbook in 1993. The procedure consists of using coloured patches and broad brushstrokes to search for the characteristic arrangement in the picture, and to leave the rest to a reworking in a larger format.

My technique requires a slow application of the colours, a spreading of one layer over another, in order to be able to control the colours on the canvas. Matisse called it "navigation". This tentative searching attracts me. This classical way of painting has many dangers and difficulties, but it always confronts me with unknown events and surprising turns. In the uncertain field of tension, I try to find the middle of the colour cosmos.

This process of finding the basic pictorial nerve has something cleansing about it. During this search, one discards fashions and meaningless spleens.

My way is to use the means of painting to depict something, to give the motif a depth, a before and after; to create a new insight and outlook, and to generate empowering silence.

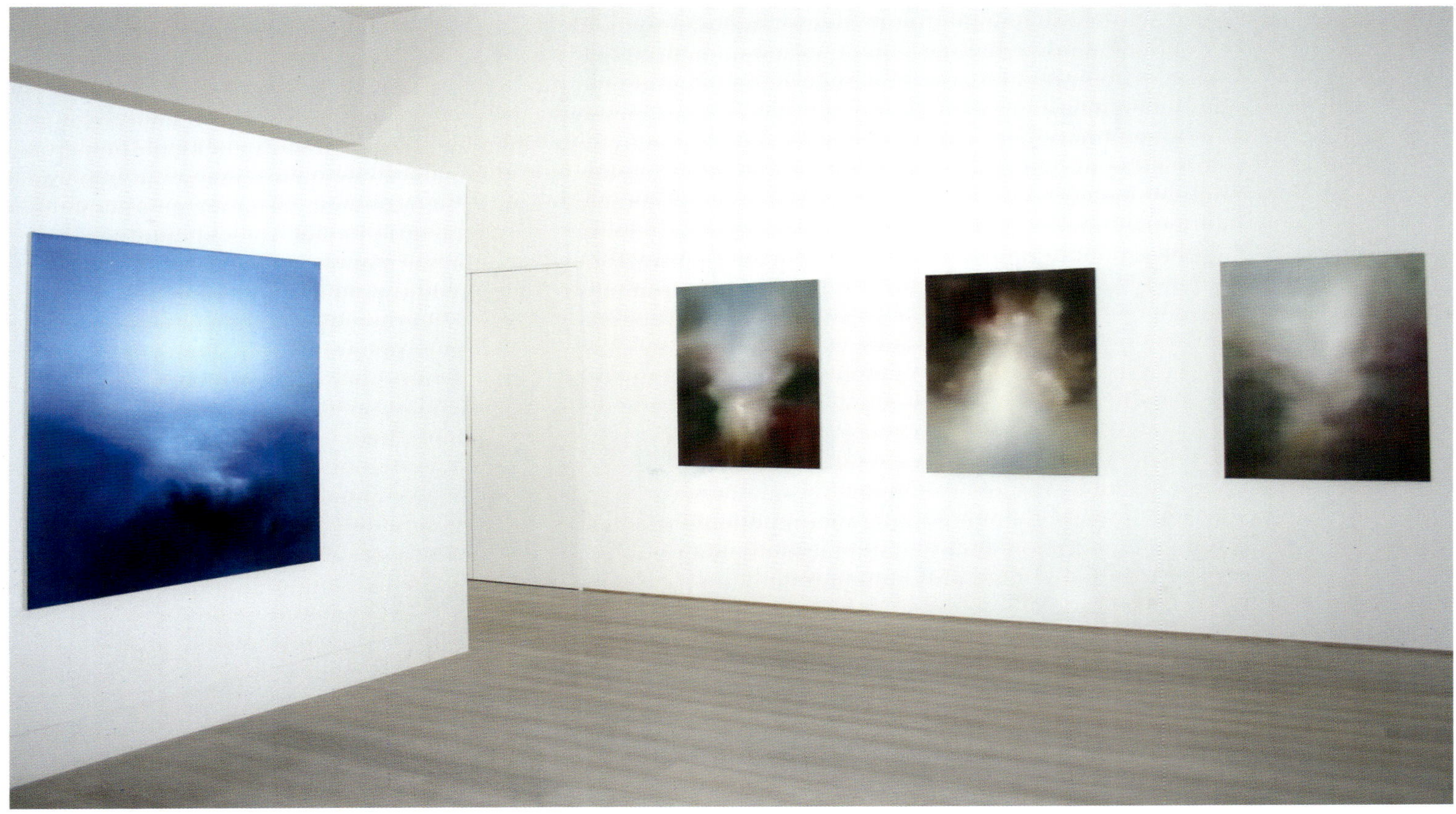

120 *V-IX-08/14*, 2014
Exhibition *Homage to Van Eyck* in Ghent
Ausstellung *Hommage an Van Eyck* in Gent

Kunst ohne Grenzen

Hommage an den Künstler
der russischen Avantgarde
K. S. Malevich

Ausstellung der internationalen
K. S. Malevich Foundation in Moskau

Helena
ГРОССМАН

2 июня - 16 июня. Центр «Дом». Москва
Большой Овчинниковский пер., д. 24, стр. 4

Exhibition at the International Malevich Foundation, Moscow
Ausstellung in der Internationalen Malevich Foundation, Moskau

121 *III-III-00*, 2000

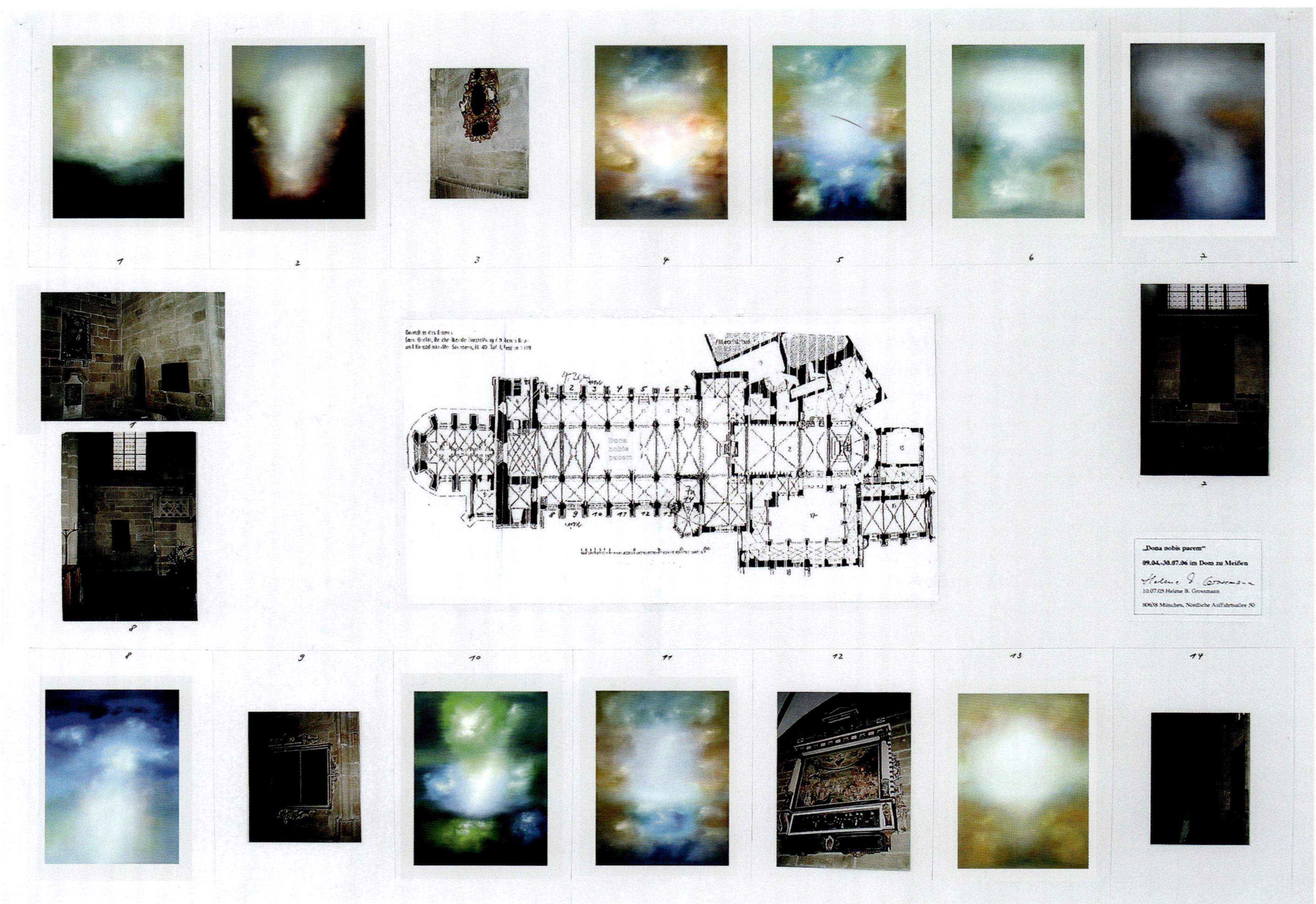

Exhibition *Licht als ewige Gegenwart* at the museum cathedral at Meißen
Ausstellung *Licht als ewige Gegenwart* im musealen Dom zu Meißen

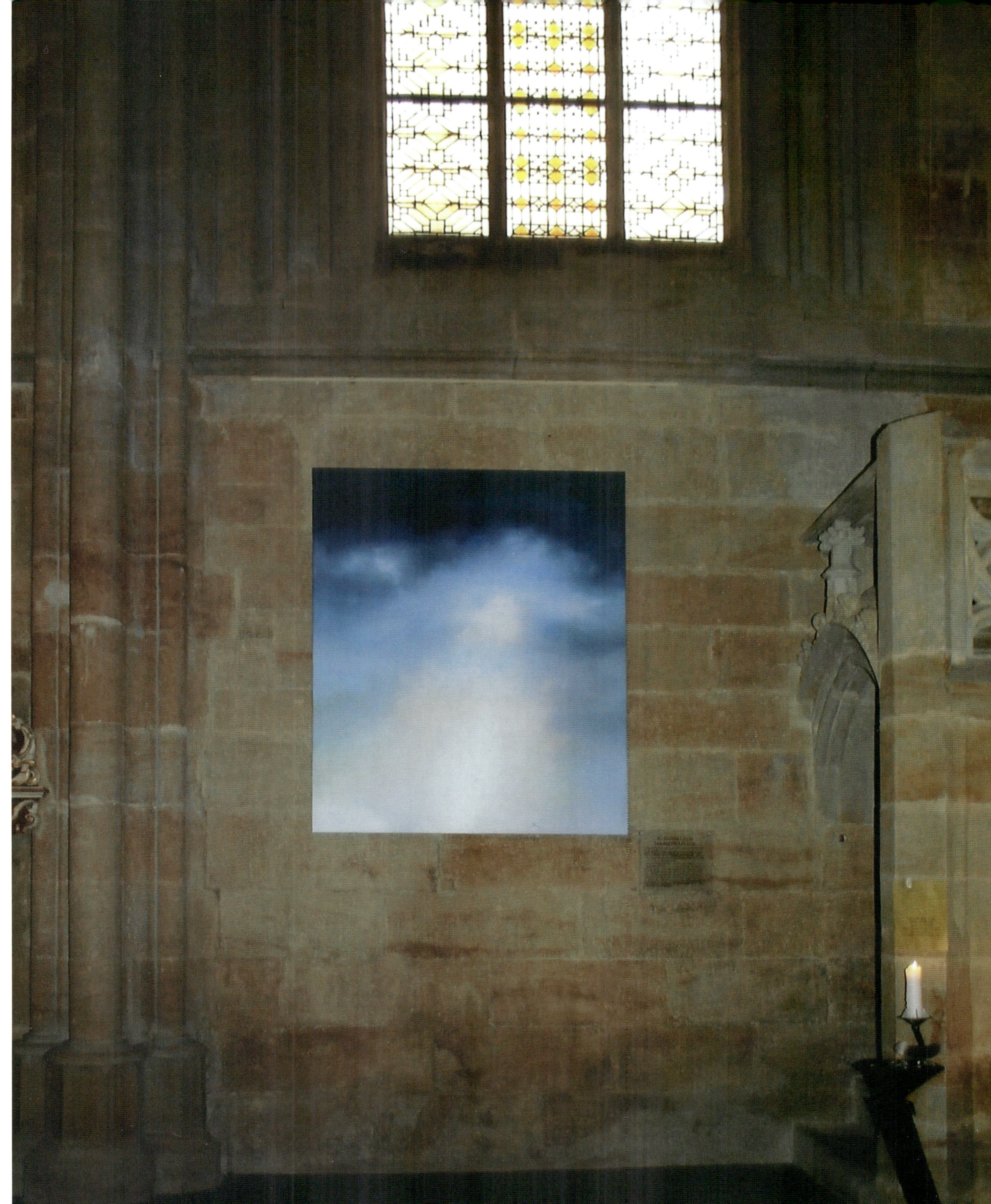

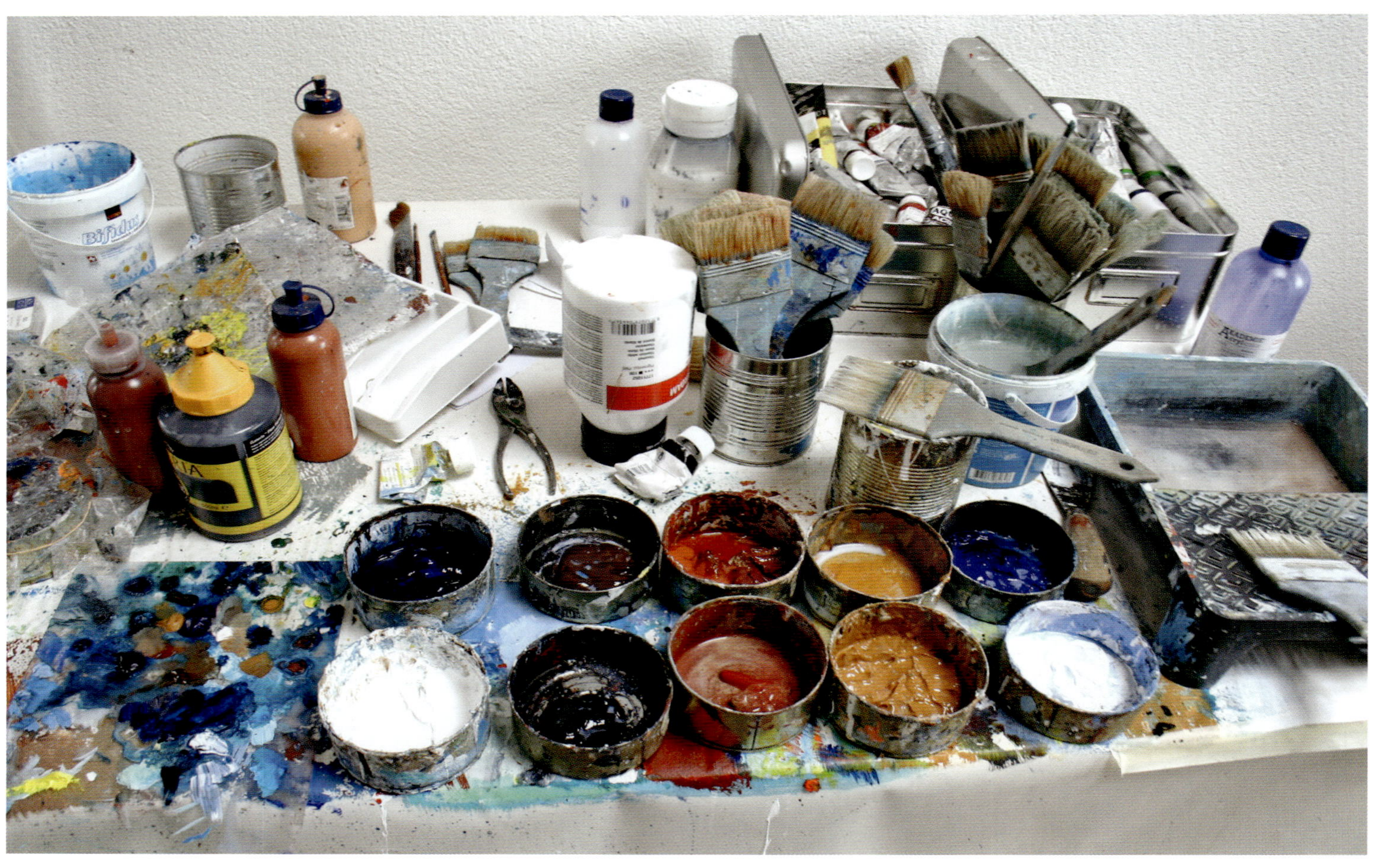

Workplace
Arbeitsplatz

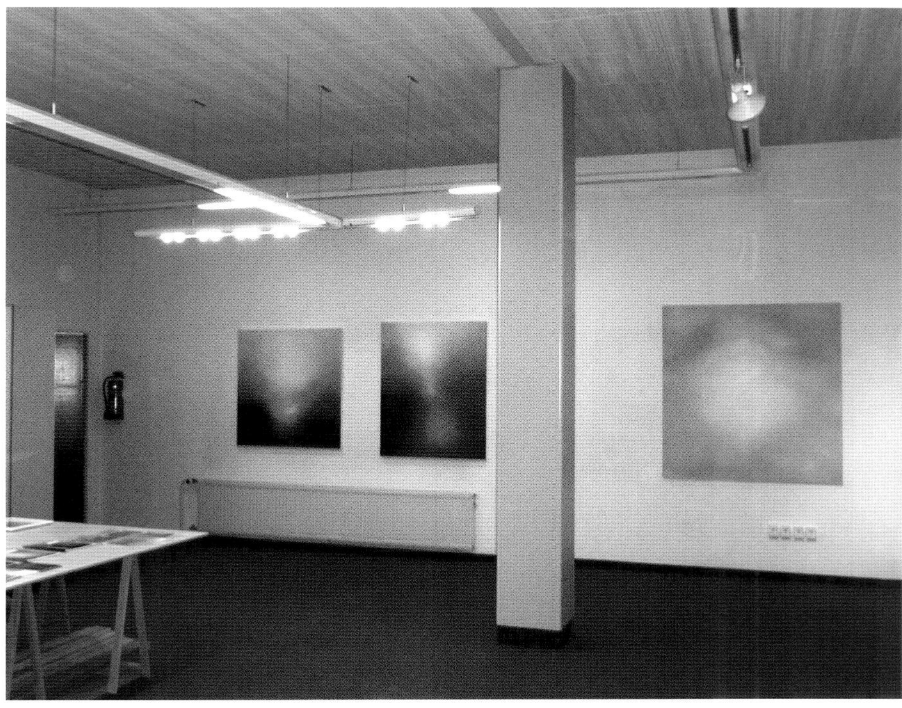
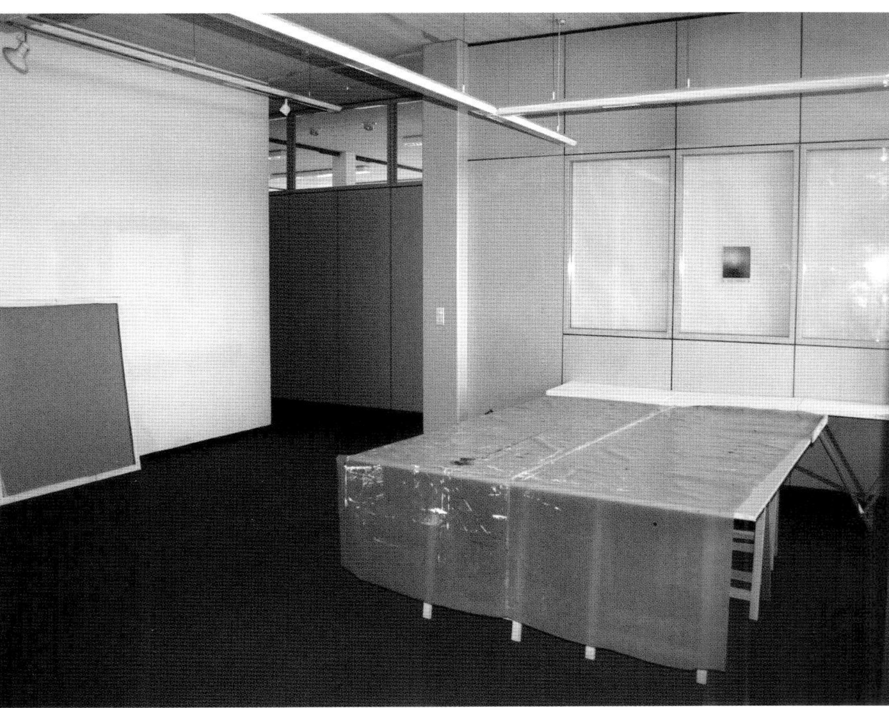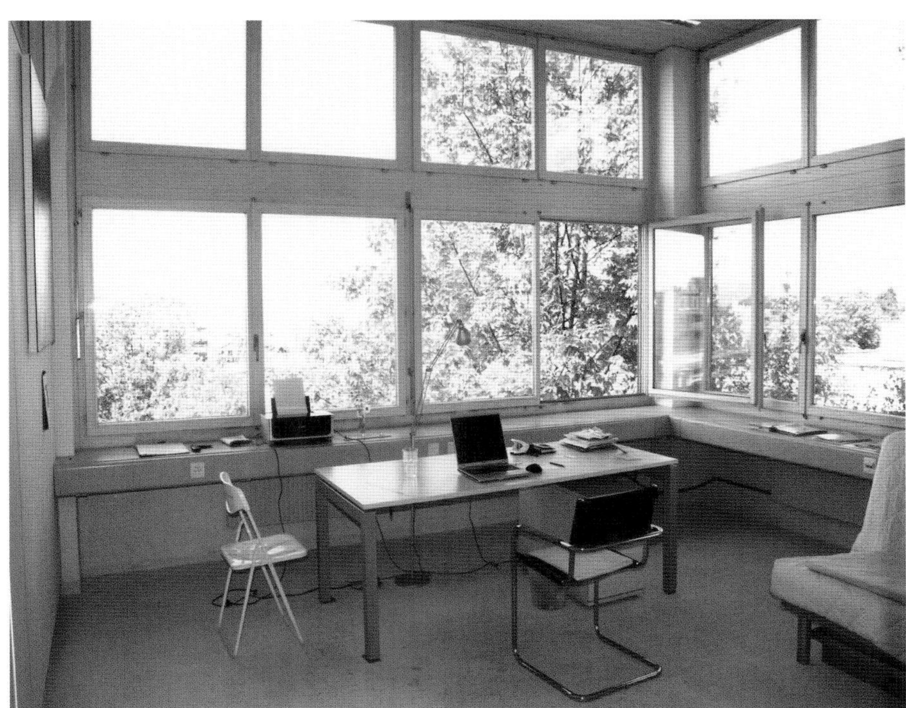

Studio impressions as artist in residence in Wollerau, Switzerland
Atelierimpressionen als Künstler in Residenz in Wollerau, Schweiz

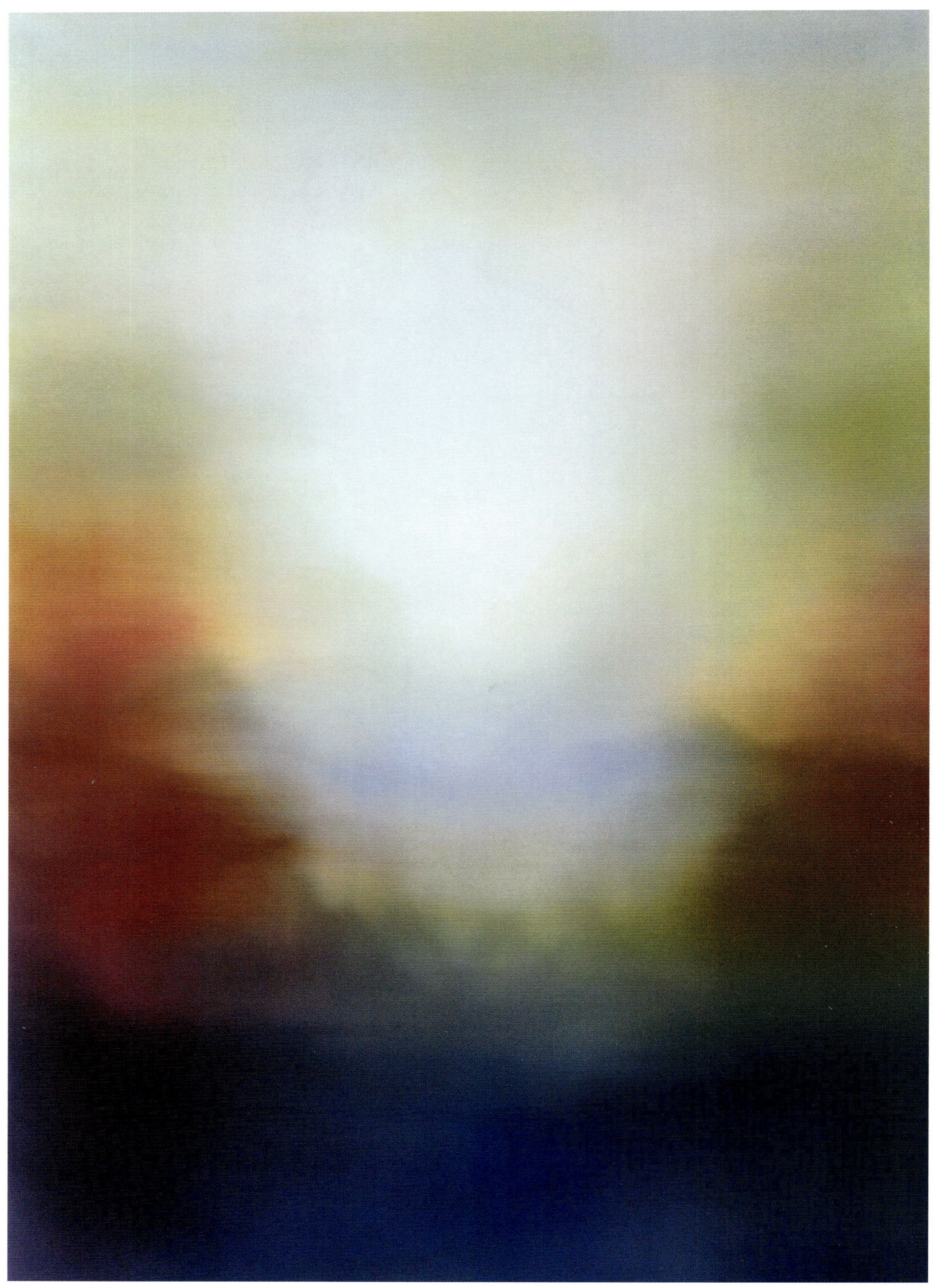

123 *In the Light of Shadow / Im Licht der Schatten*, 2016

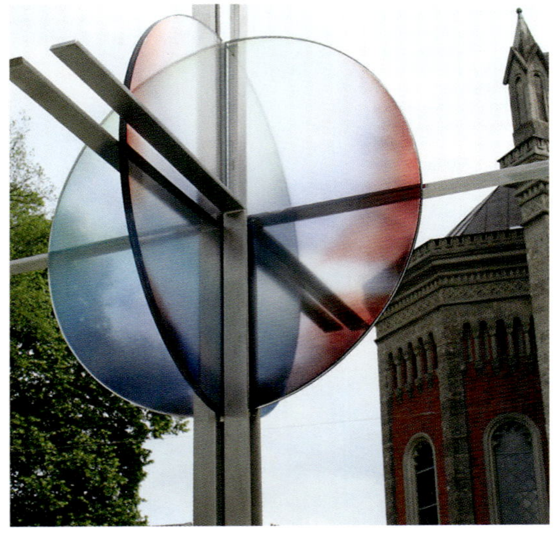

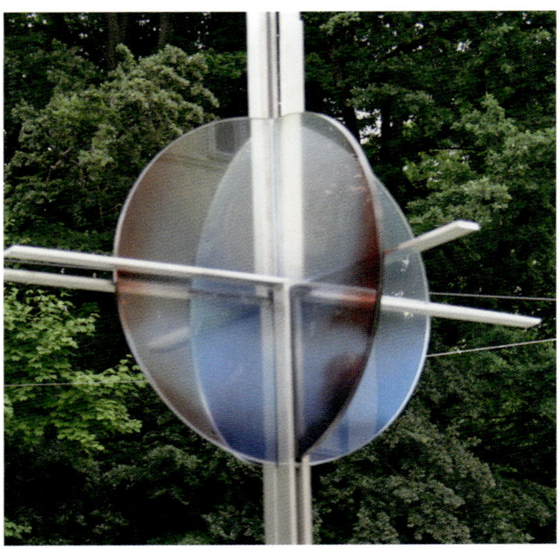

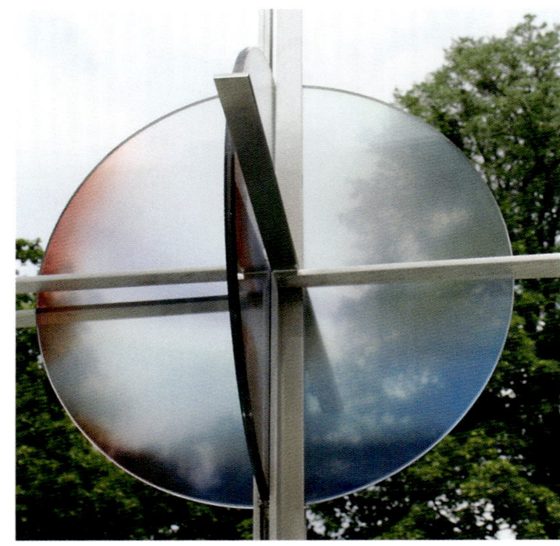

124 *Cross / Kreuz*, Christuskirche, Salzburg
125 *Glass painting / Glasgemälde*, Christuskirche, Salzburg

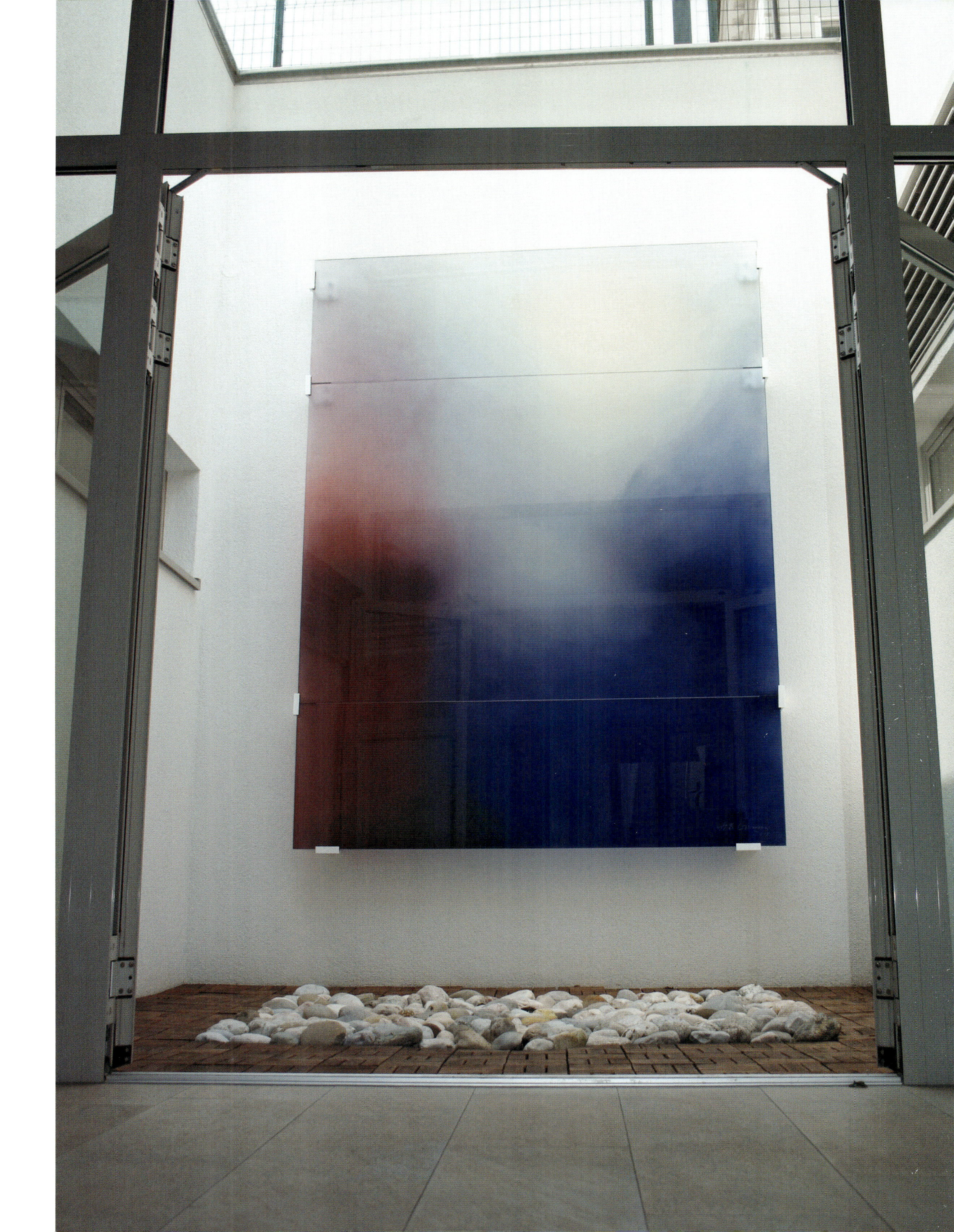

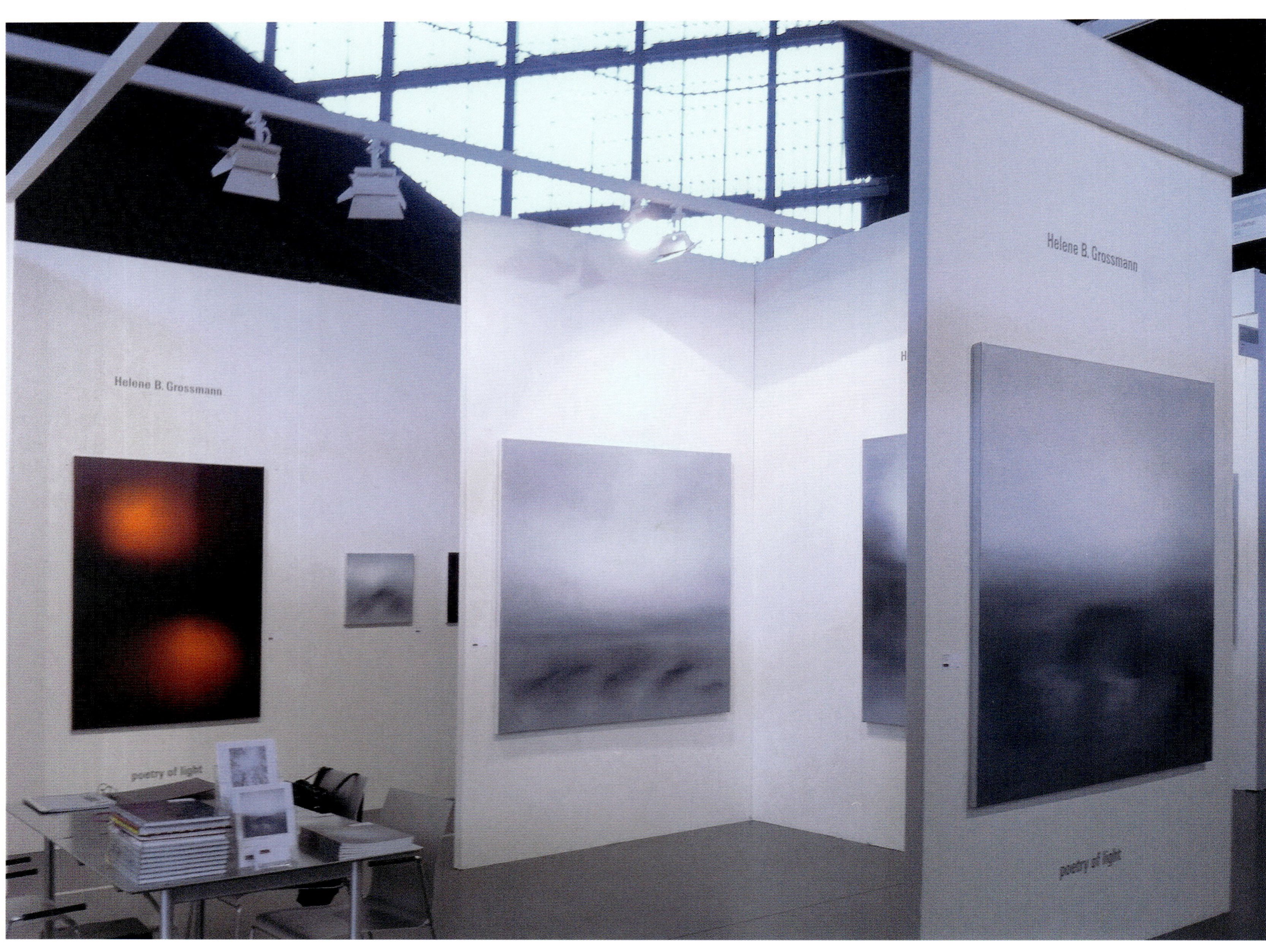

Contemporary art fair, Basel 2015
Contemporary art fair, Basel 2015

126 *Dual V*, 2015

Appendix | Anhang

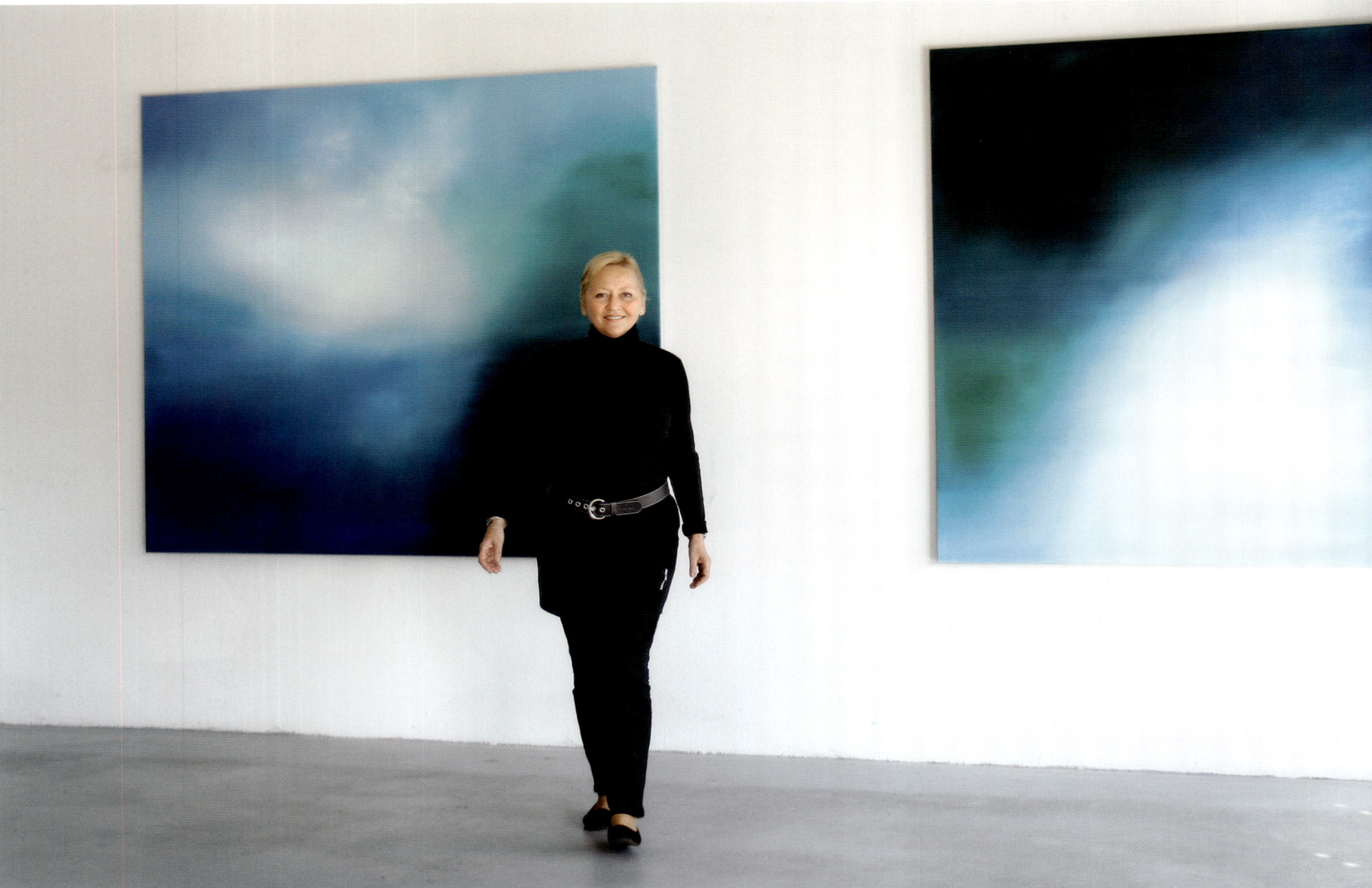

Biography

Born in Dresden

1981–85	Academy of Fine Arts, Dresden
1982/83	Study trips to central Asia and Korea
1988	Studio in Munich
1993	Part-time teaching post at Munich University
1994	Studio with grant from the city of Munich, Lothringerstrasse 13
2001	Trip to Rome, study of fresco painting
2002	Composition and execution of a ceiling fresco in Munich
2003	Working trip to the south of France
2004	Trip to Mexico
2005	Art prize for painting, awarded by the Erwin von Kreibig Museum, Munich
2009–13	Artist in Residence in Switzerland
2013	Glass picture and glass sculpture for the new Evangelisches Zentrum, Christuskirche, Salzburg
since 2007	Studios in Munich and Switzerland

Biografie

geboren in Dresden

1981–85	Hochschule für Bildende Künste Dresden
1982/83	Studienreisen nach Mittelasien und Korea
1988	Atelier in München
1993	Lehrauftrag an der Ludwig-Maximilians-Universität München
1994	Atelierförderung der Landeshauptstadt München, Lothringer 13
2001	Reise nach Rom, Auseinandersetzung mit Freskomalerei
2002	Entwurf und Ausführung eines Deckenfreskos in München
2003	Arbeitsaufenthalt in Südfrankreich
2004	Reise nach Mexiko
2005	Kunstpreis für Malerei des Erwin von Kreibig Museums, München
2009–13	Artist in Residence in der Schweiz
2013	Glasbild und Glasskulptur für das neue Evangelische Zentrum, Christuskirche, Salzburg
seit 2007	Atelier in München und in der Schweiz

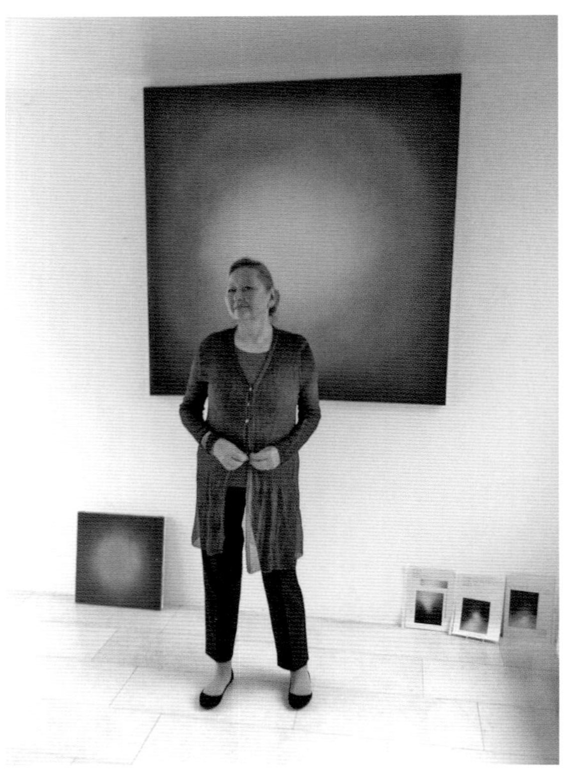

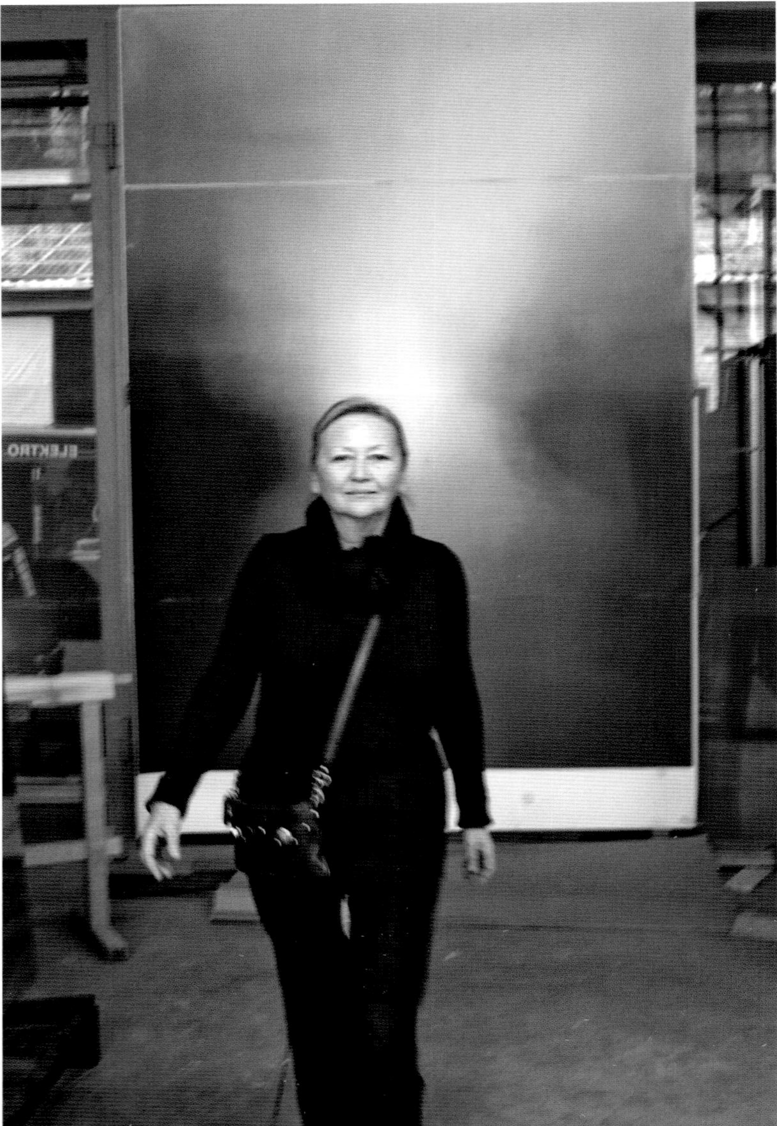

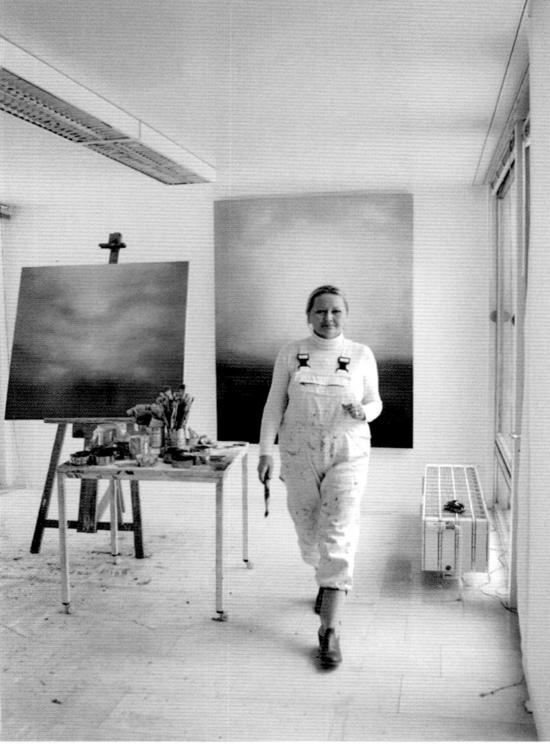

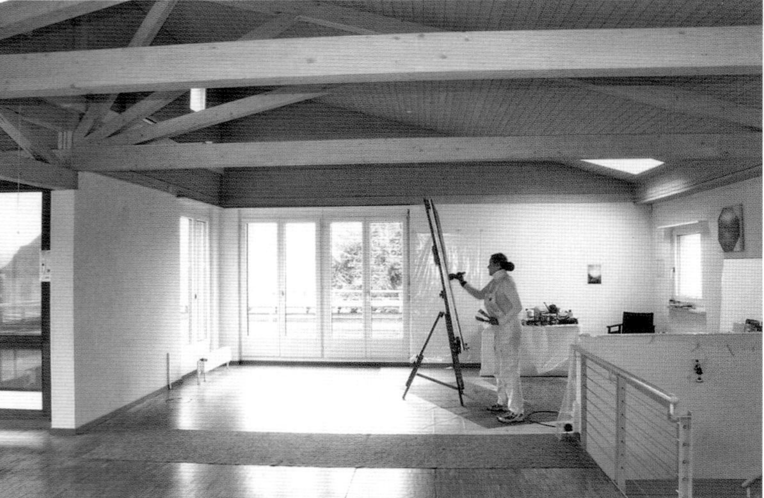

Top left and bottom left: Helene B. Grossmann in her studio in Munich
Oben links und unten links: Helene B. Grossmann im Atelier in München
Top right: Helene B. Grossmann in the Glass Studio Peters in front of the glass painting sketch for Salzburg
Oben rechts: Helene B. Grossmann im Glasstudio Peters vor dem Glasgemäldeentwurf für Salzburg
Bottom right: Helene B. Grossmann in her studio in Switzerland
Unten rechts: Helene B. Grossmann im Atelier in der Schweiz

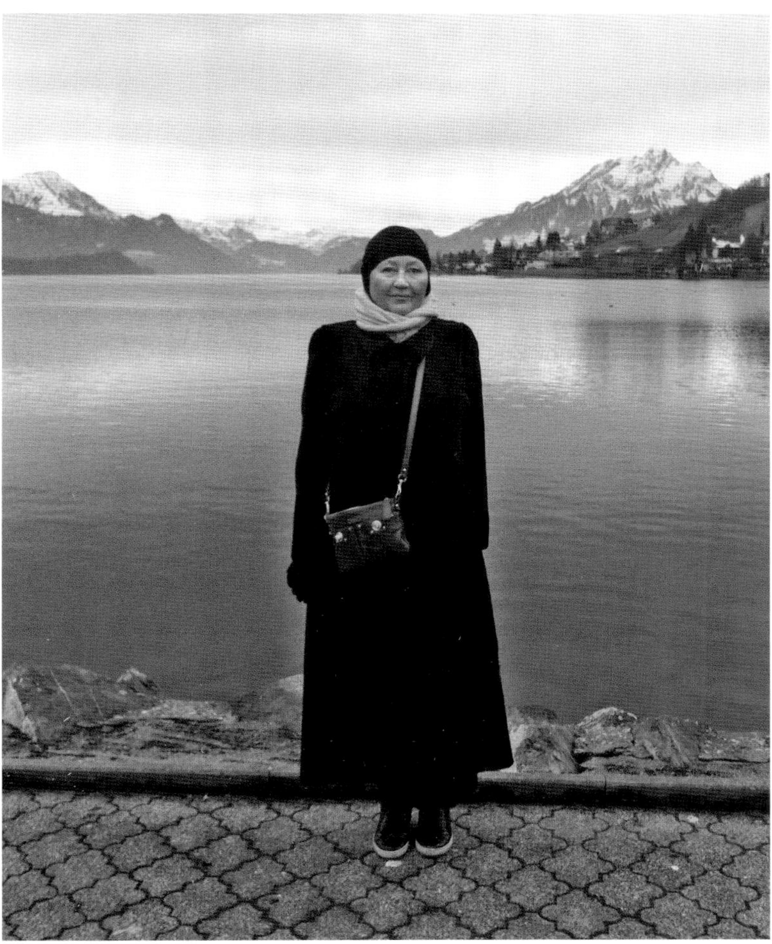
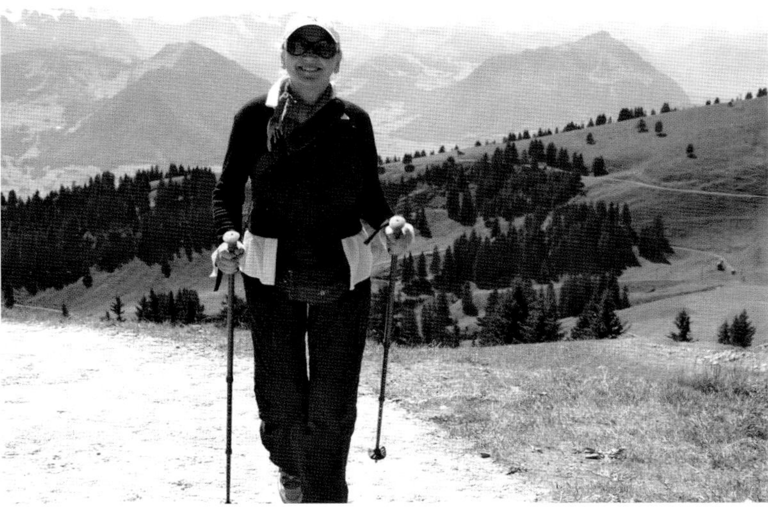
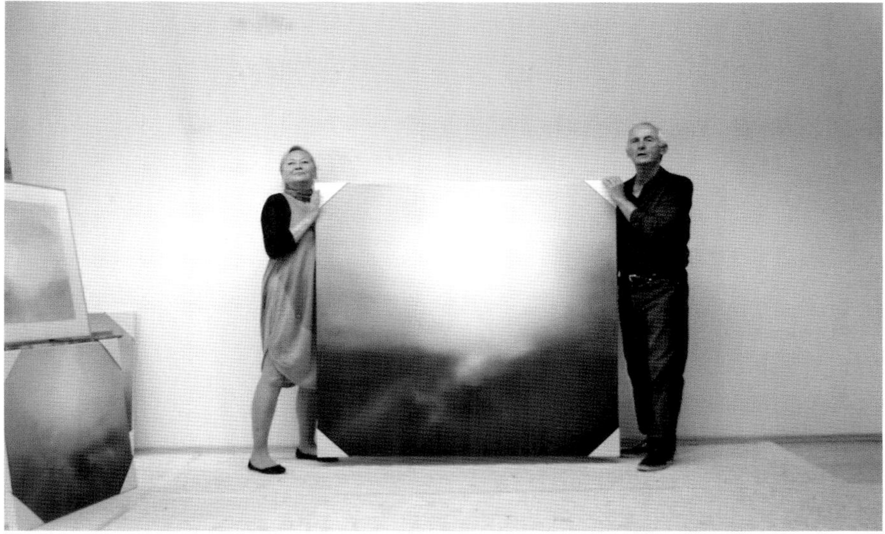
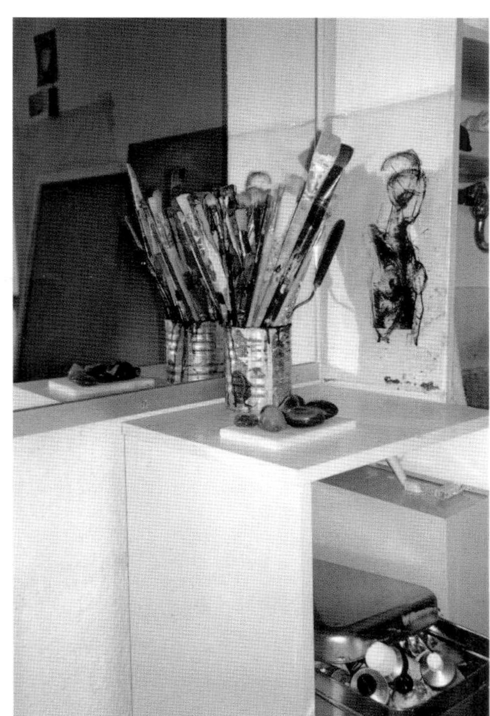
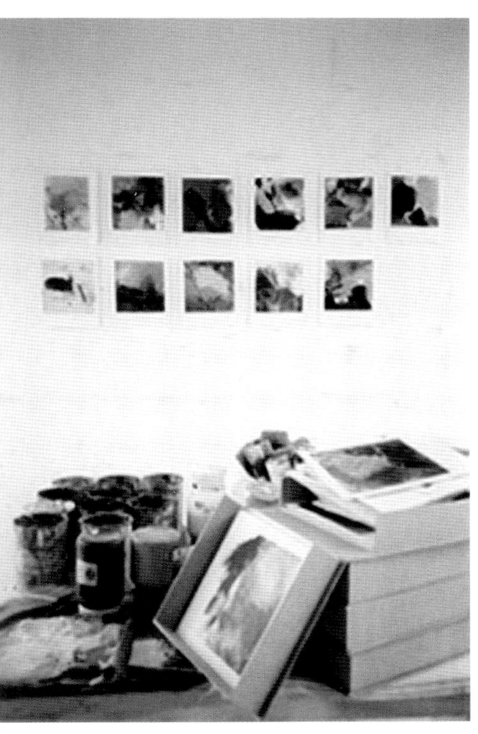

Top left: Project sojourn in Switzerland; Mount Pilatus in the background
Oben links: Projektaufenthalt in der Schweiz, im Hintergrund der Pilatus
Bottom left: Mountain impressions in Switzerland / Unten links: Bergimpressionen in der Schweiz
Top right: Exhibition installation Helene B. and Dieter Grossmann
Oben rechts: Ausstellungsaufbau Helene B. und Dieter Grossmann
Bottom: Sketchbook cassettes / Unten: Skizzenbuch-Kassetten

Solo Exhibitions (Selection) |
Einzelausstellungen (Auswahl)

2017   *Share the Light*, Galerie Mollwo, Riehen/Basel (CH)
Share the Light, Galerie Urs Reichlin, Zug (CH)

2016   *MORE LIGHT – LIGHT ONLY*, Galerie Urs Reichlin, Zug (CH)
ONLY LIGHT, Galerie Artraum Bachstein, Freiburg (D)

2015   *The Solo Project, Poetry of Light*, Contemporary art fair, Galerie Mollwo,
St. Jakobshalle, Basel (CH)
Sphären von Licht und Landschaft, Galerie Urs Reichlin, Küssnacht a. R. (CH)

2014   *LIGHT ONLY*, Galerie – art studio fael, Hannover (D)
RESPIRO – ich atme, Galerie Reichlin, Küssnacht a. R. (CH)

2013   *ONLY LIGHT*, Galerie Sybille Nütt, Dresden (D)
Vier Jahreszeiten, Galerie Urs Reichlin, Küssnacht a. R. (CH)
Das Verborgene im Wesen der Dinge, mit Werken von Jakob Weder, Galerie
im Stilhaus, Rothrist (CH)

2012   *Gemaltes Licht*, Galerie Mollwo, Riehen/Basel (CH)
ONLY LIGHT, Galerie Terminus, München (D)
ONLY LIGHT, Galerie Reichlin, Küssnacht a. R. (CH)
I'v got my eye on your art, Performance, balzer Art projects, Basel (CH)

2011   *Schweizer Impressionen*, Galerie Reichlin, Küssnacht a. R. (CH)
One-Artist-Show, Art Karlsruhe (D)

2010   *Hommage aan Van Eyck*, Galerie Pascal Janssens, Gent (B)
Licht, Galerie Fritz Winter, Diessen (D)
Faszination des Lichts, Galerie Reichlin, Küssnacht a. R. (CH)
One-Artist-Show, Art Karlsruhe (D)

2009   *Von Madrid nach Berlin*, Galerie Terminus, München (D)
One-Artist-Show, Art Karlsruhe (D)
protrahere, Galerie Sybille Nütt, Dresden (D)
Wenn Horizonte sich öffnen, Galerie Reichlin, Küssnacht a. R. (CH)

2008   *One-Artist-Show*, Art Karlsruhe (D)
Licht, Kunstverein Coburg (D)
Helene B. Grossmann – Bilder, Galerie Reichlin, Küssnacht a. R. (CH)

2007   *Helene B. Grossmann – Bilder*, Galerie Mollwo, Riehen/Basel (CH)
One-Artist-Show, Art Karlsruhe (D)
Visuelle Energie, Galerie Reichlin, Küssnacht a. R. (CH)

2006   *Pulsschlag – Malerei im 21. Jahrhundert*, Galerie Sybille Nütt, Dresden (D)
Licht als ewige Gegenwart, Ausstellungsprojekt im Dom zu Meißen (D)
Helene B. Grossmann – Bilder, Galerie Reichlin, Küssnacht a. R. (CH)

2005   *Licht*, Micus Foundation Ibiza (E)
RESPIRO, Galerie Tazl Graz (A)

2004   *RESPIRO*, Galerie Thomas, München (D)
RESPIRO, Galerie Nütt, Dresden (D)

2002   *Bilder Helene B. Grossmann*, Galerie Maria Schönenberger-Kyrimis,
           Zürich (CH)
           Kulturfokus International, Luzern (CH)
           Malerei, Kunstkreis Gräfelfing (D)

2001   *Vibrationen des Lichts*, Galerie Hartl, Poing (D)

2000   *Kunst ohne Grenzen*, Internationale K. S. Malevich Foundation, Moscow
           Kunst ohne Grenzen, Galerie A3, Moscow
           Die Welt des Lichtes und der Farbe, Galerie Beck und Eggeling, Düsseldorf (D)
           Licht und Farbe, Galerie Wolfgang Tumulka, München (D)
           Licht, Museum Weilheim (D)

1999   *Malerei*, Helene B. Grossmann, Galerie Dube-Heynig, München (D)

1998   *Helene B. Grossmann – Neue Arbeiten*, Galerie Waszkowiak, Berlin (D)
           Helene B. Grossmann – Neue Arbeiten, Galerie Königstrasse, Dresden (D)

1997   *Malerei*, Galerie Dube-Heynig, München (D)
           Neue Arbeiten, Ausstellungshalle der Bayerischen Landesbank, München (D)

1996   *Die Psychologie der Farben*, KVD Dachau (D)

1995   *Malerei – Raum*, Galerie Königstrasse, Dresden (D)
           Malerei – Raum, Ausstellungsräume der Dresdner Bank, Dresden (D)

1994   *Roter Zyklus*, Atelierhaus Lothringer-Str. 13, Galerie Artcurial, München (D)

1993   *Helene B. Grossmann – Malerei*, Kunstverein Erlangen im Palais Stutterheim,
           Erlangen (D)

1991   *Bilder und Skulpturen*, Museum Waldkraiburg (D)

1990   *Enothea*, Galerie Hornung, München (D)
           Skulpturen, Galerie am Bachfeld, München (D)

1986–1988 Ausstellungsverbot in der DDR

1985   Galerie am Schönhof Görlitz, Görlitz (DDR)
           Galerie Bautzen, Bautzen (DDR)

1984   Museum Borna (DDR)
           Galerie im Stadthaus Jena, Jena (DDR)

1982   Neue Dresdner Galerie, Dresden (DDR)

1981   Galerie Berlin, Berlin (DDR)

1980   Galerie Carl Blechen, Cottbus (DDR)

1979   Galerie Berlin, Berlin (DDR)

Group Exhibition (Selection) |
Gruppenausstellungen (Auswahl)

2016	*Kunstsalon 2016, Farbe und Raum*, Ägyptisches Museum, München (D)
	12 Künstler – 12 Sprachen, Galerie Nütt, Dresden (D)
	Best of Reichlin, Galerie Urs Reichlin, Zug (CH)
2014	*Künstler der Galerie Mollwo*, Galerie Mollwo, Riehen/Basel (CH)
	Pure Colour / Farbe Pur, WIMMERplus, Prien am Chiemsee (D)
	14 Künstler – 14 Sprachen, Galerie Nütt, Dresden (D)
2012	*Subtiles Spiel*, Galerie Mollwo, Riehen/Basel (CH)
2011	*FMDK 2011*, Schloss Mirabell, Salzburg (A)
	Künstler der Galerie Mollwo, Galerie Mollwo, Riehen/Basel (CH)
	11 Künstler – 11 Sprachen, Galerie Nütt, Dresden (D)
2010	*Künstlerhaus Wollerau*, Wollerau (CH)
	Sommer 10, 10 Künstler – 10 Sprachen, Galerie Nütt, Dresden (D)
	Künstler der Galerie Mollwo, Galerie Mollwo, Riehen/Basel (CH)
2009	*Die Sehnsucht der Luft*, Galerie Refugium, Dresden (D)
	Künstler der Galerie Mollwo, Galerie Mollwo, Riehen/Basel (CH)
2008	*Neuer Kunstsalon 2008*, Haus der Kunst, München (D)
	13 Künstler – 13 Sprachen, Galerie Nütt, Dresden (D)
2007	*Neuer Kunstsalon 2007*, Haus der Kunst, München (D)
	ICH, Galerie Nütt, Dresden (D)
2006	*Mittendrin*, Güssing, Jennersdorf (A)
	Zeitschnitt, Galerie Samuelis Baumgarte, Bielefeld (D)
	Kunstsalon 2006, Haus der Kunst, München (D)
2005	*K 2005 denkmalfarbig*, Haus der Kunst, München (D)
	Malerei und Skulptur, Kunsthalle Arnstadt, Arnstadt (D)
	Zeitgenössische Kunst, Erwin von Kreibig Museum, München (D)
2004	*K 2004 hautnah,* Haus der Kunst, München (D)
	Himmel und Erde, Schloss Seefeld, Seefeld (D)
	Jantyik Mátyás Múzeum, Békés (H)
	Galerie der Künste, Budapest (H)
2003	*K 03*, Haus der Kunst, München (D)
	Open Art – Open Future, Galerie Thomas, München (D)
	Zeitgenössische Kunst, Erwin von Kreibig Museum, München (D)
2002	*Nur Farbe*, Galerie Thomas, München (D)
	Zeitgenössische Kunst, Erwin von Kreibig Museum, München (D)
	K 2002, Haus der Kunst, München (D)
2001	*Kunstsalon 2001*, Haus der Kunst, München (D)
	Zeitgenössische Kunst, Erwin von Kreibig Museum, München (D)
	Ladengalerie Thomas, München (D)
2000	*Zeitgenössische Kunst*, Erwin von Kreibig Museum, München (D)
1999	*Künstler der Galerie Königstraße*, Galerie Königstraße, Dresden
	Zeitgenössische Kunst, Erwin von Kreibig Museum, München (D)

1998	Kunstverein Coburg, Coburg (D)
	Künstler der Galerie Dube-Heynig, Galerie Dube-Heynig, München (D)
1994	*Fünf Jahre Kunstausstellungen*, Museum Waldkraiburg, Waldkraiburg (D)
	IV. Internationale Art-Triennale, Państwowe Muzeum na Majdanku, Lublin (P)
1993	*Kunst des XX. Jahrhunderts*, Kunstausstellung Kühl, Dresden (D)
1991	*Ausgebürgert – Künstler aus der DDR*, Deichtorhallen Hamburg, Hamburg (D)
1990	*Ausgebürgert – Künstler aus der DDR*, Albertinum, Dresden (D)
	Große Kunstausstellung München, Haus der Kunst, München (D)
1982/83	*IX. Kunstausstellung der DDR*, Albertinum, Dresden (DDR)

Art Fairs | Kunstmessen

2015	The Solo Project, "Poetry of Light", Contemporary art fair, St. Jakobshalle, Basel (CH)
2009–2016	Art Miami, Miami (USA)
2013–2016	Art Karlsruhe, Karlsruhe (D)
2013	Art Expo Chicago, Chicago (USA)
2011–2014	Art Southampton, Southampton (USA)
2010–2015	Art Fair Köln, Köln (D)
2010	Munich Contempo, München (D)
2010–2013	Fine Art Fair, Palm Beach (USA)
2009	International Fine Art Fair, Salzburg (A)
2009	Liste Berlin, Berlin (D)
2007–2011	One Artist, Art Karlsruhe, Karlsruhe (D)
2006	Art of the 20th Century, New York (USA)
2005–2007	Kunst Zürich, Zürich (CH)
2004	TEFAF Maastricht, Maastricht (B)
2004–2006	ARCO Madrid, Madrid (E)
2003/04	Art Basel / Miami Beach, Miami (USA)
2003–2005	Art Basel, Basel (CH)
2002/03	Kunstmesse München, München (D)
2001	Kunst Köln, Köln (D)
1997/2001–2005	Art Cologne, Köln (D)

Works in public collections |
Werke in öffentlichen Sammlungen

Staatliche Kunstsammlungen Dresden, Dresden (D)

Deutsche Sammlung für Historische und Zeitgenössische Keramik,
    Keramikmuseum Westerwald, Höhr-Grenzhausen (D)

Allianz Lebensversicherung-AG, Stuttgart (D)

Munich Re, Münchener Rück, München (D)

Bayerische Landesbank, München (D)

Bayerische Staatsgemäldesammlung, München (D)

Museum Waldkraiburg, Waldkraiburg (D)

Literature | Literatur

Bilder und Skulpturen, 1991, Museum Waldkraiburg, Waldkraiburg

Neue Arbeiten, 1997, Bayerische Landesbank, München

Kunst ohne Grenzen, 2000, International K.S. Malevich Foundation, Moskau

Respiro, Galerie Thomas, München

Licht als ewige Gegenwart, 2005, Dom zu Meißen/Galerie Nütt, Dresden

Von Madrid nach Berlin, 2009, Galerie Terminus, München

Sammlung Gert Krogmann, 2009, Lithotec Oltmanns, Hamburg

List of works | Werkliste

1
Untitled, 2016, acrylic on canvas,
80 × 80 cm
Ohne Titel, 2016, Acryl auf Leinwand,
80 × 80 cm

2
XIX-IX-15, 2015, acrylic on canvas,
140 × 140 cm
XIX-IX-15, 2015, Acryl auf Leinwand,
140 × 140 cm

3
X-IV-08, 2008, acrylic on canvas,
50 × 50 cm
IX-IV-08, 2008, Acryl auf Leinwand,
50 × 50 cm

4
IV-VIII-08, 2008, acrylic on canvas,
200 × 170 cm
IV-VIII-08, 2008, Acryl auf Leinwand,
200 × 170 cm

5
XIX-VII-08, 2008, acrylic on canvas,
170 × 200 cm
XIX-VII-08, 2008, Acryl auf Leinwand,
170 × 200 cm

6
XXX-VII-08, 2008, acrylic on canvas,
170 × 200 cm
XXX-VII-08, 2008, Acryl auf Leinwand,
170 × 200 cm

7
XXI-I-08, 2008, triptych, acrylic on
canvas, 140 × 300 cm
XXI-I-08, 2008, Triptychon, Acryl auf
Leinwand, 140 × 300 cm

8
VII-III-16, 2016, acrylic on canvas,
160 × 160 cm
VII-III-16, 2016, Acryl auf Leinwand,
160 × 160 cm

9
Poetry of Light I, 2015, acrylic on
canvas, 80 × 80 cm
Poesie des Lichts I, 2015, Acryl auf
Leinwand, 80 × 80 cm

10
Dual I, 2015, acrylic on canvas,
120 × 100 cm
Dual I, 2015, Acryl auf Leinwand,
120 × 100 cm

11
Dual II, 2015, acrylic on canvas,
175 × 110 cm
Dual II, 2015, Acryl auf Leinwand,
175 × 110 cm

12
XV-IX-14, 2014, acrylic on canvas,
70 × 45 cm
XV-IX-14, 2014, Acryl auf Leinwand,
70 × 45 cm

13
Poetry of Light II, 2015, acrylic on
canvas, 50 × 50 cm
Poesie des Lichts II, 2015, Acryl auf
Leinwand, 50 × 50 cm

14
Poetry of Light III, 2015, acrylic on
canvas, 50 × 50 cm
Poesie des Lichts III, 2015, Acryl auf
Leinwand, 50 × 50 cm

15
Poetry of Light IV, 2015, acrylic on
canvas, 160 × 110 cm
Poesie des Lichts IV, 2015, Acryl auf
Leinwand, 160 × 110 cm

16
Still Light, 2016, acrylic on canvas,
120 × 80 cm
Noch Licht, 2016, Acryl auf Leinwand,
120 × 80 cm

17
XXVII-II-13, 2013, acrylic on canvas,
50 × 50 cm
XXVII-II-13, 2013, Acryl auf Leinwand,
50 × 50 cm

18
XXX-VIII-13, 2013, acrylic on canvas,
200 × 150 cm
XXX-VIII-13, 2013, Acryl auf Leinwand,
200 × 150 cm

19
Aurora I, X-VII-13, 2013, acrylic on
canvas, 140 × 140 cm
Aurora I, X-VII-13, 2013, Acryl auf
Leinwand, 140 × 140 cm

20
Aurora II, X-VII-13, 2013, acrylic on
canvas, 140 × 140 cm
Aurora II, X-VII-13, 2013, Acryl auf
Leinwand, 140 × 140 cm

21
Dance of the Hay Girls
Tanz der Heumädchen
Above left: *VI-VII-13*, 2013, acrylic on
canvas, 30 × 30 cm
Oben links: *VI-VII-13*, 2013, Acryl auf
Leinwand, 30 × 30 cm
Above right: *III-VII-13*, 2013, acrylic on
canvas, 30 × 30 cm
Oben rechts: *III-VII-13*, 2013, Acryl auf
Leinwand, 30 × 30 cm
Below left: *X-VII-13*, 2013, acrylic on
canvas, 30 × 30 cm
Unten links: *X-VII-13*, 2013, Acryl auf
Leinwand, 30 × 30 cm
Below right: *IX-VII-13*, 2013, acrylic on
canvas, 30 × 30 cm
Unten rechts: *IX-VII-13*, 2013, Acryl auf
Leinwand, 30 × 30 cm

22
Light Blue, 2016, acrylic on canvas,
160 × 110 cm
Light Blue, 2016, Acryl auf Leinwand,
160 × 110 cm

23
XXXI-V-13, 2013, acrylic on canvas,
50 × 50 cm
XXXI-V-13, 2013, Acryl auf Leinwand,
50 × 50 cm

24
XXV-II-11, 2011, acrylic on canvas,
140 × 140 cm
XXV-II-11, 2011, Acryl auf Leinwand,
140 × 140 cm

25
The Vltava after Smetana, 2015,
acrylic on canvas, 120 × 400 cm
Die Moldau nach Smetana, 2015,
Acryl auf Leinwand, 120 × 400 cm

26
Wave, 2009, acrylic on canvas,
155 × 300 cm
Welle, 2009, Acryl auf Leinwand,
155 × 300 cm

27
Light II, 2015, acrylic on canvas,
160 × 160 cm
Licht II, 2015, Acryl auf Leinwand,
160 × 160 cm

28
Without Borders I, 2007, acrylic on
canvas, 140 × 200 cm
Ohne Grenzen I, 2007, Acryl auf
Leinwand, 140 × 200 cm

29
Without Borders II, 2007, acrylic on
canvas, 140 × 140 cm
Ohne Grenzen II, 2007, Acryl auf
Leinwand, 140 × 140 cm

30
Without Borders III, 2007, acrylic on
canvas, 140 × 140 cm
Ohne Grenzen III, 2007, Acryl auf
Leinwand, 140 × 140 cm

31
Without Borders IV, 2007, acrylic on
canvas, 140 × 140 cm
Ohne Grenzen IV, 2007, Acryl auf
Leinwand, 140 × 140 cm

32
XXVI-VIII-08, 2008, acrylic on canvas,
140 × 140 cm
XXVI-VIII-08, 2008, Acryl auf Leinwand, 140 × 140 cm

33
XV-VIII-16, 2016, acrylic on canvas,
70 × 50 cm
XV-VIII-16, 2016, Acryl auf Leinwand,
70 × 50 cm

34
XVI-VIII-16, 2016, acrylic on canvas,
35 × 26 cm
XVI-VIII-16, 2016, Acryl auf Leinwand,
35 × 26 cm

35
XVII-VIII-16, 2016, acrylic on canvas,
35 × 26 cm
XVII-VIII-16, 2016, Acryl auf Leinwand,
35 × 26 cm

36
XVIII-VIII-16, 2016, acrylic on canvas,
35 × 26 cm
XVIII-VIII-16, 2016, Acryl auf Leinwand,
35 × 26 cm

37
XIX-VIII-16, 2016, acrylic on canvas,
35 × 26 cm
XIX-VIII-16, 2016, Acryl auf Leinwand,
35 × 26 cm

38
XXVIII-VII-13, 2013, acrylic on canvas,
110 × 110 cm
XXVIII-VII-13, 2013, Acryl auf Leinwand,
110 × 110 cm

39
Sisters
Schwestern
Left: *IV-IV-13*, 2013, acrylic on canvas,
40 × 40 cm
Links: *IV-IV-13*, 2013, Acryl auf
Leinwand, 40 × 40 cm
Right: *XI-VI-13*, 2013, acrylic on canvas,
40 × 40 cm
Rechts: *XI-VI-13*, 2013, Acryl auf
Leinwand, 40 × 40 cm

40
Swiss Impressions II, XXI-I-11, 2011,
acrylic on canvas, 120 × 100 cm
Schweizer Impressionen II, XXI-I-11,
2011, Acryl auf Leinwand, 120 × 100 cm

41
XX-VII-03, 2003, acrylic on canvas,
120 × 100 cm
XX-VII-03, 2003, Acryl auf Leinwand,
120 × 100 cm

42
Colour Pianoforte, 2010–2015, acrylic
on canvas, each 95 × 30 cm
Farbenklavier, 2010–2015, Acryl auf
Leinwand, je 95 × 30 cm

43
Light I, 2014, acrylic on canvas,
140 × 140 cm
Licht I, 2014, Acryl auf Leinwand,
140 × 140 cm

44
Blue, 2014, acrylic on canvas,
140 × 140 cm
Blau, 2014, Acryl auf Leinwand,
140 × 140 cm

45
Poetry of Light V, 2015, acrylic on
canvas, 160 × 160 cm
Poesie des Lichts V, 2015, Acryl auf
Leinwand, 160 × 160 cm

46
Poetry of Light VI, 2015, acrylic on
canvas, 160 × 160 cm
Poesie des Lichts VI, 2015, Acryl auf
Leinwand, 160 × 160 cm

47
Poetry of Light VII, 2015, acrylic on
canvas, 100 × 100 cm
Poesie des Lichts VII, 2015, Acryl auf
Leinwand, 100 × 100 cm

48
XXVI-IV-10, 2010, acrylic on canvas,
80 × 80 cm
XXVI-IV-10, 2010, Acryl auf Leinwand,
80 × 80 cm

49
VIII-II-10, 2010, acrylic on canvas,
195 × 160 cm
VIII-II-10, 2010, Acryl auf Leinwand,
195 × 160 cm

50
Leporello, acrylic on paper
Leporello, Acryl auf Bütten

51
Leonids, 2013/14, acrylic on canvas,
9 parts each 50 × 50 cm
Leoniden, 2013/14, Acryl auf Leinwand,
9 Teile je 50 × 50 cm

52
V-III-14, 2014, acrylic on canvas,
50 × 50 cm
V-III-14, 2014, Acryl auf Leinwand,
50 × 50 cm

53
VI-IV-12, 2012, acrylic on canvas,
100 × 120 cm
VI-IV-12, 2012, Acryl auf Leinwand,
100 × 120cm

54
Spring, 2016, acrylic on canvas,
140 × 140 cm
Frühling, 2016, Acryl auf Leinwand,
140 × 140 cm

55
XIX-IV-11, 2011, acrylic on canvas,
100 × 100 cm
XIX-IV-11, 2011, Acryl auf Leinwand,
100 × 100cm

56
III-V-12, 2012, acrylic on canvas,
80 × 80 cm
III-V-12, 2012, Acryl auf Leinwand,
80 × 80 cm

57
X-X-07, 2007, acrylic on canvas,
160 × 110 cm
X-X-07, 2007, Acryl auf Leinwand,
160 × 110 cm

58
XV-III-06, 2006, acrylic on canvas,
90 × 80 cm
XV-III-06, 2006, Acryl auf Leinwand,
90 × 80 cm

59
XXIII-VIII-12, 2012, acrylic on canvas,
110 × 110 cm
XXIII-VIII-12, 2012, Acryl auf Leinwand,
110 × 110 cm

60
VII-II-12, 2012, acrylic on canvas,
120 × 100 cm
VII-II-12, 2012, Acryl auf Leinwand,
120 × 100 cm

61
XIV-III-10, 2010, acrylic on canvas,
120 × 100 cm
XIV-III-10, 2010, Acryl auf Leinwand,
120 × 100 cm

62
Danae, 2015, acrylic on canvas,
160 × 120 cm
Danae, 2015, Acryl auf Leinwand,
160 × 120 cm

63
XXIX-I-12, 2012, acrylic on canvas,
140 × 70 cm
XXIX-I-12, 2012, Acryl auf Leinwand,
140 × 70 cm

64
XXIV-III-12, 2012, acrylic on canvas,
150 × 170 cm
XXIV-III-12, 2012, Acryl auf Leinwand,
150 × 170 cm

65
XV-IV-14, 2014, acrylic on canvas,
120 × 100 cm
XV-IV-14, 2014, Acryl auf Leinwand,
120 × 100 cm

66
XVI-IV-14, 2014, acrylic on canvas,
120 × 100 cm
XVI-IV-14, 2014, Acryl auf Leinwand,
120 × 100 cm

67
Poetry of Light VIII, 2015, acrylic on
canvas, 100 × 100 cm
Poesie des Lichts VIII, 2015, Acryl auf
Leinwand, 100 × 100 cm

68
Poetry of Light IX, 2015, acrylic on
canvas, 100 × 100 cm
Poesie des Lichts IX, 2015, Acryl auf
Leinwand, 100 × 100 cm

69
XII-XII-98, 1998, acrylic on canvas,
140 × 140 cm
XII-XII-98, 1998, Acryl auf Leinwand,
140 × 140 cm

70
Night Painting, 2016, acrylic on
canvas, 60 × 60 cm
Nachtbild, 2016, Acryl auf Leinwand,
60 × 60 cm

71
XVII-XI-16, 2016, acrylic on canvas,
50 × 70 cm
XVII-XI-16, 2016, Acryl auf Leinwand,
50 × 70 cm

72
III-II-11, 2011, acrylic on canvas,
120 × 80 cm
III-II-11, 2011, Acryl auf Leinwand,
120 × 100 cm

73
XI-III-11, 2011, acrylic on canvas,
120 × 80 cm
XI-III-11, 2011, Acryl auf Leinwand,
120 × 80 cm

74
Venus Flycatcher, 2015, acrylic on
canvas, 120 × 80 cm
Venusfliegenfalle, 2015, Acryl auf
Leinwand, 120 × 80 cm

75
XIX-I-15, 2015, acrylic on canvas,
100 × 90 cm
XIX-I-15, 2015, Acryl auf Leinwand,
100 × 90 cm

76
XXV-III-11, 2011, acrylic on canvas,
80 × 80 cm
XXV-III-11, 2011, Acryl auf Leinwand,
80 × 80 cm

77
II-V-11, 2011, acrylic on canvas,
70 × 50 cm
II-V-11, 2011, Acryl auf Leinwand,
70 × 50 cm

78
XIV-X-15, 2015, acrylic on canvas,
120 × 100 cm
XIV-X-15, 2015, Acryl auf Leinwand,
120 × 100 cm

79
XXVII-II-07, 2007, acrylic on canvas,
50 × 50 cm
XXVII-II-07, 2007, Acryl auf Leinwand,
50 × 50 cm

80
XI-X-11, 2011, acrylic on canvas,
50 × 50 cm
XI-X-11, 2011, Acryl auf Leinwand,
50 × 50 cm

81
X-X-11, 2011, acrylic on canvas,
50 × 50 cm
X-X-11, 2011, Acryl auf Leinwand,
50 × 50 cm

82
XIII-IV-08, 2008, acrylic on canvas,
90 × 90 cm
XIII-IV-08, 2008, Acryl auf Leinwand,
90 × 90 cm

83
Sun, 2015, acrylic on canvas,
140 × 80 cm
Sonne, 2015, Acryl auf Leinwand,
140 × 80 cm

84
II-IV-10, 2010, acrylic on canvas,
90 × 50 cm
II-IV-10, 2010, Acryl auf Leinwand,
90 × 50 cm

85
III-IV-10, 2010, acrylic on canvas,
90 × 50 cm
III-IV-10, 2010, Acryl auf Leinwand,
90 × 50 cm

86
I-IV-10, 2010, acrylic on canvas,
90 × 50 cm
I-IV-10, 2010, Acryl auf Leinwand,
90 × 50 cm

87
XV-VI-08/09, 2009, acrylic on canvas,
160 × 160 cm
XV-VI-08/09, 2009, Acryl auf
Leinwand, 160 × 160 cm

88
XXX-VIII-08, 2008, acrylic on canvas,
75 × 100 cm
XXX-VIII-08, 2008, Acryl auf Leinwand,
75 × 100 cm

89
XXV-VIII-08, 2008, acrylic on canvas,
75 × 100 cm
XXV-VIII-08, 2008, Acryl auf Leinwand,
75 × 100 cm

90
For H. H., V-IV-14, 2014, acrylic on
canvas, 120 × 100 cm
Für H. H., V-IV-14, 2014, Acryl auf
Leinwand, 120 × 100 cm

91
For G. H., 2016, acrylic on canvas,
80 × 50 cm
Für G. H., 2016, Acryl auf Leinwand,
80 × 50 cm

92
XVI-VII-10, 2010, acrylic on canvas,
120 × 100 cm
XVI-VII-10, 2010, Acryl auf Leinwand,
120 × 100 cm

93
Circle, 2013, acrylic on canvas,
12 pieces, each 70 × 50 cm
Kreis, 2013, Acryl auf Leinwand,
12 Teile, je 70 × 50 cm

94
VIII-IV-11, 2011, acrylic on canvas,
120 × 100 cm
VIII-IV-11, 2011, Acryl auf Leinwand,
120 × 100 cm

95
I-III-11, 2011, acrylic on canvas,
120 × 100 cm
I-III-11, 2011, Acryl auf Leinwand,
120 × 100 cm

96
XXII-IX-10, 2010, acrylic on canvas,
120 × 100 cm
XXII-IX-10, 2010, Acryl auf Leinwand,
120 × 100 cm

97
jan-2000, 2000, acrylic on canvas,
100 × 100 cm
jan-2000, 2000, Acryl auf Leinwand,
100 × 100 cm

98
Alpha I, Alpha II, Alpha III, 2016, acrylic
on canvas, 120 × 240 cm
Alpha I, Alpha II, Alpha III, Acryl auf
Leinwand, 120 × 240cm

99
VIII-X-11, 2011, acrylic on canvas,
70 × 50 cm
VIII-X-11, 2011, Acryl auf Leinwand,
70 × 50 cm

100
VII-X-11, 2011, acrylic on canvas,
70 × 50 cm
VII-X-11, 2011, Acryl auf Leinwand,
70 × 50 cm

101
Light and Darkness, 2016, acrylic on
canvas, 125 × 285 cm
Licht und Dunkelheit, 2016, Acryl auf
Leinwand, 125 × 285 cm

102
XXIX-VIII-09, 2009, acrylic on canvas,
120 × 100 cm
XXIX-VIII-09, 2009, Acryl auf Leinwand, 120 × 100 cm

103
I-IV-09, 2009, acrylic on canvas,
120 × 100 cm
I-IV-09, 2009, Acryl auf Leinwand,
120 × 100 cm

104
In the Footsteps of M. W. Turner I,
at the Gästival 2015, acrylic on canvas,
140 × 140 cm
Auf den Spuren von M. W. Turner I,
beim Gästival 2015, Acryl auf Leinwand, 140 × 140 cm

105
In the Footsteps of M. W. Turner II,
2015, acrylic on canvas, 100 × 120 cm
Auf den Spuren von M. W. Turner II,
2015, Acryl auf Leinwand, 100 × 120 cm

106
In the Footsteps of M. W. Turner III,
2015, acrylic on canvas, 100 × 120 cm
Auf den Spuren von M. W. Turner III,
2015, Acryl auf Leinwand, 100 × 120 cm

107
Blue Rigi by Moonlight, 2015, acrylic
on canvas, 100 × 100 cm
Blaue Rigi bei Mondschein, 2015,
Acryl auf Leinwand, 100 × 100 cm

108
XXVII-V-14, 2014, acrylic on canvas,
70 × 50 cm
XXVII-V-14, 2014, Acryl auf Leinwand,
70 × 50 cm

109
Chameleon, 2014, acrylic on canvas,
180 × 140 cm
Chamäleon, 2014, Acryl auf Leinwand,
180 × 140 cm

110
VII-III-13, 2013, acrylic on canvas,
100 × 100 cm
VII-III-13, 2013, Acryl auf Leinwand,
100 × 100 cm

111
I-VI-15, 2015, acrylic on canvas,
120 × 100 cm
I-VI-15, 2015, Acryl auf Leinwand,
120 × 100 cm

112
Light III, 2015, acrylic on canvas,
90 × 80 cm
Licht III, 2015, Acryl auf Leinwand,
90 × 80 cm

113
X-I-13, 2013, acrylic on canvas,
110 × 110 cm
X-I-13, 2013, Acryl auf Leinwand,
110 × 110 cm

114
Backlight, 2009, 2010, 2012, 2015,
acrylic on canvas, 110 × 270 cm
Gegenlicht, 2009, 2010, 2012, 2015,
Acryl auf Leinwand, 110 × 270 cm

115
Swiss Impressions I, XX-II-10, 2010,
acrylic on canvas, 155 × 180 cm
Schweizer Impressionen I, XX-II-10,
2010, Acryl auf Leinwand, 155 × 180 cm

116
Swiss Impressions III, 2015, acrylic on
canvas, 140 × 140 cm
Schweizer Impressionen III, 2015,
Acryl auf Leinwand, 140 × 140 cm

117
Dual III, 2015, acrylic on canvas,
120 × 100 cm
Dual III, 2015, Acryl auf Leinwand,
120 × 100 cm

118
Dual IV, 2015, acrylic on canvas,
120 × 100 cm
Dual IV, 2015, Acryl auf Leinwand,
120 × 100 cm

119
XXIV-VI-08/12, 2012, acrylic on canvas,
170 × 200 cm
XXIV-VI-08/12, 2012, Acryl auf Leinwand, 170 × 200 cm

120
V-IX-08/14, 2014, acrylic on canvas,
140 × 140 cm
V-IX-08/14, 2014, Acryl auf Leinwand,
140 × 140 cm

121
III-III-00, 2000, acrylic on canvas,
80 × 80 cm
III-III-00, 2000, Acryl auf Leinwand,
80 × 80 cm

122
More Sensual Light, 2016, acrylic on
canvas, 160 × 110 cm
Mehr sinnliches Licht, 2016, Acryl auf
Leinwand, 160 × 110 cm

123
In the Light of Shadow, 2016, acrylic
on canvas, 140 × 100 cm
Im Licht der Schatten, 2016, Acryl auf
Leinwand, 140 × 100 cm

124
Glass design of the cross in the
exterior of the new Evangelisches
Zentrum, Christuskirche, Salzburg
Glasgestaltung des Kreuzes im
Außenbereich des neuen Evange-
lischen Zentrums, Christuskirche,
Salzburg

125
Glass painting, 300 × 200 cm, Atrium
of the new Evangelisches Zentrum,
Christuskirche, Salzburg
Glasgemälde, 300 × 200 cm, Lichthof
des neuen Evangelischen Zentrums,
Christuskirche, Salzburg

126
Dual V, 2015, acrylic on canvas,
160 × 110 cm
Dual V, 2015, Acryl auf Leinwand,
160 × 110 cm

Christoph Vitali
Helene B. Grossmann

Voici déjà longtemps que je suis la vie et le travail de Helene B. Grossmann, avec autant d'attention que d'admiration. Au cours des dernières années, je me suis déplacé pour voir toutes ses expositions, à Küssnacht, à Bâle et tout récemment à Zoug.

Qu'est-ce donc qui rend cette artiste si importante, si considérable ? C'est indéniablement sa représentation à la fois stupéfiante et grandiose de la lumière. Elle a peint cette lumière dans d'innombrables tableaux, dans des tons de gris, de rouge et surtout de bleu, et dans des formats très divers, petits aussi bien que très grands.

Raimund Thomas, mon ami et collègue de Munich, la rapproche à juste titre de Seurat, Tiepolo, Turner et Monet… Je voudrais aller plus loin encore : Helene B. Grossmann réussit toujours à impliquer à chaque fois la lumière dans sa peinture, pour en faire le point dominant. Nous sommes alors saisis devant son travail et notre étonnement se renouvelle toujours devant sa force capitale.

Le curriculum vitæ de l'artiste mentionne le grand nombre d'expositions importantes auxquelles elle a participé, en Allemagne et en Suisse. Puisse-t-elle continuer longtemps son parcours et nous rester longtemps. C'est ce que je lui et nous souhaite de tout cœur.

Christoph Vitali est commissaire d'exposition, directeur de musée et écrivain d'art suisse. Il a été directeur de la Kunsthalle Schirn de 1985 à 1993, avant de passer à la direction de la Haus der Kunst à Munich (1994-2004). Directeur ensuite de la Fondation Beyeler à Riehen/Bâle de 2004 à 2008, il est devenu en 2008 directeur de la Kunst- und Ausstellungshalle de la République fédérale d'Allemagne, à Bonn. Christoph Vitali vit à Zurich.

Raimund Thomas
Helene B. Grossmann

Nous sommes habitués à regarder des tableaux, mais regarder ceux d'Helene B. Grossmann est une expérience d'un tout autre genre. Dès le premier contact visuel, le spectateur perd sa position d'observateur. Il est instantanément touché au plus profond de lui-même, et plongé – ou mieux encore : transporté – magiquement dans un infini de profondeur heureuse et baignée de lumière.

Et mon âme étendit
largement ses ailes,
pour voler par les pays silencieux,
comme si elle revenait chez elle.

Ainsi écrivait Eichendorff dans son poème *Mondnacht* (« Nuit de lune »). Il a vu assurément des images de ce genre, avec sa perception intuitive. Quand je reviens à mon statut d'observateur, je vois des nuages, peut-être de l'eau et de la brume, dans tous les cas un pressentiment de paysage qui se mue toutefois immédiatement en apparition primordiale, au sens figuré comme au sens propre. Ce qui saisit à nouveau et captive d'autant plus, est la lumière centrale, tantôt concentrée et aveuglante, tantôt diffuse et irradiante.

Vraiment ! Helene B. Grossmann réussit à peindre la lumière, ce fluide insaisissable, impossible à matérialiser, fugitif et pourtant si puissant. La lumière ! Quel sujet ! Bien sûr, pas celle de Rembrandt ou de Georges de la Tour : il ne s'agit pas ici d'une lumière de chandelier. Il s'agit de cette essence ultime au sens profond, dont Seurat s'est approché dans ses dessins en noir et blanc, ou bien telle qu'elle a pu être formulée de façon si fascinante par quelques-uns seulement des plus grands de la culture picturale européenne – je pense à Tiepolo, je pense à Turner et Monet.

Combien de peintres s'efforcent, depuis le début du XXe siècle, de représenter la couleur pure sans la camisole de la forme. Je ne connais personne qui ait eu l'audacieuse volonté d'apporter au spectateur le médium lumière au-delà du chemin de la peinture, voire – comme on l'a dit en introduction – de l'emporter lui-même et le transcender dans la lumière.

Cela n'est possible que sur fond de vision intuitive, d'humilité sincère, de force éruptive et de maîtrise accomplie.

Raimund Thomas est un galeriste et marchand d'art allemand à Munich, spécialisé dans l'art moderne et contemporain.

Helene B. Grossmann
Seulement la lumière

J'aimerais bien vous communiquer deux ou trois choses sur ma façon de travailler et sur mes objectifs. Mes sujets sont la lumière et l'espace chromatique. Le but est de créer des tableaux palpitants de vie dans le détail et empreints de calme dans l'ensemble. Le spectateur ne doit pas être arrimé à quelque chose, il doit pouvoir s'ouvrir, l'esprit libre, aux processus naturels de son approche.

Mes travaux sont donc en rapport avec la nature même de la peinture, avec la lumière et avec la couleur. Depuis mes études, j'essaie de matérialiser la lumière par la technique picturale. Je me suis longtemps occupée de la réfraction des couleurs, donc de leur variabilité dans le tableau. Dans la plupart des cas, on voit moins à première vue et le coloris des tableaux ne se développe qu'après coup. Cette variabilité est également soumise aux moments du jour et aux conditions de lumière. On découvre perpétuellement quelque chose d'autre, avec les changements d'atmosphère.

C'est un exercice d'équilibre délicat entre abstraction et objectivité. Pour toute objectivité, il existe un modèle. Il n'y en a pas pour l'abstraction : c'est la réalité elle-même.

J'essaie d'exprimer des sentiments humains élémentaires, en cherchant à réactiver l'espace entre observateur et tableau. Avec l'aide de la lumière, les observateurs font l'expérience d'une perspective qui est au-delà de l'espace réel.

La conception de la plupart de mes tableaux naît de façon si complexe que je peux difficilement moi-même l'expliquer avec des mots.

La base de chaque tableau est mon carnet de croquis. On peut en voir une partie sous la mention « Grafik ». J'ai appelé ce carnet de croquis *Kalendertage* (Jours calendaires). Ce sont des travaux préparatoires très abstraits et la fixation d'expériences par écrit. J'ai commencé ce genre de carnet de croquis en 1993. Le processus préparatoire consiste à chercher par des taches de couleur et des traits rapidement jetés la disposition caractéristique dans le tableau, avant de soumettre la suite à une révision dans un format plus grand.

Ma technique exige un lent traitement des couleurs, une application couche par couche, afin de pouvoir gérer les couleurs sur la toile. Matisse appelait cela « navigation ». Cette quête tâtonnante m'intéresse. Cette approche picturale classique recèle de nombreux dangers et difficultés, mais elle me confronte en permanence avec des événements imprévus et des tournants surprenants. J'essaie de trouver dans le champ de l'incertitude le centre du monde chromatique.

Ce processus pour trouver le ressort fondamental de la peinture a quelque chose de purifiant. Avec cette recherche, on se débarrasse des modes et des spleens inutiles.

Mon chemin consiste à mettre quelque chose en image avec les moyens de la peinture, afin de conférer au motif une profondeur, un avant et un après. Pour créer une nouvelle perspective et un regard nouveau, et produire un silence qui donne de la force.

Biographie

Naissance à Dresde

1981-1985	École supérieure des Beaux-Arts, Dresde
1982-1983	Voyages d'études en Asie centrale et Corée
1988	Atelier à Munich
1993	Chargée de cours à la Ludwig-Maximilians-Universität de Munich
1994	Atelier subventionné par la Ville de Munich, Lothringer 13
2001	Voyage à Rome, étude et travail de la fresque
2002	Conception et réalisation d'une fresque de plafond à Munich
2003	Séjour de travail dans le Sud de la France
2004	Voyage au Mexique
2005	Prix de peinture de l'Erwin von Kreibig Museum, Munich
2009-2013	Artiste en résidence en Suisse
2013	Vitrail et sculpture en verre pour le nouveau Centre évangélique de la Christuskirche, Salzbourg
Depuis 2007	Ateliers à Munich et en Suisse

Imprint

Published by:
Hirmer Verlag GmbH
Nymphenburger Strasse 84
80636 Munich

Concept: Helene B. Grossmann
Authors: Raimund Thomas,
Christoph Vitali

Photographs: Dieter Grossmann

German copy editing and proof
reading: Alexander Langkals,
Landshut
English translation: James Perry
and Michael Scuffil, Leverkusen
English copy editing and proof
reading: Jane Michael, Munich
French translation: Denis-Armand
Canal, Paris
French copy editing and proof
reading: Martine Passelaigue

Hirmer Project Management:
Rainer Arnold
Layout and Typesetting:
Tanja Bokelmann, Munich
Lithography: Reproline Mediateam,
Munich
Font: Proxima Nova
Paper: Magno Satin 200 g/m^2
Printing and binding: Passavia
Druckservice, Passau

Printed in Germany

Bibliographic information published
by the Deutsche Nationalbibliothek
The Deutsche Nationalbibliothek
lists this publication in the Deutsche
Nationalbibliografie; detailed
bibliographic data is available on the
Internet at http://www.dnb.de.

Image credits for all reproduced
Works: © Helene B. Grossmann
Dust jacket and cover image:
XXX-VII-08, 2008

© 2017 Hirmer Verlag GmbH,
Munich, Helene B. Grossmann,
the authors.

ISBN 978-3-7774-2849-9

www.hirmerverlag.de
www.hirmerpublishers.com
www.helenegrossmann.com